The Troubles with Democracy

Off the Fence: Morality, Politics, and Society

The series is published in partnership with the Centre for Applied Philosophy, Politics, and Ethics (CAPPE), University of Brighton.

Series editors:

Bob Brecher, professor of moral philosophy, University of Brighton
Robin Dunford, senior lecturer in globalization and war, University of Brighton
Michael Neu, senior lecturer in philosophy, politics, and ethics, University of Brighton

Off the Fence presents short, sharply argued texts in applied moral and political philosophy, with an interdisciplinary focus. The series constitutes a source of arguments on the substantive problems that applied philosophers are concerned with: contemporary real-world issues relating to violence, human nature, justice, equality and democracy, self and society. The series demonstrates applied philosophy to be at once rigorous, relevant, and accessible—philosophy-in-use.

Recent titles in the series:

The Right of Necessity: Moral Cosmopolitanism and Global Poverty
Alejandra Mancilla

Complicity: Criticism between Collaboration and Commitment
Thomas Docherty

The State and the Self: Identity and Identities
Maren Behrensen

Just Liberal Violence: Sweatshops, Torture, War
Michael Neu

The Troubles with Democracy
Jeff Noonan

The Troubles with Democracy

Jeff Noonan

ROWMAN &
LITTLEFIELD
INTERNATIONAL

London • New York

Published by Rowman & Littlefield International Ltd.
6 Tinworth Street, London SE11 5AL, United Kingdom
www.rowmaninternational.com

Rowman & Littlefield International Ltd. is an affiliate of Rowman & Littlefield
4501 Forbes Boulevard, Suite 200, Lanham, Maryland 20706, USA
With additional offices in Boulder, New York, Toronto (Canada), and Plymouth (UK)
www.rowman.com

British Library Cataloguing in Publication Data Available
A catalog record for this book is available from the British Library.

ISBN 978-1-7866-0427-9 (hardcover)
ISBN 978-1-7866-0428-6 (paperback)

Library of Congress Cataloging-in-Publication Data Available

ISBN: 978-1-78660-427-9 (cloth : alk. paper)
ISBN: 978-1-78660-428-6 (pbk. : alk. paper)
ISBN: 978-1-78660-429-3 (electronic)

♾ ™ The paper used in this publication meets the minimum requirements of
American National Standard for Information Sciences—Permanence of Paper for
Printed Library Materials, ANSI/NISO Z39.48-1992.

Contents

Introduction

Democracy Today

Liberal political theorists are anxious that liberal-democracy is in trouble. Political scientists Roberto Stefan Foa and Yascha Mounk suggest that support for existing political institutions is collapsing in Europe and America. The rise of right-wing populist forces signals a willingness to entertain authoritarian alternatives. In their 2016 paper they claim to have made the "deeply disturbing" discovery that "citizens in a number of supposedly consolidated democracies in North America and Western Europe have not only grown more critical of their political leaders . . . they have also become more cynical about the role of democracy as a political system . . . and more willing to express support for authoritarian alternatives."[1] They argue that citizens—and, apparently, especially the young—seem to be drifting away from a commitment to liberal-democracy. "In virtually all cases," they argue, "the generation gap is striking, with the proportion of younger citizens who believe it is essential to live in a democracy falling to a minority. What is more, this disaffection with the democratic form of government is accompanied by a wider skepticism towards liberal institutions."[2] However, they give no argument to support their identification of "liberal institutions" and "democracy."

Thinkers outside the liberal mainstream are also concerned that the liberal-democratic capitalist world has crossed a threshold. Giorgio Agamben worries that we now live in a "state of exception" in which a permanent crisis, fanned by the flames of the "War on Terror" and fear of infiltration by Islamic terrorists, has in effect suspended the rule of law and constitutional norms.[3] In an analogous vein, Colin Crouch speaks of a "post-democratic order," in which democratic values decline because citizens are no longer engaged in the drama of self-government. They withdraw to the private sphere and let politicians make the decisions.[4] "The people" are reduced to a slogan invoked to justify whatever decision unaccountable executives and politicians take. Elections are bought; politicians are in the pocket of big business; all parties converge toward a formless "center" that simply complies with techno-economic dictates; whole populations are surveyed and monitored; racialized populations are surveilled, policed, imprisoned in penitentiaries or, in the case of migrants, concentration camps, where they can be harassed, beaten, or murdered. Those with some money are free to shop, the rest are monitored and humiliated for the sake of increasingly meager welfare payments.

These trends are not inventions, but they are also one-sided. They ignore equally powerful counterevidence coming from other surveys and the street that people are mobilizing to assert democratic power against the undemocratic implications of liberal and capitalist institutions and norms. Right-wing populists might be in power, but they have spawned, especially in the United States, a vigorous opposition, also centered on youth. A University of Chicago poll found that 62 percent of Americans ages eighteen to thirty-four—the very age suffering the most from student debt and precarious employment—believed a strong government was needed to handle the economic crisis.[5] Belief that a strong government is needed to counter the very undemocratic forces of the market might be illiberal, but it is hardly undemocratic. We know from history that if markets are unregulated, the majority of people suffer; if governments can intervene to ensure better outcomes for the majority, that outcome is democratic. The mistake is to confuse democracy with liberal-democracy. I will argue that the future of democracy depends upon finding ways to go beyond the democratic limitations of liberal-capitalist society. Liberalism and democracy agree that people are equal, but democracy, I will argue, goes beyond abstract principle to find ways to ensure that people's real interests are not only voiced but also satisfied by public policy.

The last decade is hardly the first crisis of democracy. There was never a democratic Golden Age, and people have always had to fight for their voices to be heard and their real needs satisfied. Winning constitutional rights has been a tremendous step forward for the majority of people, but democracy requires more than constitutional rights. It requires *social and economic institutions and norms* that ensure, so far as possible, that people are not dominated by a minority ruling class or economic forces beyond their control. Democracy is not just liberal political argument and choice, it is the institutionalization of our power as social self-conscious human beings to determine our collective life. It does not solve every problem on its own, but it ensures that everyone's interests are fully expressed and everyone who is affected by a decision can participate in making it. A more democratic society would still have *to choose* to transition to clean energy, for example; but in a more democratic society, the choice would not be swayed by the outsize power of fossil fuel corporations. It is possible to choose badly in a democracy, but that is different from not really being able to choose at all because you have the right to vote but no effective social power. The struggle for democracy, I will show, is a struggle for effective social power.

The key task for real democrats, therefore, is to ask ourselves why right-wing populists have been successful. Foa and Mounk find part of the answer, but they do not understand its implications. "Even as democracy has come to be the only form of government widely viewed as legitimate, it has lost the trust of many citizens who no longer believe that democracy can deliver on their most pressing needs and preferences."[6] But it is not "democracy" that has failed to deliver, it is political parties and corporations that have failed to meet citizens' needs, all the while encouraging forms of production and consumption that undermine the long-term future of human life on the planet. The solution, then, is to build new political parties and social and economic systems, and that is the unexamined demand beneath the populist upsurge. Democratic activists need to respond with positive ideas that that can win back the people swayed by populist mythologies.

If democracy is going to advance, then it needs to solve a problem most proponents of liberal-democracy never address. The democratic value of self-determination depends on collective control over universally required life-resources and major social institutions. Liberal-capitalist institutions have developed to *prevent* collective control over resources and economic institutions. Where resources are collectively owned and controlled, they can be used to produce life-goods that satisfy people's core needs and enable them to realize their core human capacities. The problem is that such use contradicts the master right of capitalism: private property in those same resources, and the exploitation of labor and nature to produce money-value.[7] Hence the fundamental contradiction that democrats must confront is between what John McMurtry calls the "life-value" of nature, labor, productive enterprises, parliaments, and social institutions, and their capture by capitalist money-value.[8] Life-value simply means the contribution that any good makes to the satisfaction of fundamental human needs and the free expression of intellectual, creative, and affective human capacities. No one can be free who cannot live, or whose life is mere service to a ruling class and the social forces its competitive struggles unleash. If democracy enables human freedom for each and all, then it demands collective control over the natural and social conditions of life support, exercised through public institutions governed by those whose lives are shaped by and within them. If that is what we mean by democracy, liberal-capitalist society has never been, and cannot become, democratic.

Democracy is born of constant struggles of the exploited, oppressed, and alienated; their achievements have been partially institutionalized in liberal-democracies but are also always tenuous. The strength of democracy is thus always dependent on the efforts of those most deprived of power to fight to protect past gains and conquer new territory. Many crucial victories have been rolled back or weakened in the past forty years; right wing undemocratic forces have been in the ascendancy for much longer than the brief reign of Donald Trump. But democracy as the demand for collective self-determination has not been defeated—there are still myriad struggles, led by workers, women, racialized groups, demonized sexual identities, the disabled, refugees, and anyone else marked for domination. The future of democracy, I will argue, depends on each of these groups discovering the common ground that unites them, and fighting together on that basis.

This book will argue that democracy demands more than equal rights and parliamentary elections. It grows up from our relationship with the natural world and shapes all major social institutions, not just political institutions. Its foundation is the shared life-interest of all people in being able to access the goods, resources, relationships, and institutions they require to freely develop their creative capacities and express their voice in the deliberations through which law and public policy are shaped. Given the practical imperative of discovering common ground,

I will focus on normative rather than organizational issues. New unified movements will depend on solidarity, and solidarity can only be built between different groups who learn to recognize in one another common unmet needs. Political philosophy can only make the case that there is such common ground; on its own it is incapable of organizing movements. There is no master plan for political organization; success depends on knowledge of local histories that no general philosophy can master. Thus, I hope my argument contributes to the development of new democratic movements by providing a deeper understanding of the universal values and common purposes that have—if I am correct—always nourished democratic struggle.

Chapter 1 will spell out my understanding of democracy as a social form in which all major social institutions are steered by life-value principle and law and policy decided by collective deliberation. A brief examination of a variety of struggles in different historical periods uncovers a unifying theme: Democratic struggles are always *against* forms of social power that systematically deprive some group of citizens of access to goods, resources, relationships, and institutions they need to live fully and freely, and *for* forms of collective control over those resources, etc. Success in those struggles satisfy the natural and social conditions of self-determination. No one is vulnerable to exploitation or domination who is in control of their means of life and self-realization. The historical survey thus provides evidence for the reality of a shared life-interest in democratic institutions that is both the source of democratic struggle and their justification against the private, exclusionary interests they target.

The dominant interpretation of democracy, liberal-democratic theory, paints a different picture. While it is not always indifferent to the role that need-satisfaction plays in democratic life, it typically grasps this role one-sidedly, as a passive function of citizenship rights that leaves underlying structures of social power unchanged. Chapter 2 explores the complex history of liberal-democracy (including its close analogue: republican theories of democracy). While liberalism has made indispensable contributions to democratic theory, it consistently leaves out the need for democratic control over *all* major social institutions, economic institutions included.

The deepest threat to democratic self-determination is thus the way in which class power, synthetically connected with the historically developed forms of racialized and gendered dominance, has captured universally required life-resources and normalized their exploitation for the accumulation of money-value. The much lamented—even by mainstream economists—rise in income inequality is an effect of this structural cause. Chapter 3 will critically examine the mainstream worry about inequality, explain its depth cause, and expose the real harm it causes to its victims and democratic values.

The spectacular rise in inequality, coupled with the false belief that some undeserving special interests are being coddled at the expense of "the people," lies behind the upsurge in populist movements represented most dramatically by the victory of Donald Trump in the 2016 US presidential election. Chapter 4 will examine the right-wing populist upsurge but argue, against Foa and Mounk, that it does not spell the end of democracy but is itself a distorted expression of democratic power. It represents popular power unmoored from the deeper commitment to *universal* and *comprehensive* need-satisfaction and turned against demonized enemies (the racially subaltern, the immigrant, the foreigner). The solution is not a return to failed liberal-democratic normalcy but the reorientation of the democratic energy unleashed in the movements toward the creation of new movements that serve the universal interest in comprehensive need-satisfaction, not the disguised elite interests of the populist demagogue.

Chapter 5 will examine contemporary theoretical and practical alternatives to liberal-democratic normalcy. Theoretically, the focus will be on the idea, articulated first perhaps by Claude Lefort and essential for understanding influential "agonistic" theories of democracy, that democracy should be understood as the struggle of minorities for a social space that respects pluralistic values rather than (as I maintain) a universal set of values and institutions satisfying shared conditions of self-determination and freedom.[9] The idea here is that struggles for democracy are not for some *thing*, but to open a closed space to voices traditionally silenced. Democracy, at its best, is a cacophony of public arguments and never a settled institutional reality. These agonistic theories of democracy have their practical analogue in "horizontalist" practices of direct democracy (think of Occupy, for example), which eschew efforts to recapture state and social institutions and look to build parallel spaces for self-determination.[10] While there is much to learn from agonistic theory and horizontalist practice about the limitations of actually existing democracies, both ultimately fail because they misunderstand the way in which democratic pluralism presupposes shared needs and goals, and the reasons democracy requires unified movement capable of taking control of social, political, and economic life.

The final chapter will synthesize the lessons learned in the critical chapters of the book into an argument about the need for unified movements, focused on ensuring need-governed access to the material sources of self-determining power by means of democratic control over all major social institutions. This project retains the historical links between the history of democracy and revolutionary opposition to minority class, race, and sex control over the resources that all human beings require to survive and thrive. It rejects the insurrectionary impatience of nineteenth- and early twentieth-century vanguard parties. The lesson the historical failure of those movements teaches is that the radical transformation of society is too complex a task to be centrally managed and accomplished through a single blow. It requires recursive learning informed by positive feedback loops that can only be ensured and established by the introduction of fundamental changes over an open-ended time frame. This process will always encounter opposition and disagreement. History teaches that opponents can never be completely "liquidated," so they have to be, ultimately, convinced. Struggles against structurally entrenched coercive power are necessary, but democratic power does not flow from the barrel of a gun; instead it flows from the concerted demands of people fighting for that which they need to live as full and free human beings.

NOTES

1. Robert Stefan Foa and Yascha Mounk, "The Democratic Disconnect," *Journal of Democracy*, vol. 27, no. 3 (July 2016), 7.

2. Robert Stefan Foa and Yascha Mounk, "The Signs of Deconsolidation," *Journal of Democracy*, vol. 28, no. 1 (January 2017), 6.

3. Giorgio Agamben, *The State of Exception* (Chicago: University of Chicago Press, 2004).

4. Colin Crouch, *Post-Democracy* (Cambridge, UK: Polity Press, 2004).

5. Steve Chapman, "Why Young Americans Are Drawn to Socialism," *Reason* (May 21, 2018); https://reason.com/archives/2018/05/21/why-young-a mericans-are-drawn-to-sociali (accessed September 19, 2018).

6. Foa and Mounk, "The Democratic Disconnect," 16.

7. I have traced this history in more detail in an earlier work. There is no need to repeat the analysis here. The present argument focuses on challenges to democracy that have arisen since that book was published, and develops a positive argument based upon a reevaluation of the centrality of public institutions to democratic life absent from the earlier argument. See Jeff Noonan, *Democratic Society and Human Needs* (Montreal: McGill-Queen's University Press, 2006), 1–53.

8. John McMurtry, *Philosophy and World Problems, Volume 1: What is Good? What is Bad? The Value of all Values Through Time, Place, and Theories* (Oxford: EOLSS Publishers, 2011), 213–15.

9. See Claude Lefort, *The Political Forms of Modern Society* (Cambridge, MA: MIT Press, 1986), 270.

10. The classical argument in favor of horizontalist practices is John Holloway, *Change the World without Taking Power* (London: Pluto Press, 2005).

Chapter 1

Democracy and Self-Determination

The meaning of the idea of democracy is simple enough—rule of the people. Institutionalizing that idea has proven to be the main difficulty. For who are "the people" whose moral equality is implied by the idea of democratic citizenship? Moreover, what are the social conditions that must be satisfied if their equality is to mean equal ability to satisfy their core human needs and live meaningful and valuable lives? Unless it relates to life's real needs and possibilities, equality is just a platitude uttered by rulers secure in their unequal power. One must also ask, what limits to their power must the people recognize, respect, and agree to impose upon themselves if they are not to undermine the environmental conditions of their very existence, or cause unmanageable social and cultural conflict? I think of the history of democratic struggles as attempts to answer those questions. The best answers, I will argue in this book, have two dimensions.

On the one hand, they explain why most past barriers to the recognition of the moral equality and shared life-interests of people have been illegitimate. They reveal that these barriers have not been rooted in any real incapacity on the part of ordinary people to participate in the public affairs. Rather, they simply targeted specific groups for exclusion and domination because of a demonized characteristic which—in the eyes of those with power—rendered them incompetent to help rule. Democratic struggles exposed these aristocratic excuses as false. Of course, not every argument is of equal validity, and not every perspective is equally consistent with the shared life-interests of citizens. Democracy does not eliminate the need to evaluate perspectives and policies in light

1

of everyone's shared life-interests. The history of democratic struggle is not a struggle against the need to test claims for truth. It is a struggle against elites who claim that their private interests are the truth. Hence, as a political struggle, the history of democracy proves the moral equality of people and institutionalizes the right of everyone to participate in the decisions that shape their lives.

That alone is not enough to ensure that "the people" rule. From a social perspective, democratic struggles have also changed the way resources are utilized and valued. Instead of being for the sake of the self-aggrandizement of the high-born and rich, democratic struggles insist that resources are first of all life-resources, whose value is to satisfy everyone's fundamental needs, and which must be appropriated in ways consistent with universal need-satisfaction and the long-term ability of nature to sustain life. It is true that early struggles for democracy did not always recognize the general need for human economies to situate themselves within a broader natural world that sets limits to production, consumption, and waste. The past forty years of environmental crisis have made clear that economic systems must be "life-coherent": supportive of the satisfaction of human needs and human flourishing while at the same time ensuring open-ended ecological integrity.[1]

From the beginning, democracy had to confront the assumption that aristocracy—rule of the best—was natural and democracy unnatural. Despite the derision and opposition of the aristocracy, democracy did manage to consolidate itself in some city states in ancient Greece, and the memory has never been forgotten, even though the ancient experiment lasted only a couple centuries. Since ordinary working people are always the majority, and they stand to benefit most, they carry within them, in their having a voice they need to express, even when—as for most of history—they have not been allowed to express it, the possibility of democratic resurgence. Even if they have not read it, their struggles give rise to the demand to realize the basic value of democracy that Thucydides invoked in "Pericles' Funeral Oration." "We are called a democracy," he wrote, "for the administration is in the hands of the many, not of the few. . . . There exists equal justice for all . . . poverty is not an obstacle, but a man may benefit his country whatever the obscurity of his condition."[2] Note that he does not say "Athens," but "we." Democracy is not a property of an abstract entity like a nation or a city-state, it is a relationship among people who treat one another as equals and organize their institutions to ensure that "the administration" is in the hands of the many.

The rejection of noble birth as a criterion of participation was a revolutionary idea: "The question raised by critics of democracy is not only whether people who have to work for a living have time for political reflection, but also whether those who are bound to the necessity of working in order to survive can be free enough in mind . . . to make political judgments. For Athenian democrats, the answer is, of course, in the affirmative."[3] The democratic achievement of the Athenians was extraordinary—the only known experiment with democracy in the ancient European and Asian worlds, and the last one until the rebirth of democratic politics in the English, American, and French Revolutions.[4]

Extraordinary it was, but also contradictory. It ran up against all three problems noted above. It answered the question about the scope of "the people" too narrowly. While working people were judged competent to speak, women and slaves were not. Hence the contradiction of classical politics: Economic barriers to political participation were abolished for Athenian peasants and workers, but citizenship was not extended to women and slaves. Moreover, it did not extend the principles of democratic rule into the household or the economy. Women and slaves were kept in subjection in the household, and while property was abolished as a condition of citizenship for men, it was not abolished altogether. Finally, it did not extend to Athens's relations to other cities and empires. Democracy at home was compatible with imperialism abroad. Athens could be as brutal to neighbors as any oligarchic or aristocratic state, "rationally" deliberating as a democratic collective whether to enslave and exterminate whole peoples.[5] Ultimately it was warfare that ended the Athenian democratic golden age.

The end of Athenian democracy was not the end of democracy. The idea that the people could rule was never forgotten. The history of struggle for democracy is also, at the same time, the history of trying to resolve the contradictions the original experiment exposed—to extend the scope of the people to include excluded groups, to extend democratic rule to all major social institutions, and to ensure that democratic governance is compatible with peaceful relationships within and between societies and does not undermine the ecological conditions of life on earth. Democracy has such a long history not only because the majority of people have an abiding interest in establishing it but also because it allows for argument and struggle about its proper scope in ways that more authoritarian structures cannot. Overcoming its contradictions does not lead to its abolition, as with authoritarian regimes, but its growth.

Most democratic theory has focused on political institutions: constitutional and common law bases of rights, the nature of representation, the logic of public political argument, the role of political parties, and the importance of the separation of powers. Attention to what I will call the social conditions of democratic life—the extension of democratic power into the family, economy, and social institutions—generally has typically been the problem of system critics (paradigmatically, Marxists, feminists, anti-imperialists, gay rights activists, black power militants). Their democratic credentials are held suspect by mainstream defenders of political democracy. Nevertheless, these radical critics call into question the adequacy of political democracy, but they do so in the name of better satisfying the conditions of democratic social life.

Political democracy demands equal rights to office and opportunity. If the availability of those offices and opportunities depends on an economic system that prioritizes private profits over the satisfaction of people's needs, or if it evaluates people according to cultural codes that mark some groups as inferior and incapable of doing certain jobs, and if people, regardless of their sex or racialized characteristics, are dependent on finding work in order to live, having money in order to become educated, and have no say in what they do or how they do it at work, then, even if they enjoy rights to vote and demand equal treatment, they will not be self-determining, and the society will not be democratic.

Political democracy is not an end in itself. Its value is instrumental to the realization of the human capacity for self-determination. History shows that the real goal of democratic struggles is not representation or constitutionally limited government but effective collective control over the institutions in which life-horizons are shaped. In turn, the end of democratic control over social institutions is the freedom of individual members of the groups that compose society to fully realize their creative capacities, making their lives meaningful, and contributing to the well-being of others, both in the present and in the future. This view can be substantiated by examining some paradigm democratic struggles.

DEMOCRACY AS A SOCIAL FORM:
HISTORICAL OVERVIEW

It is abundantly clear from the facts of cultural difference and historical change that human beings are not inert physical structures that are
merely acted upon by external forces but social self-conscious agents
whose creative activity maintains, produces, and changes the social
world. Social worlds are framed by natural laws and forces, but they
are properly steered by principles and laws that are products of human
practice. Political democracy presupposes this general human capacity to transform the natural world according to plans of our own. This
general capacity includes the ability to regulate social life according
to norms we self-consciously formulate, and this ability includes the
ability to evaluate those norms in terms of second-order principles (of
consistency, justice, goodness). Those second-order evaluations can
in turn inform movements for social change when they reveal that the
way things work is not the way they ought to work. The "ought" is the
metaphysical dividing line between natural events and political change:
Things happen in nature, but only human beings make things happen
because an active group among them believes that change ought to
happen.

Of course these capacities are not exercised in a vacuum. Nor do we
make history in circumstances of our own choosing.[6] Revolutions do
not happen for exclusively moral reasons; society must be in a state
of structural breakdown before second-order critiques of first-order
principles emerge and become effective. At the same time, revolutions
are not natural occurrences like volcanic eruptions. They are moments
of political creativity that involve "the vast masses of human beings in
action," in which the latent political agency of people formerly treated
as nothing but the objects of power become subjects of their own history.[7] In other words, struggles to democratize the social world are the
struggles of people to overcome the structural barriers to their capacity
to determine the laws and principles that govern their lives. Implicit
in this idea—but difficult to realize in practice, as we will see—is the
belief that the laws people will choose for themselves will equally serve
everyone's real interests in satisfying their needs and helping shape
collective life. Democratic law thus ought to overcome the alienation
between self-determination and power. When it is the work of citizens

themselves, to obey the law is to obey their own will, which is just another way of saying that they determine themselves and the terms under which they live together.

If we examine the history of democratic theory even briefly, we see the value of self-determination repeatedly invoked or implied. Although Plato was a critic of democracy, he argues that democracy arises from a revolution in which the poor overthrow their rich oppressors. "I suppose democracy comes about when the poor are victorious, killing some of their opponents and expelling others, and giving the rest an equal share in ruling."[8] The poor treat their oligarchic masters as an alien weight pressing down on them, impeding their ability to live freely, and they remove that weight through collective action. The struggle for democracy is impelled by the desire to realize their latent human capacity to determine their own lives.

A similar idea is at work in the different historical circumstances and political philosophy of John Locke. The democratic moment in Locke's work is found in the defense of revolution that concludes the *Second Treatise of Government.* He argues that revolutions against tyrannical rule are rare but inevitable when the abuse is long standing, because essentially free people eventually find tyranny unbearable. "For when the people are made miserable and find themselves exposed to the ill usage of arbitrary power, cry up their governors, . . . the same will happen. The people, generally ill-treated, and contrary to right, will be ready, on any occasion to loose themselves of a heavy burden that sits upon them."[9] Our capacity to determine our own conditions of life for the sake of ensuring that it is free underlies the right to rebellion. Our place in life is not fixed, according to Locke, and any power that tries to keep people wed in place for the sake of its own alien interests deserves to be overthrown.

In both Plato and Locke, democracy is linked to the power to overcome oppression, a power I am calling the power of self-determination. An important threshold is crossed when political theory and practice rejects the legitimacy of naturalized moral hierarchies and demonstrates that human beings *in fact* create their own societies. If it is true that human beings have the power to create their own societies and decide how they should be governed, then any group or social structure that actively prevents other groups from exercising their power of self-determination is oppressive. The contrary of democratic society is an oppressive society. Oppressive societies would not be *oppressive* if people lacked this power of self-determination. If one agrees there is such a thing as oppression and it ought to be overcome, then one must agree that the oppressed are capable of self-determination. However, both Plato and Locke, ancient democracy and emergent liberalism, drew the bounds of "the people" narrowly. The Greeks included laborers but excluded women and slaves. Locke excluded everyone except propertied men, and even the more radical Leveler movement during the English Civil War, which argued against property as a condition of citizenship, did not explicitly demand the inclusion of women in the circle of self-determining agents.[10] The problem here is not unique to the details of ancient Greek democracy or early liberalism, but expresses a contradiction between two forms of universality internal to the history of democracy: the contradiction between a false universalization of one arbitrary aspect of identity (class membership, sex, race) as definitive of humanity, and the concrete universality of shared needs and the capacity for social self-conscious agency. The false universal is ideological; its function is to justify the subaltern status of different classes, races, and sexes and their exclusion from political, economic, and cultural power by portraying them as less than human. Concrete universality, on the other hand, underlies all coherent criticisms of domination and oppression. Even when such criticism is launched from within the particular history of one group only, the capacity for self-determination the group activates in practice is universal, because it derives from the human powers to imagine and build worlds. Their oppressors deny they have this capacity; successful struggles prove the oppressors wrong.

Well, what of the unsuccessful struggles, a critic might rejoin? Do they prove that those who are struggling to make their voices heard have no legitimate claim? The Spartacus slave revolt failed. Did that prove they really *ought to have been enslaved*? The answer is no. Even the fact of organization, rejection, resistance, and the expression of the positive demand to be heard is proof that the dominated, oppressed, and exploited are equally social self-conscious people with their oppressors. Truly "inferior" people would never rebel. Over the long term, history provides sufficient evidence that all historically oppressed groups organize against the structures and groups that dominate them. Struggle and victorious struggle are different. Success might take a number of attempts, and even then might be partial. The capacity for self-determination, which is what is crucial here, is demonstrated by the reality of the struggle.

The material demands that underlie these struggles are the political and normative substance of radical criticisms of the limitations of liberal-democratic capitalist society. Marxism, feminism, and antiracist, anticolonialist theories all assert, even if sometimes in the language of class, sex, or race and not "humanity," that liberal-democratic capitalist society was not fully democratic because structural forms of exploitation, alienation, and oppression impeded the ability of the members of some groups to determine their life-horizons.

Marx's critical comments on "bourgeois democracy" and the totalitarian disaster of communism in the twentieth century lead to a colloquial misunderstanding of Marx as an antidemocratic thinker.[11] In truth, Marx began his career as a radical democratic critic of Prussian authoritarianism and continued throughout his life to try to understand the social and political conditions in which the universal human power of self-determination could be realized in the lives of each and all. As he put it, his goal was to help create a society in which "the free development of each is the condition of the free development on all."[12] The democratic implications of this goal are clear once we trace its origins back to Marx's critique of Hegel's conception of the free society.

For Hegel, a free society was one in which the people recognized the law as their own work. Marx accepts this generic definition, but argues that the people can only recognize the law as their own work if they are its authors. A free state must therefore be democratic. "In democracy none of the elements attains a significance other than what is proper to it. Each is in fact only an element of the whole *demos*. . . . The constitution appears as what it is: the free product of men."[13] When we obey laws of our own creation (or that accord with a constitution that was our own creation), we obey only ourselves, not an alien, coercive force, and are thus free: *self*-determining.

However, the freedom implicit in political democracy can only become explicit in the lives of the people when they control the material conditions of their lives in addition to being the authors of the laws. Contrary to liberalism, Marx maintains that the equal rights of citizenship are a necessary but not sufficient condition of democratic self-determination. Careful study of the actual operations of liberal-democratic norms led Marx to argue that class structure operates as a constraint on the ability of working people to effectively participate in political life and an unspoken but real limitation on the ability of political decisions to alter and remove class structure. The liberal revolutions of the eighteenth century abolished class as a condition of citizenship, but they did not abolish class as a coercive power over the working majority. "The limits of political emancipation are evident at once from the fact that the *state* can be a free state without man being a free man."[14] That situation can arise because "the political annulment of private property not only fails to abolish private property but even presupposes it. The state abolishes, in its own way, . . . distinctions of wealth . . . as non-political distinctions when it proclaims . . . that every member of the nation is an equal participant in the national sovereignty. Nevertheless, the state allows private property . . . to act . . . in [its] own way."[15] Private property determines the operations of the economic, or "private," sphere of society in which the profit-seeking choices of those who own productive assets give rise to social forces that shape the life-chances of workers who have no legitimate say in the use of those assets or the governance of the firms that control them.

At root, Marx is arguing that individual freedom depends on collective self-determination, which is impossible if a minority class controls the resources, wealth, and institutions that everyone's lives depend on. The development of liberal-democracy in capitalist society proves that political revolutions that extend the rights of citizenship are not sufficient conditions of democracy. The way in which the distinction between public and private is drawn in liberal capitalism ensures that the class with preponderant economic power can coercively determine the life-horizons of workers, even if they do not formally exclude workers from government. Their interests rule because formally democratic political institutions preserve and protect explicitly undemocratic economic institutions and forces, and those institutions and forces dominate the lives of those who must work within them to support themselves. Marx concludes that the democratization of the economy is a necessary condition of a democratic society.

Marx was not unaware that capitalist society was also patriarchal and racist, but his systematic contribution to democratic practice focused on the need to overcome class-based barriers to self-determination. Given that he did not explicitly thematize race and sex as structural causes of oppression, later Marxists often spoke as though class is one thing and race and sex something else entirely. Clearly, such formulations are both empirically untrue and politically problematic. Empirically, working class people are not aracial and sexless. Indeed, most of the world's workers are not white, and so—simply as a matter of empirical adequacy to reality—race, class, and sex have to be thought of together. Politically, the matter is more difficult, since not all criticisms of racial and sexual oppression lead in fully democratic directions. Liberal critiques of oppression prioritize the removal of formal barriers to participation, but reject arguments that white supremacy and patriarchy are deep structures that can only be overcome through radical social change. Furthermore, there have been important historical conflicts between radical critiques of white supremacy and patriarchy on the one hand and Marxist critiques of class exploitation and alienation on the other. These have arisen because empirically inadequate assumptions about working class race and sex identity have fed arguments that only class struggle can overcome the systematic barriers to oppression (i.e., that struggles against white supremacy and patriarchy, as important as they are, are not radical enough on their own).[16] As David Roediger argues in this regard,

> when these arguments press furthest . . . we are presented with the view that neoliberal elites countenance demands based on race, sex, and gender in order to divert attention from the real inequalities of class. Such a conspiracy theory trades on the kernel of truth that elites . . . do . . . attempt to shift the terms of struggles . . . into soporific categories of the "value of diversity" and "multiculturalism." . . . But this hardly makes popular antiracist struggles irrelevant or inimical to addressing class oppression.[17]

Indeed, since workers have concrete racial and sexual identities that structure their concrete lives *as workers*, antiracist or antipatriarchal struggles have to have socioeconomic impacts and goals, even though they are not reducible to them.

Where sex or race either excludes people from the circle of citizenship, or if it continues to impose additional burdens and inequalities by consigning them to the private sphere even after formal citizenship rights have been extended, then sexual and racial oppression are further structural impediments to collective self-determination. Whatever the actual demands that different feminist, anticolonialist, and antiracist groups have made, as *democratic* struggles they expose the way in which collective self-determination is impossible unless subaltern sexual and racialized groups are able to speak fully and freely, in their own voice. My own position, which I will develop more fully in the final chapter, is that the construction of solidarity, while always difficult, depends ultimately on our capacity to see beneath and within the set of demands that any group makes—the universal demand that the conditions for the full and free realization of the human power of self-determination be satisfied. The given demands vary depending on who is making them; they are complex and develop historically, but they are not ever mere "particulars" to be elevated to a higher universality via translation to one political language (say, Marxism) or another (say, radical feminism).[18] All demands for the satisfaction of fundamental human needs, inflected by the concrete identity of those whose lives they shape, are universal. Men have no need for access to abortion, and women have no need for prostate screenings, but both need health care. The political key is to work beneath the manifest form to the universal life requirement it expresses.

In order to prove to sexists and racists that they too are subjects, women and racialized people need to tell their own stories, articulate their own demands, and express the concrete ways in which their human needs have been denied and how they might be satisfied. If "the people" is composed of people who belong to oppressed groups, then the individuals who belong to them must be able to voice the specific ways in which they have been harmed and deprived. Humanity is, recall, a concrete universal, sameness of self-determining potential in different forms and expressions. What the struggles of women and racialized people prove, therefore, is not that self-determination is a false ideological universal that must be rejected in the name of democratic diversity but that democratic diversity depends on ensuring the satisfaction of the particular demands of historically oppressed groups *so that* their individual members can realize the potential for self-determination they share in because they are human beings.

Just as self-determination is the through-line that links ancient and modern, liberal and socialist theories of democracy, so too is it the through-line that links different permutations of feminist and antiracist struggle to each other, *and to the broader transhistorical struggle for democracy.* That the more radical versions of feminism and antiracist struggle see this connection most clearly is not surprising, because this clarity of vision is a function of their seeing how liberal forms of feminism and antiracism repeat the error of liberalism itself: limiting self-determination to the sphere of political rights. Of course, equal citizenship rights are an important step toward democratic self-determination, but democratic self-determination requires more than just political rights. Thus bell hooks, a strong critic of liberal feminism, argues that feminism is not just about equality under the law but, more deeply, "a struggle to end sexist oppression; therefore it is necessarily a struggle to eradicate the ideology of dominance . . . as well as a commitment to rearrange society so that the self-development of people can take precedence over imperialism, [and] economic expansion."[19] Self-determination for women requires a transformation of the line between public and private, a politicization of the sexual and familial that ends patriarchal control over women's bodies and self-understanding, and not just legal equality to compete with men within exploitative and oppressive structures.

An analogous argument can be made about anticolonial and antiracist movements. They too have identified a structural barrier to all-around need-satisfaction that impedes the full and free expression of racialized people's life-capacities. The struggle against racism, like the struggle against sexism and class exploitation, is, viewed from the democratic perspective, a movement that activates the self-determining power of racially oppressed people in movements against the structures that prevent them from satisfying their needs and freely realizing their individual goals and projects. On the anticolonialist side of antiracist struggle, Frantz Fanon provides the clearest understanding of their animating universal value. For Fanon, the very fact that colonized people can organize and fight back proves the humanity their racist oppressors deny them. "The native . . . laughs to himself every time he spots an allusion to the animal kingdom in the other's words. For he knows he is not an animal, and it is precisely at the moment that he realizes his humanity that he begins to sharpen the weapons with which he will seize his victory."[20] If recognition of humanity is the precondition of fighting back, it must be the case that "humanity" here means "power of self-determination." Once colonized people have recognized their humanity, they begin to fight back, and that fight is for democratic social forms within which that self-determining power can be realized as free individual life.

The same deep truth can be found in struggles against domestic racist structures. One hundred years before Fanon, Frederick Douglass noted the exact same link between recognition of humanity and self-determination. At the moment when he and others planned to escape from their plantation, they had to steel themselves for dangers they would face: "The strength of our determination was about to be tested . . . we had talked long enough; we were now ready to move . . . and if we did not intend to move now, we had as well . . . sit down, and acknowledge ourselves fit only to be slaves. This, none of us were prepared to acknowledge."[21] The true slave, as Aristotle argued, is a tool that uses other tools; someone that looks like a human being but is incapable of self-determination.[22] Douglass and his comrades confront this possibility: If they are too scared to seize freedom, then they would be Aristotle's true slave. But they discover that whatever the risk, freedom is worth it. Once they have recognized their humanity, there could be no other choice but to accept the risks and flee. Douglass was not, as Fanon was, a revolutionary, looking instead to the liberal principles of the American Constitution as the political justification for the struggle against racism and slavery. Yet he locates the impulse to freedom deeper than politics—in the power to determine our own conditions of life, a power slavery systematically *denies* but cannot *destroy*.

Kenyan political philosopher Makau Mutua understands the universal value of self-determination with unmatched clarity. Mutua argues that the right to self-determination is the most fundamental of all rights. When people are denied the power to determine their own collective life, then the abstract individual rights typically assumed to be fundamental by white liberals are meaningless because they operate in a field that is globally oppressive. "It is my argument that the most fundamental of all human rights is the right of self-determination, and that no other right overrides it."[23] Since human beings are social, individual freedom depends on collective freedom to decide the institutional structures within which individual lives are lived. If these institutional structures are imposed, by colonial or other forms of alien power, then the individuals living within those structures are unfree, whatever latitude for abstractly individual action they are given. Hence struggles for individual freedom always involve struggles to overcome the alienation of social power from collective decision making.

The principle of self-determination also provides us with the norm that we need to criticize actually existing societies, whatever they call themselves. Arbitrary political power, class exploitation, patriarchy, and racism are organized according to distinct logics, but they all have the effects of depriving those who suffer under them from accessing the resources and controlling the institutions they need to access and control if they are to determine their life-horizons. Societies become more democratic the more these distinct forms of exploitation, alienation, and oppression are *comprehensively* overcome. They are more comprehensively overcome when the systematic burdens and harms they impose upon people are eliminated. Materially speaking, these are eliminated when everyone can access what they need to realize their full potential as social self-conscious agents. These material harms are eliminated *democratically* when the major social institutions are governed by the deliberative power of self-organized citizens, and not the imperious commands of a ruling class or the mechanical force of reified social dynamics. In a fully democratic society, citizens satisfy their needs through their own productive labor, whose collective product is under their control, and whose use is decided on the basis of the recognized and acknowledged priority of need-satisfaction. Democratic citizens are not the objects of charity or welfare, but the subjects of their own reproduction, development, and flourishing.

LIFE-REQUIREMENTS
AND SELF-DETERMINATION

Democracies satisfy the fundamental conditions for the collective self-determination and individual self-realization of their members. However, no one is *born* a self-determining agent. We are born dependent on our mothers, the broader community in which she lives, and the biosphere upon which all life depends. The second and third forms of dependence never disappear, even if certain forms of egocentric blindness to life's conditions encourage forms of action that ignore them. Yet these forms of dependence are not necessarily oppressive, but simply frames within which we can become self-determining agents, if we respond appropriately to the challenges they pose.[24] If we live by the illusion that we are abstract egos with no obligations to anyone save those with whom we explicitly contract, then we will not only impoverish our relationships but, more seriously, allow those with greater bargaining power to rule society. If, by contrast, we recognize that we must live together, we can find the intrinsic good of social connection and consciously reorganize our major social institutions on its basis. The goal is to ensure that *collectively*, we govern in our shared real interests so that individually we can develop our cognitive, creative, and emotional abilities as fully as possible, limited by the demands of a healthy environment and the interests of others, but not undemocratic classes and social forces.

In general, the problem of democratic social life is the problem of how to organize major social institutions so as to recognize and serve the underlying social good of collective self-determination and, by extension, the shared good of enabling individuals to shape their own life-projects and life-horizons. Actual institutional design and change must take into account a mass of empirical details that philosophical examination of general problems must set aside. More importantly, since people are not generic mannequins but develop as human beings in definite cultures, histories, and languages, institutional change must take account of (but not be hostage to) these actual histories. The practical relevance of political philosophy is to identify and make a convincing case for the existence of the underlying social good and urge it as an organizing frame for and an orienting value of practical struggle for democratization. That is my aim here.

Making that case requires us to leave the realm of abstract values and examine the concrete, material, biosocial requirements of human life. Collective self-determination presupposes democratic control over the resources and institutions that produce the means of satisfying these requirements. Individual self-realization presupposes collective self-determination. If the resources and institutions that produce the means of satisfying our life-requirements are controlled by a minority class and their use determined by that class's decisions in response to reified social powers (such as market forces in a capitalist society), then the majority is dependent on the minority and *everyone* on those reified forces. Society is not self-determining, whatever its constitution might say, and is not, therefore, democratic. Individuals in that sort of society are thus doubly dependent, first on the ruling class and second on the state of the reified forces. This double dependence will be amplified for subaltern identities when class structure takes on patriarchal and racist tones. Unlike our dependence on the biosphere or general

interdependence on one another, these forms of dependence are illegitimate because they are harmful to those who live under them and are,
in principle, unnecessary. Illegitimate independence is overcome when
control over the resources and institutions that produce and distribute
key life-requirements is democratized. I will examine the question of
how new democratic movements to overcome illegitimate dependence
can be built in chapter 6. Here the key questions are: What are these
core human life-requirements, and what are the major social institutions
involved in their production and distribution?

Let us begin with a noncontroversial starting point. Democratic
forms of social life presuppose that their members are alive. Hence the
most basic political question that one can ask is: What are the basic
conditions of being alive? The question is political and not biological or
medical because human beings do not live on raw nature, but produce
the goods and services their lives require. Even in the case of hunter-
gatherer societies, the work of hunting and gathering must be distributed and coordinated and some means of distributing the findings or
killings worked out and agreed upon. When I speak of the "biosocial"
nature of human beings, I mean that for us, natural elements and forces
and our biochemistry are always expressed and experienced as a social
reality, shaped (but not invented) by physical and symbolic labor. Since
we are equally biological and social, our fundamental needs are both
biological and social.

The question "What are the conditions of being alive as a human
being?" is thus equivalent to the question, "What are our fundamental
human life-requirements?" To answer this question we must first distinguish needs as fundamental life requirements from needs that are
instrumental parts of particular projects from the unlimited number
of shapes our desires must take. We find the principle of distinction
in the higher degree of life-necessity that attaches to fundamental
needs. This higher degree of life-necessity is captured perfectly by
John McMurtry's N-criterion, which asserts: *"x is a need if and only
if, and to the extent that, deprivation of x regularly results in reduction of organic capacity."*[25] Consumer demand for commodities of all
sorts vastly outstrips the scope of our needs in this sense. So too, no
general philosophy of needs can comprehend, in advance, the tools and
instruments the successful realization of particular projects will require.
No democratic society can be obligated to satisfy what is in principle

limitless (consumer demand) or anticipate what any particular person will need to fulfil specific life-projects. The democratic problem is not to give the people what they want or every single thing they might need as a tool, but to ensure that the general conditions for collective self-determination and social self-conscious agency are satisfied for each and all. Those general conditions coincide with our fundamental natural and social life-requirements.

Whatever else anyone wants to do in life, he or she must be alive in order to do it. Hence democratic societies must ensure that everyone is furnished with the basic material inputs their organism requires: food energy, water, breathable air, clothing, homes, social spaces that are free from violence, and preventative and restorative medicine. These must be provided in ways that are environmentally sustainable over an open-ended future. To ensure that systems of production are coherently integrated with the carrying capacity of the environment, the broader culture affirms as good, forms of life that do not valorize wasteful forms of resource use.

It is true that human beings do not just eat; we create cuisines that are shaped as much by symbolic factors as nutritional values. Whether we get water from streams or bottles depends on the type of society we live in. Some people prefer naturopathic or traditional medicine to the scientific variety. These differences of need-satisfier are real, but the underlying needs are the same.[26] You can test it if you like. Decide that you do not need water of any sort, and test the hypothesis. I assume there will be no takers for the challenge (save perhaps someone who is suicidal). My argument accepts the reality and value of distinct cultural shapes of life, but, as shapes of *life*, they all depend on and grow up out of our natural history and the basic needs central to it.

Of course there is much more to life than the satisfaction of core physical needs. Democracy has not been an object of struggle for more than two millennia just because people need to eat. People also demand to develop and flourish as self-creative individuals. Humans have an evolved neural architecture that is capable of symbolic thought, imaginative transcendence of the given, planning, communication, artistic creation and scientific understanding and invention, mutualistic relationship, pleasure, care, solidarity, and joy. The realization of these properly human potentialities depends on the satisfaction of fully social life-requirements. They are as exigent conditions of *human* life as breathing and drinking are conditions of biological life. When social institutions are organized primarily to safeguard the unequal wealth and property of a ruling class and the structures and dynamics that enrich them, they deprive the majority of the sociocultural and political goods they need to live freely and fully as social self-conscious agents.

Sarah Clark Miller articulates clearly the connection between human needs and agency in her important work on the ethics of needs. "Fundamental needs," she writes, "are the needs that threaten agency in the sense that if they are not met, the serious harm of compromised agency will result."[27] Where my analysis differs from Miller's is in terms of focus and implications. For Miller, the reality of needs grounds a moral claim on others to help satisfy it. I agree with this broad claim, but my focus here is not on the relationship between needs and correlative *individual* duties, but on systematically unmet needs and democratic struggles to change social institutions charged with satisfying the most fundamental and universal of them. There is an ethical core to my position, but it is a *materialist* ethics, an ethics of struggle and social change, not an ethics of individuated obligation, at least not when public goods and the use of collectively produced wealth is at issue.[28]

The hinge between our basic biological needs and properly sociocultural and political needs is the emotional need for love and nurture. The institution that is initially responsible for the satisfaction of this need is the family. However, by "family" I mean only a structured organization of care, concern, and love. The family can be heterosexual and nuclear, same sex, single parent, or various forms of extended family. It could be constructed by people who are otherwise strangers under situations of severe emotional stress (such as between street people who band together). What is essential is that people have their needs for emotional care, love, and support met in a regular way by people they can trust. The political importance of the family was powerfully demonstrated by the universal repugnance shown toward the Trump administration's tearing children away from parents accused of illegally crossing the US border. What was at stake was not some antediluvian myth of the sacrosanct nuclear family but knowledge of the profound harm and trauma children suffer when they are torn away from loving parents (caregivers). The history of residential schools for indigenous Canadian children proved the same point, over a much longer time frame: Children are brutally harmed in their psychological development when they lack structured care and concern.[29]

The connection between family health and the economic system shows the problem of consigning family to the private sphere. Just as its ability to satisfy children's material needs depends on its place in economic life, so too, its emotional need-satisfying ability depends on the values of the broader culture. Where a patriarchal command imperative rules, the family becomes a site of abuse and domination. As Carol Gilligan and David A. J. Richards argue, "patriarchy precludes love between equals, and thus it also precludes democracy, founded on such love and the freedom of voice it encourages . . . the repression of free sexual voice plays . . . a central role in sustaining patriarchal modes of authority . . . recovery and the expression of such voice plays an important role in resistance."[30] Where children grow up in families where free sexual voice and egalitarian relationships structure the relationships between the adult partners, they learn the values of dialogue and reciprocity. Where patriarchal authority rules, they learn the power of command. Only the former is conducive to a democratic society.

As important as family life is, human beings must develop beyond its enclosure to live in the wider and more complex social world. Hence, we must discover and develop our capacities for thought, imagination, and creative construction through education. Like families, educational systems are contradictory. Educational institutions should be broadly understood to include cultural institutions like galleries and museums, community centers, public science centers, and all manner of informally organized groups structured by mutual interest. As important as all these institutions are, still by far the most important educational institution is the school. On the one hand, schools can be structures of control and hierarchical authority. However, we must not be led from this negative possibility to the belief that education is not a fundamental human social need. Just as we cannot be fully emotionally healthy and capable of recognizing and responding to others' emotional needs without the example of egalitarian and living relationships at home, so too, we cannot fully develop our intellectual and practical capacities without education. As is the case with families, the problem is not education as such but the way in which its institutional form is used to transmit existing system values in a repressive way. To educate is not to *train*; it is to open people to the possibility of thinking and doing differently. Built into every genuine educational experience, therefore, is the experience of using our intellectual and imaginative powers to think differently than we initially expected, to challenge the given, and to demand an account from authorities who say things must be as they are. Legendary educator Myles Horton, leader of the Highlander School, brings out the intrinsic connection between education and thinking beyond the established universe of theory and practice:

> I remember that somebody said that I was cruel. I was dealing with a group of young people and one of the girls cried because she said I made her very unhappy and that I should make people happy, not suffer. I said, well, . . . when they grow physically they have joy and pain. . . . Growing is a painful process, but they have joy in being young. I mean, what you are doing with the mind is the same . . . you should stretch people to their limits and our limits.[31]

A democratic society requires public schools, adequately furnished with the informational resources contemporary society demands, in which all students have an equal opportunity to develop their cognitive and imaginative capacities. At the same time, these schools must be governed by the imperative to prepare people to think and argue for themselves, in the service of the truth, not self-aggrandizement or personal advantage. The goal must be citizens who to think in the interest of discovering more comprehensive truth, not conformity with power. The goal here is not the anarchistic abolition of schools (as suggested most famously by Ivan Illich) but their democratization: the overthrow of schooling from within by the democratic displacement of administrative power within and the social power of money without.[32]

Individuals cannot be adequately furnished with basic material resources, families function as egalitarian centers of nurture and love, and schools cannot function as institutions in which imaginative and cognitive capacities freely develop unless the economic system through which wealth and income is generated is steered by the goal of satisfying people's needs. The capitalist system does satisfy some people's needs, but it leaves others completely deprived, the majority living in grossly unequal circumstances in comparison with the wealthy, demands money in exchange for most life-goods, and allows almost no democratic freedoms at work. It is not class interests outweighing all other interests that makes the economic system central to the struggle for democracy. Rather, it is that because life depends on access to core need-satisfiers, if we are dependent on an economic system that compels us to act in conformity with its imperatives in order to live and develop, and these imperatives dominate even democratic political decisions, then society cannot be democratic, even if its constitution says it is. My point was shockingly illustrated by the German finance minister, Wolfgang Schäuble, at the height of the Greek financial crisis. After Syriza was elected on a promise to renegotiate the terms the European Central Bank had imposed on Greece, Schäuble retorted: "Elections change nothing. There are rules."[33] The main rule is that capital must circulate freely to find the highest return. Everyone and everything must be determined by that imperative.

If our rights are thus conceived as rules that permit behavior *only within the limits tolerated by this imperative*, they are clearly inadequate guarantors of democratic society. Political and civil rights can be used in such a way that they mask the coercive and undemocratic operations of economic and social power behind the scenes. It does not follow that rights are nothing but such tools of coercive power. The history of struggle for rights as a central component of democratic struggles is proof enough that people need formal legal principles that protect spaces for thought, speech, self-expression, and so forth. What a democratic society requires is not monocultural uniformity, but an understanding that the value of rights is to protect the ability of people to become unique centers of social self-conscious agency so that they can contribute their talents and ideas to the democratic steering of society. At the same time, the democratic content of rights is not that they carve out a private sphere into which no one else may penetrate, but that they allow each person to contribute his or her voice to debates about what rules, principles, laws, and policies should govern our collective life. They enable the public realm, they do not hive individuals off from it. Unless everyone can make their argument, society cannot be self-determining, since the self-determination of a complex society depends on everyone explicitly agreeing to abide by the decision, and people cannot be expected to abide by a decision if they have been excluded illegitimately from the deliberations.

There is a final, all-encompassing human need that is touched by all the previous needs but which is not reducible to any of them: the need for free time. If the meaning and value of our lives depends in general on what we are able to do and experience within it, then the primary concern of any human being must be the amount of time a given form of social organization demands for forms of activity (like alienated labor) that lack life-value. Self-determination has an irreducible temporal dimension. The more time that is compelled from us in service to powers that treat us as fungible objects, the less time for self-determining activity we necessarily have. I have dealt with the nature and problem of free time as a comprehensive condition of good human lives elsewhere.[34] Here I want to confine my focus to its properly political dimensions.

It is clear that the determination of law and policy, the governance of major social institutions, and the direction of economic forces toward democratically agreed upon, need-satisfying, capacity enabling goals would make serious demands on the lifetime of individuals. If the need to work consumes so much time that people have none left over (after they rest and restore themselves) to devote to thinking about and participating in the debates through which political, social, and economic life is governed, then democracy will be seriously constrained. At best, people will consent to expert opinion in periodic elections. Democratization, therefore, must go hand in hand with a renewed effort to reduce the working day and week, freeing time for democratic participation in major social and political institutions. Such use of free time should not be seen as a constraint on individual freedom but, again, as with civil and political rights, an enabling condition of individual contribution to collective self-determination.

However, democratic self-determination faces a deeper temporal challenge than the amount of time people must work. Since the eighteenth century, capitalist society has been impelled by a techno-economic imperative of social acceleration. In a world where firms and countries are all in competition with one another, speed of decision making is a crucial competitive advantage. Social acceleration is the direct temporal antithesis of democratic deliberation. Democratic deliberation operates according to an open temporal matrix; it goes on until all positions have been fully heard and decision is taken. The temporal logic of social acceleration is closed; the decision must be taken in the least amount of time. That structure is closed because it *must* exclude that which is essential in democratic deliberation: reflection on ends or goals. Instead it must assume the given goal (winning the competition) as fixed and, simply, calculate (with automated means if possible) the quickest route to the goal. Hartmut Rosa explains the challenge this temporal structure poses for democracy. Social acceleration has disconnected the "diverse institutionalized structures of political will formation, decision-making, and decision-implementation in representative-democratic systems" from the "rhythm, tempo, duration, and sequence of social developments."[35] Unless the contradiction between these two temporal systems—the open matrix of political argument and the closed structure of competitive decision making—can be resolved in favor of the former, wider and deeper democratization will be impossible.

I regard questions of political possibility and impossibility also as problems about time. That which is impossible in one era proves possible in another. It seems impossible to slow down the pace of social and economic life within the complex of forces that exist today. Small inroads can create sufficient space for bigger imaginations, and bigger imaginations can continue to pry open more space for creative practical changes. Nevertheless, we are not dealing at present with practicalities but needs, and it is clear that human beings need time, in general, to act and experience, but also, in particular, to participate as democratic subjects.

The struggle to free life-time from domination by alien powers and alienated labor is the implicit unifying ground of all struggles for self-determination. Even when they are not explicitly struggles to shorten working time, all struggles that achieve their goal of freeing the satisfaction of natural and social needs from the coercive domination of market forces and oppressive forms of domination have the effect of freeing life-time for self-directed development. If, for example, a student must work forty hours a week in alienated labor to pay their tuition, this is forty hours lost to other, nonalienated, self-determined uses. If in response to student struggles, the government uses its taxing power to raise sufficient revenue to eliminate tuition fees, the student would be able to free those forty hours of life-time from alienated labor and devote it to studies, cultural experiences that support that education, and his or her relationships. If, to give another example, there is a gender and racial wage gap, then, on average, members of the subaltern sexes and races will have to devote more time to alienated labor just to reproduce themselves and their families. Successful struggle to overcome those wage gaps (and the sexist and racist ideologies that legitimize them) thus frees time for each member of the subaltern group.

As the unifying ground of struggle, this underlying structure of human natural and social needs does not deny social and cultural and individual differences, but explains how they arise from the same creative capacities acting in different contexts. Unless we are in control of the processes through which our needs are satisfied, we are reduced to the objects of the powers that control them, which will in turn control what anyone can do or be. When we gain control, we gain the power of choice and self-determination. For example, if you are in prison, the warden will decide what you will eat, and if he wants to feed vegetarians meat, their only alternative choice will be to starve. If we collectively ensure food security for all, and recognize that our need to eat comes with moral and cultural contours, we can create a system where everyone satisfies their need to eat in their own way. So too with every other core human need. It is a need because our lives and social self-conscious agency depend on satisfying them. That does not entail any one particular means of satisfaction. Liberal-democracy, however, has consistently portrayed demands that society focus first of all on need-satisfaction as contrary to the interests of free individuals. I will consider the problem of the liberal understanding of democracy in the next chapter.

NOTES

1. John McMurtry, *Philosophy and World Problems, Volume 1: What is Good? What is Bad? The Value of all Values Through Time, Place, and Theories* (Oxford: EOLSS Publishers, 2011), 243.

2. Thucydides, "Pericles Funeral Oration," University of Minnesota Human Rights Library, http://hrlibrary.umn.edu/thucydides.html (accessed March 22, 2017).

3. Ellen Meiksins Wood, *Citizens to Lords: A Social History of Western Political Thought from Antiquity to the Middle Ages* (London: Verso Books, 2008), 39.

4. I say "European and Asian" to hold open the possibility that one might find in indigenous peoples of Africa and (what is today) North and South America forms of life democratic arrangements that remained unknown or at least untheorized in Western and Eastern philosophy and political theory. I will return to the importance of indigenous peoples' struggles in chapter 6.

5. In the Melian dialogue, for example, Thucydides reports on the argument between Athenians and the rebellious Melians. The subject: the justice of putting the men of the rebellious city to death and enslaving its women and children; https://www.shsu.edu/~his_ncp/Melian.html (accessed April 4, 2017).

6. Karl Marx, "The Eighteenth Brumaire of Louis Napoleon," *The Marx-Engels Reader*, Robert C. Tucker, ed. (New York: W. W. Norton, 1978), 595.

7. Sheldon Wolin, "Constitutional Order, Revolutionary Violence, and Modern Power: An Essay of Juxtapositions," *Fugitive Democracy and Other Essays*, Nicolas Xenos, ed. (Princeton, NJ: Princeton University Press, 2016), 435.

8. Plato, *The Republic*, G. M. A. Grube, trans., revised by C. D. C. Reeve (Indianapolis, IN: Hackett Publishing, 1992), 227 (557a).

9. John Locke, *Second Treatise of Government* (Indianapolis, IN: Hackett Publishing, 1980), 113.

10. For Leveler demands and principles see Christopher Hill, *The World Turned Upside Down* (Harmondsworth, UK: Penguin, 1975), 38.

11. August H. Nimtz Jr. dispels this myth once and for all by a meticulous reading of the actual history of Marx and Engels's engagement with democratic politics and the deeply democratic commitments of their own practice. See August H. Nimtz Jr., *Marx and Engels: Their Contribution to the Democratic Breakthrough* (Albany, NY: State University of New York Press, 2000).

12. Karl Marx and Friedrich Engels, *Manifesto of the Communist Party* (Moscow: Progress Publishers, 1986), 54.

13. Karl Marx, "Contribution to the Critique of Hegel's Philosophy of Law," *Karl Marx Friedrich Engels: Collected Works*, vol. 3 (New York: International Publishers, 1978), 29.

14. Karl Marx, "On the Jewish Question," *Karl Marx Friedrich Engels* (New York: International Publishers, 1978), 152.

15. Ibid., 153.

16. See, for example, David Harvey, *Seventeen Contradictions and the End of Capitalism* (Oxford, UK: Oxford University Press, 2014), 166.

17. David Roediger, *Class, Race, and Marxism* (London: Verso Books, 2017), 11.

18. Ibid., 157.

19. bell hooks, "Feminism: A Movement to End Sexist Oppression," *Feminisms*, Sandra Kemp and Judith Squires, eds. (Oxford, UK: Oxford University Press, 1997), 24–25.

20. Frantz Fanon, *Wretched of the Earth* (New York: Grove Press, 1963), 42–43.

21. Frederick Douglass, *A Narrative of the Life of Frederick Douglass, An American Slave* (New York: Penguin, 1982), 125.

22. Aristotle, "Politics," *The Basic Works of Aristotle*, Richard McKeon, ed. (New York: Random House, 1966), 1133 (1254b, 15–20).

23. Makau Mutua, *Human Rights: A Political and Economic Critique* (Philadelphia: University of Pennsylvania Press, 2002), 108.

24. I explore the connection between these "frames of finitude" and good human lives in *Embodiment and the Meaning of Life* (Montreal: McGill-Queen's University Press, 2018).

25. McMurtry, *Philosophy and World Problems*, 110. McMurtry first formulated this criterion in his 1998 work, *Unequal Freedoms* (Toronto: Garamond, 1998), 164.

26. The term "need-satisfier" comes from the work of Len Doyal and Ian Gough, *A Theory of Human Need* (New York: Guilford Press, 1991), 168. I explore their argument in more depth and explain how my own position differs in *Democratic Society and Human Needs*.

27. Sarah Clark Miller, *The Ethics of Need: Agency, Dignity, and Obligation* (London: Routledge, 2012), 17.

28. A full explanation of this materialist ethics would take us too far afield. See Jeff Noonan, *Materialist Ethics and Life-Value* (Montreal: McGill-Queen's University Press, 2012).

29. The evidence for this claim is elaborated in detail in the final report of the Canadian Truth and Reconciliation Commission on Residential Schooling. The full report can be found at http://www.trc.ca/websites/trcinstitution/index.php?p=890 (accessed August 8, 2018).

30. Carol Gilligan and David A. J. Richards, *The Deepening Darkness: Patriarchy, Resistance, and Democracy's Future* (New York: Cambridge University Press, 2009), 19.

31. Myles Horton and Paolo Friere, *We Make the Road by Walking: Conversations on Education and Social Change* (Philadelphia: Temple University Press, 1990), 175.

32. Ivan Illich, *De-Schooling Society* (London: Marion Boyars, 2002).

33. Wolfgang Schäuble, quoted in Gavin Hewitt, "Greece, The Dangerous Game," British Broadcasting Corporation, February 1, 2015; https://www.bbc.com/news/world-europe-31082656 (accessed July 8, 2017).

34. Noonan, *Materialist Ethics and Life-Value*, 78–84.

35. Hartmut Rosa, *Social Acceleration: A New Theory of Modernity* (New York: Columbia University Press, 2015), 252.

Chapter 2

Liberalism and Democracy

The classical liberal principles of equality, individual rights, consent to government, and the rule of law are typically understood as synonymous with democracy. Despite this assumed synonymy, I will argue that there are fundamental tensions between the *democratic* value of collective self-determination and the classical liberal interpretation of individual rights and liberty. From the democratic perspective, self-determination is first of all a shared achievement that depends on collective control over universally required life-resources and their use in life-sustaining and enhancing ways. In liberalism, on the contrary, individuals are abstracted from the social whole and rights institutionalized in ways that contradict collective self-determination. In practice, historically, the liberal opposition between collective self-determination and the right to private property has meant the subordination of the democratic power of the whole to the economic power of the class that controls universally required resources and institutions.

This tension marks the development of liberalism on the international scale as well. As Beate Jahn has shown, as far back as Locke, a complex dialectic of national development and colonial domination shaped the emergence of liberal-democratic capitalist societies. "Colonialism," Jahn notes, "played a crucial role for economic development in Europe. . . . It allowed the domestic poor and politically disenfranchised to emigrate and thus relieved the political pressure on the government. And it allowed the government to export its poor . . . [and] provided common political ground for rich and poor alike."[1] The common ground was an alliance against the indigenous population now subordinate to colonial power. The internationalization of liberal-democracy, therefore, intensifies rather than solves its domestic contradictions.

These tensions have left liberalism susceptible to change through democratic struggles. The complex history of liberalism from the late seventeenth century until today is a series of theoretical and practical attempts to coherently synthesize the democratic implications of its understanding of equality with the undemocratic implications of its understanding of liberty. The results have been uneven. It would be ahistorical to argue that liberalism is completely undemocratic. It is obvious that part of what oppressed groups have fought for are inclusive interpretations of the political and civil rights denied them. Moreover, while democracy requires that people have determining power over the major social institutions that shape their life-horizons, this principle is not incompatible with representative institutions. People cannot be constantly engaged in political deliberations and still have time for other meaningful forms of self-realization. Finally, to say that individual self-determination is not a property of abstract individuals but an achievement of democratic social organization is not to say there should be no private sphere of life. The democratic goal is not to abolish privacy and individuality, but rather to ensure that both take forms that cohere with the general demands of environmental integrity, social peace, and universal flourishing.

I will argue that the key problem with liberal-democracy originates in the classical liberal conception of individual liberty and the social conditions in which it developed. In its canonical form, liberalism argued that the natural liberty and equality of individuals established strict limits to state power, whether democratic or not. The private sphere included both family and economic life. The father should rule the family, and the property owner should rule the economy. Political incursions into the private sphere are tyrannical. In the earliest years of liberalism, when the African slave trade flourished, the principle of private property extended to other human beings. Hence, this way of drawing the line between public and private meant that the liberty of white propertied men was purchased at the cost of the oppression of women in the family; slaves on the plantations of the American South, Brazil, and the Caribbean; and the exploitation of workers of all sexes and races in emergent capitalist industry.

One does not have to be an expert logician to see that a philosophy of freedom that asserts the equality of all "men" (i.e., human beings) and yet treats women, blacks, and propertyless males as mere objects to be used is self-contradictory. The Levelers, who argued for universal manhood suffrage in the English Civil War, liberal feminists like Mary Wollstonecraft and Olympe de Gouges during the French Revolution, anticolonial revolutionaries like Toussaint Louverture in San Domingo (Haiti), and abolitionists in antebellum America were all quick to expose these contradictions. Their struggles are the practical basis for the self-transformation of classical liberalism. This self-transformation redrew the public-private distinction, widened the franchise to include all adult human beings, and redistributed income and enacted affirmative action programs in the service of material, not merely moral and legal, equality. Nevertheless, despite these developments, even contemporary egalitarian, cosmopolitan liberalism has never fully resolved its contradictions. All liberalisms confine democratic power to political institutions and social democratization to the regulation, rather than transformation, of institutional sources of coercive power. This chapter will focus on the reasons all forms of liberalism are inadequately democratic limitations of liberalism. I will begin with classical liberalism and then explore its progressive democratization over the past three centuries by egalitarian liberals, republicans, and cosmopolitan liberals.[2]

CLASSICAL LIBERALISM

From its origins, liberalism has had an ambivalent relationship with democracy. Recognizably liberal ideas about individual freedom and equality began to emerge around the time of the English Civil War, but their first systematic articulation, in the work of Thomas Hobbes, yielded a theory of undivided sovereignty, preferably in the person of an absolute monarch. John Locke's *Second Treatise of Government* would become the first classical liberal text. Locke's major concern was not popular self-government but the consent of free and equal people to political authority. Locke assumed that people were more interested in increasing their wealth than directly exercising political power. Locke's argument elevated the natural rights of male property owners over popular participation and allowed the principle of private property to extend to lands expropriated from colonized peoples, and even some people themselves (slaves).[3] There are democratic elements to his position, but it is more a theory of limited government than democratic self-determination.

Locke's classical liberal conception of freedom, equality, and natural rights prioritizes the value of private life over collective action. Politics is not an intrinsically valuable human activity; there is no celebration of the intrinsic value of collective self-determination. There are threats to health and wealth that people must defend against, but the focus of classical liberalism is on the danger of state power, not the value of citizens deciding together how their common life will be governed. The limits of even democratic government are established by natural rights to the security of the person and private property. "Man being born," Locke argues, "with a title to perfect freedom, and an unconstrained enjoyment of all the rights and privileges of the law of nature, equally with any other man . . . hath by nature a power, . . . to preserve his property, that is, his life, liberty, and estate. . . . Because no political society can be . . . without having in itself the power to preserve property . . . there only is political society where everyone of the members hath quitted this natural power, resigned it up into the hands of the community."[4] The self-determining power of the property owners is exercised by erecting barriers to *any* power, from above or below, interfering with their natural rights.

There is, nevertheless, a democratic moment: Political power originates from the consent of the people. The undemocratic underside is more powerful. It reveals that political power is barred from governing areas of *social* life that can exert coercive power over those members of the "community" who have no formal share of political power. Hence the immanent contradiction: An exclusionary class project of white men to safeguard their property is identified with the "community" as a whole. They reduce the majority to the status of silent objects of power, even though everyone is supposedly born free and equal.

In its earliest years, liberalism remained blind to that contradiction and focused its attention on the problem of limiting democratic power. In the American Revolution it was James Madison who saw most clearly the tension between democratic power and individual liberty. He argued that a free state cannot allow the untrammeled collective power of citizens to decide every issue. If that were permitted, then the workers and the poor would always carry the legislative day, using their political power to "confiscate" the property of the rich, destroying their liberty, and undermining the very purpose of political power: to protect property. He disguises this argument as a critique of political factions, but his real concern is to check the democratic power of the propertyless majority.[5] "The most common and durable source of factions has been the various and unequal distribution of property. Those who hold, and those who are without, property have ever formed distinct interests in society."[6] If the majority have democratic power to determine legislation, they will use it in the material interests to redistribute property in violation of the liberal principle of absolute security of property. "The apportionment of taxes . . . provides the greatest opportunity and temptation . . . to a predominant party, to trample on the rules of justice."[7] If slaves were given the vote, they would obviously abolish slavery. If the poor were given the vote, they would tax the rich to alleviate their poverty. Both votes would be contrary to the laws of justice in Madison's view, even though they would be democratic.

The contradiction immanent to the classical liberal conception of equality catalyzed the struggles of excluded workers, women, slaves, members of other subaltern racialized groups, and minorities for inclusion and substantive freedom. Initial success on the part of working class men in England did not resolve the ambivalence but only heightened classical liberal fears. By the time John Stuart Mill was working in the mid-nineteenth century, the franchise had been extended to working males, who seemed inclined to bring Madison's prophecies about progressive taxation to reality. Rather than see this willingness of the majority to involve itself in politics as a victory for human freedom, Mill worried that when democracy violates the security of property, it risks becoming tyranny (of the majority).[8] Hence the problem for Mill was how to limit the class power of democratic majorities, at least until they are sufficiently enlightened to understand that the real foundation of a free society is individual liberty.

The problem is not that Mill was unaware of the way in which structural forces of a capitalist and patriarchal society can undermine the liberty of workers and women, rendering ideological the hymns that the ruling class sings to freedom and liberty. In his essays on socialism he recognizes that capitalism is brutally exploitative and undermines the value of workers' formal equality.[9] He looks forward to a time when social evolution has overcome all structural impediments to the full flourishing of workers' personalities.[10] With his partner Harriet Taylor, he helped shape the principle of the liberal feminist critique of patriar-chy.[11] Still, despite these real democratic elements of his work, when pushed up against the wall of class power by movements from below, Mill chose property over democracy.

In his reflections on democratic government, Mill's main concern is to avoid "class government." He establishes an equivalence between ruling class and working class government. Both are illegitimate, he claims, because both conflate the general public interest with their own exclusive class interest. "Democracy," he claims, "is not the ideally best government, unless this weak side of it can be strengthened."[12] Mill's solution is to obviate the danger of class government by reducing the value of the working class vote through a system of weighted voting. The details are of no interest here. Noting it highlights the problem: At moments of intense conflict between security of property and demo-cratic self-determination, even the most democratic classical liberals have sided with property, with the undemocratic power of white men.

Contradictions either destroy a theory or force it to change. In the case of classical liberalism, it changed. In the twentieth century, egali-tarian liberal philosophers abandoned the formalist conception of equal-ity typical of classical liberalism and reformulated it as a substantive value, opening the door to a more democratic liberalism.

EGALITARIAN LIBERALISM

The common complaint against classical liberalism is that its concep-tion of moral equality was inconsistent with its strong defense of prop-erty rights. If people were morally equal, they should not be subject to arbitrary power. If some control that which others need to survive, those others will be, in effect, dependent on the owners, regardless of their moral and legal status. The inability of classical liberalism to deal with the problem of substantive, structural inequalities—inequalities not due to accidental features like luck but built into the basic organization of socioeconomic life—underlies the Marxist critique of classical liberal-ism, as we saw in chapter 1.[13] It has also prompted a self-criticism that has proven enormously influential, so much so that—in the United States at least—"liberalism" and wealth redistribution are nearly syn-onymous today.[14]

In practice, the development of egalitarian liberalism was forced by a series of struggles against the underlying structures of material inequality protected by classical liberal conceptions of private property. Philosophically, its predominance in the latter half of the twentieth century is largely due to the work of John Rawls. In many respects Rawls's *Theory of Justice* was a product of its times, an attempt to provide a unifying ethos that could restore harmony to the fractious American republic after the tumult of the civil rights movement, black power, women's liberation struggles, the anti–Vietnam War movement, and student rebellions of the 1960s. Rawls's proposed solution has also had universal implications, not least of which is a resetting of the dominant interpretation of individual rights and the social conditions of equal liberty.

In order to assess the democratic value of Rawls's work, we need to examine three key aspects: (1) Rawls's understanding of self-determination, (2) the role of the difference principle in establishing material equality, and (3) the role the political agency of the subaltern plays in establishing material equality.[15]

From the standpoint of democratic theory, the most important section of *Theory of Justice* is the least commented on: part three. Here Rawls digs beneath the machinery of justification to discuss the deepest values of liberal society. He turns to the work of Wilhelm von Humboldt for the idea of society as a "social union of social unions." In this view, a free society is one that enables its individual members to fully realize their talents. Individuals see their own good expressed as the contribution their life makes to society and the good of other individuals.

> Thus we can say, following von Humboldt, that it is through social union founded upon the needs and potentialities of its members that each person can participate in the total sum of the realized assets of the others. We are led to the notion of a community of humankind the members of which enjoy one another's excellence and individuality elicited by free institutions, and they recognize the good of each as an element in the complete activity the whole scheme of which is connected to and gives pleasure to all.[16]

Rawls's formulation lacks the poetic concision of "from each according to his [and her] abilities, to each according to his [and her] needs," but the underlying idea is the same. In contrast to what Rawls calls "private society," citizens of a democratic society do not see their good as exclusively their own, but understand that it depends on social organization and desire that their life make a positive difference to others' lives.[17] In other words, at the level of fundamental value commitments, Rawls sees democratic society as I do: as a form of social life in which decisions about resource use are made collectively in the interests of individuals as social self-conscious self-determining agents, who in turn see themselves as individual members whose good requires that they contribute back to the community.

The centrality of this conception of society as a cooperative enterprise for mutual self-development has led some recent interpreters to claim that Rawls is better understood as a socialist rather than a liberal defender of the welfare state. William A. Edmundson maintains that Rawls was a "reticent socialist" who rejected both laissez-faire and welfare state capitalism because both failed to secure the social conditions for the self-realization of all citizens. In Rawls's just society, everyone had to have real equality of opportunity to flourish, and that goal could only be secured if private property was limited to personal property for use. Major public assets and industries would be state owned. "The expressive significance of social ownership flows directly from Rawls' most famous conception: that of society as a cooperative scheme for mutual advantage."[18] Social ownership is a condition of realizing this democratic conception of society, because private ownership of the means of production allows "owners to hoard or dispense of their winnings as they see fit," leaving "losers" once again as "dependents," not equal participants in social life.[19] Rawls's idea for social ownership is nationalization, on the model of postwar British social democracy, and he says nothing of substance about the political means of arriving at that goal.[20] It is this silence as to means of transition, combined with his insistence on the need to rely on markets to allocate resources and investments and his elevation of the importance of fixed constitutional principles over social power from below, that limits the democratic value of his socialism (or, perhaps better, social democracy).

At best, Rawls would be a proponent of a version of what Hal Draper called "socialism from above."[21] The influence of postwar British social democracy and its model of state ownership reveals that what Rawls had in mind is not social ownership of the means of production as Marx envisaged it, democratic stewardship of the economy in the twin interests of need-satisfaction and capacity development, but state management from above. While this model might solve some problems of more laissez-faire versions of capitalism, it does not necessarily democratize firms or economic life as a whole, and it is difficult to square with Rawls's repeated affirmations of the necessity and efficiency of markets. This is not the place for a detailed critique of the possibility of "market socialism," but the problem that markets pose for the socialist goal of directing the economy to preconceived just ends is that they generate their own forces when allowed to operate as the institutions by which society allocates its resources.[22] Where markets allocate resources, they allocate them to the most "efficient" use, which in capitalism means the most profitable use. A socialist market, presumably, would substitute "need-satisfaction" for "profit," *but that substitution is impossible without planning, and planning, by definition, replaces market forces as the primary allocative institution.* Rawls nowhere acknowledges this contradiction, nor does Edmundson discuss it or try to resolve it. The important point here is political and not economic. If markets are allowed to allocate resources, they will allocate them according to the reified power they generate, and not according to goals democratically decided on.

We can see the impact of this problem if we look at what Rawls actually says about economic matters in *Theory of Justice*. He does not argue that citizens should organize and reappropriate the life-serving resources of nature and the wealth produced by their collective labor from the ruling class, but instead relies on a bureaucratic redistributive system justified by his "difference principle." The difference principle asserts that inequalities of wealth and income are permitted if, and only if, they are in the interests of the least well-off.

Assuming the framework of institutions required by equal liberty and fair equality of opportunity, the higher expectations of those better situated are just if and only if they work as part of a scheme which improves the expectations of the least advantaged members of society. The intuitive idea is that the social order is not to establish and secure the more attractive prospects of those better off unless doing so is to the advantage of the less fortunate.[23]

Whether he is a reticent socialist or not, Rawls clearly relies here on an assumption familiar from mainstream economics that connects motivation to produce with expected income. In this view, the rich are the more productive members of society, but they will lack incentive to be productive unless they are rewarded with higher income. In practice, as we know from actual history, they will always argue for the lowest possible rate of taxation on grounds that Rawls seemingly allows them to occupy: Economic "efficiency" will be compromised if the rich cannot enjoy the full fruits of their investment. Hence it is unclear in practice just how great inequalities could be under Rawls's scheme, but it is clear (if actual debates about appropriate tax rates are our guide) that wildly different conclusions can be drawn from the premise that *some* inequality is required as motivation for higher levels of productive effort.

There is a deeper problem with Rawls's position. Regardless of whether one sees the motivation argument as sound psychology or self-serving ideology, it is clearly inconsistent with the explanation of motivation in a democratic society discussed above. On that view, people thought of themselves as equal members of a community and were motivated to do whatever they did because they saw their talents as contributions to the overall good of the community and other people as equal members of it. Here, without saying so, Rawls clearly assumes that the rich are class conscious and act primarily in their interests as owners of capital and productive resources. They may agree to redistributive taxation, but it is clear that the difference principle assumes strong class differences and does nothing to overcome them, socially or psychologically.

Defenders of Rawls such as Edmundson may argue that this objection really amounts to nothing, that what matters in the end is redistribution and not how it is justified. However, democratic self-determination is not grounded simply in redistribution after the fact (although progressive taxation is crucially important as a step in the right democratic direction). A fully democratic society has to overcome class differences, because where there are class differences there are deep inequalities of social power. Where there are deep inequalities of social power, those who have less or none are dominated, and where any group is dominated, the society cannot be a self-determining whole. Both *Theory of Justice* and *Political Liberalism* ignore the problem of mobilizing workers and subaltern groups (which are unmentioned in either *Theory of Justice* or *Political Liberalism*). Instead of arguing that social movements have the responsibility to identify and correct impediments to the full realization of democratic values—and, indeed, celebrating these as the engine of democratic change—Rawls looks to a bureaucratically managed welfare system that redistributes an undefined amount of income downward, without any explicit input form the "least well-off" themselves. Hence, Rawls gives us redistribution on terms that the ruling class can accept: enough to maintain social piece, but not enough to seriously disrupt the foundations of class power in private ownership and control over universally required life-resources. Such limits are necessary to ensure the possibility of what Rawls calls in *Political Liberalism* "overlapping consensus," but it is purchased at the cost of democratic struggle. "What is crucial," he argues, "is always to recognize the limits of the political and the practical. First, we must stay within the limits of justice as fairness as a political conception of justice that can serve as the focus of an overlapping consensus."[24] In concrete terms this means compromise on the fundamental issue of who controls that which all need to survive and develop, and that compromise means that *in reality*, as opposed to ideal theory, those resources will remain in private hands.

Thus, instead of a social union of social unions in which each devotes itself to the good of all, receiving what they need and contributing back to the common wealth through their own projects, we have a class society that limits the scope and efficacy of subaltern agency. Sheldon Wolin identifies the problem precisely: Rawls relies on "policy makers to keep democracy at bay."[25] He elaborates:

> The "consistent" solution is an apolitical philanthropy and no more democratic: "Social and political inequalities whether great or small," are to be adjusted "to the greatest benefit to the least advantaged members of society." Rawls acknowledges that the formula is "hardly clear" . . . but one consequence is clear: the least well off will be passive recipients who will have their material lot eased because a redistributive mechanism acceptable to the "haves" is in place.[26]

Democratic control over the use of universally required life-resources, the deepest social condition of democracy, and one explicitly affirmed by Rawls in part three of *Theory of Justice*, is thus not satisfied by the socioeconomic policy actually demanded by *Theory* and *Political Liberalism*. Rawls demands equality in the distribution of "primary goods." These are goods that rational people want because they "have a use whatever a person's rational plan of life: rights, income, and opportunities.[27] However, this equality is not achieved or maintained by democratic control over natural wealth and economic institutions.

An analogous problem undermines the democratic value of the thinker who has pushed Rawls's political liberalism as far as it can go in the interests of substantive equality and individual self-determination, Martha Nussbaum. Her "capabilities approach" to social justice argues that it demands more than mathematical equality of access to Rawls's primary goods.[28] Following Amartya Sen, she sees the goal of social life as maximizing the freedom to "do and be" the things that citizens have reason to do and be.[29] In order to maximize the space of civic freedom, governments must ensure that all conditions for the satisfaction of a comprehensive set of "capabilities" are met for all citizens. Her approach was developed when she was working in close connection with feminist activists in the Global South.[30] This work sensitized Nussbaum to the way in which gross material inequality undermines agency, and the way in which sex exacerbates material inequality. There is a much sharper rhetorical edge to Nussbaum's work than that of Rawls.

The fundamental principle of the capabilities approach is that social legitimacy depends on ensuring individual freedom.

> The Capabilities Approach can be provisionally defined as an approach to comparative quality-of-life assessment and to theorizing about basic social justice. It holds that the key question to ask . . . is, "What is each person able to do and be?" In other words, the approach takes *each person as an end*, asking . . . about the opportunities available to each person. It is *focused on choice or freedom*, holding that the crucial good societies should be promoting for their people is a set of opportunities, or substantial freedoms, which people then may or may not exercise in action.[31]

There is much to commend in this approach, zeroing in as it does on the good life as free activity, and free activity as conditioned by the scope of access to natural and social means of life. Yet, like Rawls, Nussbaum sees need-satisfaction as a wholly passive affair: Societies will pursue *"for* their people" substantive freedoms [emphasis added]. That goal is very different from democratic self-organization and collective control over the natural and social means of life and self-development. Democracy affirms the agency and subjecthood of people; Nussbaum invokes it at the level of individual life-project but denies it at the level of basic socioeconomic forces, which remain under the control of a minority. Nussbaum also invokes quite standard liberal fears of democratic exuberance. Like Mill, she is concerned that the unbridled use of democratic power can cause social injustice. Hence she looks to the constitution and the courts, rather than political self-education, as the cornerstone of protection for the capabilities approach. "I have . . . connected the capabilities list to the part of the nation's written constitution . . . that elaborates citizens' fundamental entitlements. I have offered a set of capabilities-based templates for the work of the US Supreme Court."[32] There is not one word here about the role that democratic struggles have played historically in giving voice to unmet needs. There is certainly value to having core material entitlements anchored constitutionally, but, as Wolin reminds us, constitutions can substitute themselves for democratic power. He is criticizing American liberals generally, but he could just as easily have been criticizing Nussbaum when he wrote that "Constitutional democracy is democracy fitted to a constitution . . . it is democracy without the demos as actor."[33] Like classical liberals, Nussbaum looks to the constitution not as the active expression of individuals politically constituting themselves as a people (as Marx did), but as a constraint on democratic action:

> The empowerment of people through democratic procedures is a shared aim of most people working on the Capabilities Approach. . . . Too frequently, however, the word "democracy" is insufficiently defined. Most modern democracies have a place for rights entrenched beyond the reach of majority vote, and I would argue that if democracy means "the people rule," such entrenchment is a necessary feature of democracy, since it protects fundamental aspects of self-rule. . . . In other words, democracy should not be understood as mere majoritarianism.[34]

She is right to affirm the need for entrenched political rights and reject naive views about the natural virtue of citizens. Yet her argument here runs in the wrong direction. The real problem today is not runaway majorities stripping minorities of their rights, but an entrenched minority appropriating more and more of the world's resources and wealth to itself. It controls all major institutions, including political institutions, by virtue of its socioeconomic power; can afford to and does in fact live apart from public institutions and shared life-horizons; and devotes its immense power to keeping people and their demands at bay. The US Supreme Court (especially as it is constituted under Trump) is not going to solve this structural problem. Vigorous democratic action that goes after the problem at its roots is required. This struggle must have global as well as national and local dimensions. The need for global action is at the center of the "cosmopolitan" interpretation of egalitarian liberalism.

COSMOPOLITAN DEMOCRACY

Cosmopolitan theories of democracy arose in the 1990s in response to globalization. Globalization interlinked nation-states on multiple levels—economic, military, environmental. cultural-symbolic, and epidemiological—in ways that overtaxed the powers of nation-states acting in isolation. In liberal-democratic countries, globalization called into question their traditional basis of legitimacy: popular sovereignty. If national institutions had to continually adjust to international pressures, then the ability of a sovereign people to govern themselves was undermined. In non–liberal-democratic countries, increased trade contact and real-time multimedia communication meant they could not hide their deviation from liberal-democratic norms. They faced intensifying pressure from human rights activists to conform their institutions to liberal-democratic standards. Human rights became the basis for a cosmopolitan theory of legitimacy. No nation-state was legitimate, cosmopolitan theorists argued, unless it protected and promoted human rights. Human rights were contrasted with the "Westphalian model" of national sovereignty in effect since the end of the Thirty Years' War in 1648. In that model, national sovereignty was absolute and interference with the internal affairs of a sovereign state nominally forbidden.

On the one hand, cosmopolitanism calls for international democratic development in response to the growth of global forces that cannot be controlled by nation-states acting alone. On the other hand, it calls for internal democratic development in those nation-states that have not yet become liberal-democracies. Underlying both demands is the classical liberal principle of the moral equality of human beings. In the words of David Held, one of its leading proponents, cosmopolitanism defends the values of "equal moral worth, equal liberty, the equal political status of all human beings, [and] the common heritage of human kind." Taking these values seriously means "a new conception of internationalism . . . [that attempts] to entrench them, in core political, social, and economic institutions."[35] If, within liberal nations, race, sex, and class have been rejected as morally arbitrary, then it must follow, for analogous reasons, that national citizenship be rejected as a justification of inequality. If it is wrong for nation-states to, say, not provide women and men with the same educational opportunities, then it is also wrong to deny Kenyans and Canadians the same educational opportunities, because it is in virtue of our capacities as human beings, and not our sex or citizenship, that we need education.

Cosmopolitan theorists thus recognize shared human interests grounded in a set of shared needs. These needs inform a set of demands for an institutional structure that ensures these needs are regularly met. Equality must be substantive and decided by whether those core needs are fully satisfied or not. The ubiquity of democratic struggles motivated by systematic deprivation of needs is sufficient evidence in support of the claim that human beings have shared interests in a need-satisfying social infrastructure, their real and valuable differences notwithstanding. The real difference between cosmopolitan theories and my position concerns the issue of whether the standard interpretation of human rights principles as globalized versions of liberal rights are sufficient for the realization of the democratic values cosmopolitans affirm.

For cosmopolitan thinkers, human rights form the normative *and* practical basis of a new global order. Their notion of human rights is modeled on the rights of citizenship typical of liberal-democratic constitutions.[36] They express our common needs as universally legitimate demands that ought to exercise a compelling force on all governments to either meet those needs or change. Since human rights include political rights, they exert a universal democratizing force that is equally exacting wherever it is expressed. Neither single countries nor the global order is legitimate unless it is steered by the democratic decisions of the people it affects. That is what James Bohman means when he says that human rights are "justice-making."[37] The justice they make is on one level distributive; on the other, political. Full social justice anywhere demands that people's needs are satisfied *so that* they are able to participate politically. "What are specifically human *political* rights," James Bohman asks, "if human rights confer the status of membership in the human community? Political human rights confer more than simply the status of being human, as is evidenced by the enumeration of many different human rights, including the right to participate in decision-making."[38] Since no nation-state acting alone can control global economic and cultural forces, new global institutions are required to satisfy the demands of human rights. In line with the normative and critical goals of my argument, I will stick to cosmopolitan principles and avoid discussion of different possible models of cosmopolitan governance.

Democratic legitimacy depends on policy and law being responsive to consciously articulated citizen interests. If reified social forces overwhelm the deliberative power of citizens, the society is not fully democratic, regardless of what its constitution says. If the cause of reified social power is a *global* economy, the democratic solution must involve expanding democratic power currently dammed up within national silos. Nancy Fraser puts the point clearly: Democracy is "a function of two distinct elements . . . the translation condition and the capacity condition. According to the translation condition . . . communicative power . . . must be translated . . . into binding law. . . . According to the capacity condition, the public power must be able to implement the discursively formed will to which it is responsible."[39] If capital is free to range across borders in search of the most profitable investment, then the democratic power of the public sphere must be "transnationalized" or the capacity condition cannot be satisfied and democracy undermined by globalization.

The problem with cosmopolitan theories of democracy is analogous to that of egalitarian liberalism. Everyone understands that human beings have fundamental needs, that reified market forces and competition over profits threaten the ability of people to satisfy their needs, and that those who are dependent on capitalist labor markets or welfare systems to satisfy their needs cannot be fully self-determining. None goes further than demanding politically steered redistribution on Keynesian, social democratic lines. Indeed, Held subtitles his important cosmopolitan manifesto, *Global Covenant,* "The Social Democratic Alternative to the Washington Consensus." Obviously, progressive taxation and income redistribution are important steps toward a democratic economy, and a democratic economy is an essential element of a fully democratic society. The deliberative powers of people can only be effective, however, if citizens actually control the resources they need. Unfortunately, globalization has intensified the dependence of local communities on global markets, a problem that is especially severe in the Global South (and indigenous communities in the Global North). In the absence of locally grounded democratic movements to take back control of life-resources, the actions of non-governmental organizations bent on spreading cosmopolitan democracy can appear as a further *undemocratic* limit on the political agency of local people.

As the past forty years of neoliberal assaults on social democracy have proven, as long as society contains opposed class interests, gains made against the ruling class's control over universally required life-resources are always tentative and threatened.[40] The key issue, one not adequately dealt with by cosmopolitan liberals, is the limited impact of state regulation and redistribution *when it is treated as a variable whose success can be calculated independently of the strength of social movements from below.* When class struggle shifted decisively in favor of the rulers, gains that social democrats had achieved were ruthlessly rolled back. As Ingo Schmidt convincingly argues, neoliberalism and the end of the Cold War decisively shifted the political context in which Western European and Canadian social democracy operated. "The weakening of the social democratic left made it next to impossible for social democrats as a whole to resist capitalist quests for concessions. The social democratic right had always been reliant on internal counterweight on the left in its dealings with capital. After the left had lost the internal battle, the right was no longer in a position to negotiate with the capitalists. . . . As a consequence, social democrats turned from struggling for social reforms to minimizing concessions to capitalists."[41] Whether Syriza in Greece, Podemos in Spain, Die Linke in Germany, and the Labour Party under Corbyn signal the start of a long-term resurgence of the social democratic left or not, the key problem for future democratic development is the reactivation of social movements capable of making real inroads against the actual control of universally required life-resources. Successful experiments in cooperative ownership, workers' democratic self-management, and collective control of community institutions from below, *combined with* legislation and regulation from above, would signal the beginning of a transformative social process. I will return to this crucial issue in chapter 6.

To conclude this section, we need to think about the other key plank of the cosmopolitan platform: new transnational institutions. Here an analogous problem opens up: the gap between the potential of transnational regulations to control capitalist globalization and the absence of nourishing movements from below needed to give those institutions democratic legitimacy. As the slow crisis of the European Union under relentless pressure from an expanding populist antimigrant platform in Britain, Hungary, Germany, Poland, and Italy shows, the creation of supranational institutions can promote shared standards and policies without "transnationalizing" a democratic public sphere at all. While the European Union has facilitated trade, common standards, and open borders, it is nevertheless often perceived by the citizens of its member states as aloof and bureaucratic. There is no better evidence of its undemocratic element than the way in which it crushed the Greek people's demand for an end to imposed austerity. The opposition between the Greek people and the leadership of the European Union is only one instance of many collisions—Brexit being the latest—between popular demands and European policies. This has led Alex Callinicos to conclude that "the EU is a thoroughly anti-democratic set of institutions. The fury with which its leaders greeted the Greek referendum of July 2015 is typical—and understandable. Most times an EU treaty has been put to a popular vote it has been rejected."[42] Real problems with the European Union do not mean that democratic international or global institutions are impossible, but they do show that so long as they are, and are perceived to be, an elite project, they will continue to run democratic deficits.[43] In my own view, the interests of global democracy must begin by strengthening local and national forms of democratic control over local and national institutions. International institutions cannot be democratic unless they develop organically from local conditions and reinforce people's control over their life-supporting resource base.

It is true that the nation-state and capitalism coevolved, and that nation-state institutions can be used to protect as well as control the reified powers of capitalist markets. At the same time, if capital is successfully met with organized democratic power everywhere it tries to flow, and if that power is anchored in actual control over fundamental life-resources, it cannot undermine the people's power of self-determination. *If* transnational institutions evolve out of local control over local life-conditions, then they will serve purposes of global democratization. What matters most is that people control their fundamental means of life and the social institutions that govern their use. As a matter of material fact, all resources are located in some specific location, which is why *local control* is primary. Global forces exist and can operate in undemocratic ways just because local populations are expropriated (subjected to "accumulation by dispossession," in David Harvey's apt phrase), and thus made dependent on international flows of investment.[44] Of course, while local victories remain local, they are vulnerable to reaction (the history of Latin American struggles for democracy against US imperialism is an instructive example), but the very fact that they are attacked proves that the primary threat to global capital is local democratic control over life-resources. *All* democratic gains are vulnerable to reaction; the more universal they become (the more social spaces that are democratically self-determining and not dependent on international capital flows), the more secure each is. Let us now turn to the republican conception of democracy to see if it solves the problems that beset the history of liberal-democracy.

REPUBLICAN DEMOCRACY

Institutionally, there is little distinction between liberal and republican theories of democracy. Both insist on constitutionally entrenched rights, parliamentary bodies, the rule of law, the separation of powers, and regulated markets as essential for democracy. Where they differ is on the question of the practice of democratic freedom. Republicans have a more robust conception of political freedom, which generates more exigent demands on both people and governments. Republicans demand that citizens be active in the assertion of their political freedom and that governments be checked in their centralizing and bureaucratizing tendencies by popular activism. Republicanism draws its politics from a two-millennia history of popular self-organization against autocracy and monarchy, from the Roman Republic, through the medieval Italian city-states, to the English, American, and French Revolutions.

The through-line linking these historically specific political experiments is the value of non-domination. Non-domination is distinct from the liberal value of noninterference. If any value defines republicanism, it is non-domination. "In both classical and contemporary republicanism, the value of political liberty or freedom serves as the organizing principle. Accordingly, let us say that republicanism is any political doctrine in which a principle providing freedom from domination is given a central place . . . we can regard domination as a sort of dependency on arbitrary power."[45] The key question from my perspective concerns the republican understanding of the causes of arbitrary power.

To begin, we must understand the difference between the republican theory of freedom as non-domination and the liberal theory of freedom as noninterference. The difference is rooted in the idea of freedom as the power to choose between available options. What matters most for a free agent, republicans argue, is the availability of options to choose from, not simply being unhindered in choosing the one that you ultimately desire. As Philip Pettit explains in his recent systematic defense of republican democracy:

> When you perform as a deliberative agent, you think of yourself as someone able to choose between available options, someone on whom the choice depends. You conceive of yourself . . . as the . . . author of whether the world will be one in which this option materializes or one in which some alternative materializes. This self-conception is inconsistent with indifference to the prospect of any option being hindered, even one you are unlikely to take.[46]

For Pettit, the classical liberal tradition, from Hobbes through Locke to Bentham, rejects interference with choosing the option you want to choose, but not with restrictions on the range of choices. If options you would not choose are not put on the table, there is no loss of freedom, according to Pettit's version of liberal theory, whereas there is a loss of freedom from his republican perspective. What matters for republicanism is not first and foremost the desirability of that which is chosen, but the constraints or lack of constraints on the range and power of choice.

The importance of this difference becomes clear when we examine it in concrete political terms. Insisting on freedom as non-domination allows republicanism to develop a more sophisticated understanding of the ways in which arbitrary power can interfere with choice. Pettit distinguishes between powers that *invade* choice and powers that *vitiate* choice. Powers invade choice when they directly prevent people from choosing between options. In the case of invasion, the agent's will is directly dominated by political power. "Whenever another power or body imposes their will on you, allowing you to choose only within the limits that they dictate, their hindrance constitutes an invasion of your choice."[47] Invasion of choice is always illegitimate because it subordinates the agency of citizens to external powers.

Vitiating interference is not so direct, but it is also illegitimate. Powers vitiate choice when they unduly restrict the range of options from which you can choose, but otherwise leave the choice to you. Hence we see the problem with classical liberal theories of freedom as noninterference. There is no direct interference in the case of vitiating interference, but there is still domination because you are prevented from choosing between a full slate of options. Vitiation occurs when you are deprived of full knowledge of the available choices or deprived of the resources that are the material conditions of choice. If universities charge tuition that is determined by what the market will bear and not by what the poorest but qualified students can pay, the poor student's choice is vitiated, even if it is not dominated. Students can choose between universities, but if they cannot pay any of them, they cannot attend. "What sort of factors will count as vitiation? . . . Any factors that deprive you of resources required for freedom in that choice, or that limit the use to which you can put those resources, without imposing the will of another as to what you should do."[48] Invasion is the more severe form of domination, but it is crucial to note that vitiation is also an illegitimate impediment to full political freedom. If democracy maximizes the space of political freedom, then it must overcome both forms of interference, so far as possible.

Although Pettit does not put the point in exactly these terms, his distinction between invasion and vitiation tracks the difference between domination by people and domination by impersonal forces. A totalitarian government actively prevents people from exercising civil and political rights and directly punishes dissenters. This power is personal and overt, embodied in the leader of the government and exercised by the police and courts in a way that is meant to intimidate. In contrast, no one directly impedes students in the example above from going to university, and no one tries to intimidate them from making the choice. Yet, if a student were to ask his or her boss for a raise to pay tuition, the boss would respond that however much he or she would like to see the student go to school, wage rates are set by competitive pressures and a raise is thus quite impossible. The boss as a person is not responsible for the wage rate or tuition costs, both of which are set by market forces beyond any one person's control. Nevertheless, the student still cannot go to school. The strength of Pettit's argument when measured against classical liberalism is that it recognizes both forms of domination, whereas the second is invisible to classical liberal theory. However, Pettit's proposed solutions to vitiating interference do not deal adequately with its social causes.

The republican solution to all forms of domination is more or less the same as the egalitarian solution. Pettit agrees that there are fundamental human needs that must be met if people are to live freely. The starving person, the illiterate, the person imprisoned on political charges clearly cannot live freely. Free people need material resources and rights. Pettit spells out the set of core needs he believes must be satisfied in a theory of social justice, the details of which need not concern us here. What is important for our interests is the principle the theory rests upon. "The ideal suggests that citizens should be guaranteed resources and protections in the same range of choices—the basic liberties—on the basis of public laws and norms. . . . Social justice, so interpreted, would require each citizen to enjoy the same free status, objective and subjective, as others. It would mandate a substantive form of status equality."[49] Substantive status equality means that every citizen can look every other citizen in the eye and feel their civic equal. No one is so poor or ill-educated that he or she needs to defer to "their betters," everyone has the basic confidence to stand up for themselves and assert their position on matters of public concern, and none are subordinated to the will of a superior class. This form of status equality would make direct invasions of choice impossible, but would it be sufficient to solve the problem of the vitiating force of reified social power?

I do not think it would be sufficient. Like egalitarian and cosmopolitan liberals, Pettit has nothing to say about the governance of non-political institutions. Thus, he does not explicitly address the structure of power in business firms or bureaucratic institutions like hospitals and schools. But if we need education and health care, and if we have to work for a living but our choices play no directing role at work, in school, or in the hospital, then we can certainly suffer domination there, and Pettit's critique of domination is silent. Perhaps there are minimum wage laws that ensure a living wage. Excellent. But a life above the poverty line is not fully free if workers have no say in the pace of work, its organization, the skills it demands, or its general availability. Maybe tuition is set at a price all can afford, or is abolished altogether. Again, excellent; but if the course offerings are determined by the "skills" that labor markets are buying, then student choice is vitiated by the collusion between market forces and school administrators. Huge zones of our lives are lived under institutions that are not directly political but can still exercise coercive power against us, and Pettit's theory of freedom as non-domination has nothing to say about them. Political regulation from above, not democratic transformation from below, is his solution. It is certainly more democratic than laissez-faire, but not as democratic as necessary to ensure self-determination.

Instead, self-determining agency stops at the steps of Parliament or Congress. Citizens *will have their needs satisfied*, but not through their own democratic control over natural resources, the productive enterprises that convert them to required goods, and the panoply of other social and cultural institutions that define the human world. "The overall thrust of the argument," Pettit writes, "is that democracy is defined, not by the presence of electoral institutions, but rather by the fact that people exercise control over government, enjoying equally accessible influence in the imposition of an equally acceptable direction."[50] This is a fine definition of democracy for political institutions, but a theory of democracy as freedom as non-domination cannot stop at the level of government. What about the influence of the boss, the university administrator, the hospital board, or the welfare clerk? All of those exercise coercive, undemocratic power. All those offices should be targeted for democratic transformation by a complete and consistent theory of democracy as freedom, as non-domination. As with its liberal cousin, the republican conception of democracy limits its scope to political institutions, providing a rich conception of political democracy but leaving too many sources of undemocratic, alien power unexamined and unchanged.

Liberals and republicans are not *wrong* about the value of constitutions, separation of powers, and the rule of law to democracy. The classical liberal idea of the moral equality of persons and the right of the governed to create and consent to their governors were the seeds from which existing democracy grew. Latent in these ideas is the master democratic value of self-determination. Political power grows out of the real ability of people to determine their own lives; any power that impedes rather than enables this capacity for self-determination is illegitimate. As we have seen, classical liberals drew the circle of "the people" too narrowly. They did not recognize the democratic claims of colonized people to their traditional lands, and they excluded women and working men from citizenship. However, the struggles of the excluded for inclusion have helped address that contradiction. Still, struggles for inclusion are not sufficient to ensure the full democratization of liberal-capitalism. Classical liberalism also failed to see the way in which material inequality can, in practice, undermine moral equality. The law might rule over all equally, but if you have to pay for lawyers, the interests of the one with the most money will tend to prevail. Egalitarian and cosmopolitan liberals have addressed this shortcoming in the classical view with demands that fundamental needs be recognized and satisfied as material conditions of genuine equality and equal democratic participation. This demand is echoed by republicans, who add to the egalitarian argument a more robust conception of freedom and more strident calls for political action against invasive and vitiating interference with the popular will.

Liberals and republicans thus make significant contributions to democratic theory and existing democratic practice. However, unless deeper social changes are made, actually existing political democracy leaves too much of life hostage to reified powers and breeds the sort of cynical indifference to democracy that Foa and Mounk identified. Of all the problems reified market forces are causing, none is more important than the extraordinary degree of material inequality that separates the so-called 1 percent from everyone else. The causes of its acceleration over the past forty years and the damage it causes to existing democracy is the subject of the next chapter.

NOTES

1. Beate Jahn, "Rethinking Democracy Promotion," *Review of International Studies,* vol. 38, no. 4 (2012), 701–2.

2. Deliberative democracy could also be seen as a species of egalitarian liberalism. In earlier work, I have criticized Habermas's version of it on grounds similar to those I will advance against all species of liberalism here. (See Noonan, *Democratic Society and Human Needs,* 174–84. While I think those arguments remain valid, I have also come to think that no theory of democratic society can do without the practice of deliberation as the political means of freely determining law and policy. The key problem, as I now see it,

is not with deliberation as a practice of arriving at common ground, but its restriction to political institutions only. I will develop the systematic arguments about deliberation and all-around social democratization in chapter 6.

3. See John Locke, *Second Treatise of Government* (Indianapolis, IN: Hackett, 1980), 25–29. Here Locke dismisses indigenous title because he thinks they waste the land. Since they do not increase its monetary value by exploiting it for private profit, they forfeit any title they might claim. Locke himself was deeply implicated in both the slave trade and the colonization of America. See the discussion in Jahn, "Rethinking Democracy Promotion," 697–98.

4. Locke, *Second Treatise of Government*, 46.

5. Madison's critique of faction is an oblique reference to Machiavelli's warning centuries earlier that faction is fatal to democracy. See Nicolo Machiavelli, *The History of Florence and Other Selections*, Myron P. Gilmore, ed. (New York: Washington Square Press, 1970), 214–15.

6. James Madison, "The Federalist, No. 10," *The Federalist* (Cleveland, OH: Meridian Books, 1965), 59. Madison's arguments helped support the constitutional principle of indirect election for president. Americans do not vote directly for president but for electors from the Electoral College, who commit their state's share of Electoral College votes to the candidate who gets the most votes in the state. This system can lead to the election of presidents with less than a majority of the popular vote, as was the case with Donald Trump in 2016.

7. Ibid., 60.

8. The phrase comes from Alexis de Tocqueville. See Alexis de Tocqueville, *Democracy in America*, Richard D. Heffner, ed. (New York: Mentor Books, 1956), 114.

9. John Stuart Mill, *On Socialism* (Buffalo, NY: Prometheus Books, 1987), 68.

10. Ibid., 131.

11. John Stuart Mill and Harriet Taylor Mill, *Essays on Sex Equality*, Alice S. Rossi, ed. (Chicago: University of Chicago Press, 1970).

12. John Stuart Mill, *Considerations on Representative Government* (Indianapolis, IN: Bobbs-Merrill, 1958), 128.

13. On the difference between structural deprivation and luck see G. A. Cohen, *Rescuing Justice and Equality* (Cambridge, MA: Harvard University Press, 2008), 300–2. Cohen's "luck egalitarianism" was one of several positions advanced in the "equality of what debate" that began in the 1980s. Key contributions include Amartya Sen, *Equality of What? The Tanner Lectures on Human Values*, Scott McMurrin, ed. (Cambridge, UK: Cambridge University Press, 1980); Ronald Dworkin, "Equality of Resources," *Philosophy and Public Affairs*, vol. 10 (1981), 271–302; Richard Arneson, "Equality and Equality of Opportunity for Welfare," *Philosophical Studies*, vol. 55 (1989), 106–39.

14. For an examination of the profound changes in the interpretation of the American constitution, from its classical liberal origins to the modern progressive-egalitarian liberal reading, see Richard A. Epstein, *The Classical Liberal Constitution: The Uncertain Quest for Limited Government* (Cambridge, MA: Harvard University Press, 2014).

15. It is impossible to examine the whole argument of *Theory of Justice* here or explore fully its connection to the later *Political Liberalism*. My focus will be confined to those aspects of Rawls's work directly relevant to the issue of the ambivalent relationship between liberalism and democracy.

16. John Rawls, *A Theory of Justice*, revised edition (Cambridge, MA: Harvard University Press, 1999), 459.

17. Ibid., 458.

18. William A. Edmundson, *John Rawls: Reticent Socialist* (Cambridge, UK: Cambridge University Press, 2017), 185.

19. Ibid., 77.

20. Ibid., 49.

21. Hal Draper, "The Two Souls of Socialism," *Marxists Internet Archive*; https://www.marxists.org/archive/draper/1966/twosouls/ (accessed October 12, 2017).

22. The most detailed model of "market socialism" is found in Alec Nove, *The Economics of Feasible Socialism* (London: Allen and Unwin, 1983). For a decisive critique of this model and a detailed explanation of the fatal contradictions between socialism and market allocation, see Pat Devine, *Democracy and Economic Planning* (Cambridge, UK: Polity Press, 1988).

23. Rawls, *Theory of Justice*, 65.

24. John Rawls, *Political Liberalism* (New York: Columbia University Press, 1996), 182.

25. Sheldon Wolin, "The Liberal/Democratic Divide: On Rawls' Political Liberalism," *Fugitive Democracy* (Princeton, NJ: Princeton University Press, 2016), 271.

26. Ibid.

27. Rawls, *A Theory of Justice*, 54.

28. I have explored in greater detail than I can here the differences between her capabilities approach and my conception of democratic society in Jeff Noonan, "The Contradictions of Nussbaum's Liberalism," *International Critical Thought*, vol. 1, no. 4 (2011), 427–36.

29. See Amartya Sen, *Development as Freedom* (New York: Knopf, 1999), 74–76.

30. The first capabilities list is worked out in Martha Nussbaum, *Women and Human Development* (Cambridge, UK: Cambridge University Press, 2000), 78–80.

31. Martha Nussbaum, *Creating Capabilities: The Human Development Approach* (Cambridge, MA: Harvard University Press, 2011), 18.

32. Ibid.,166.
33. Wolin, "Fugitive Democracy," op. cit., 102.
34. Nussbaum, *Creating Capabilities*, 179.
35. David Held, *Global Covenant* (Cambridge UK: Polity Press, 2004), 162.
36. Louis Henkin, "International Human Rights as 'Rights,' *Human Rights*, J. Richard Pennock and John W. Chapman, eds. (New York: New York University Press, 1981), 263.
37. James Bohman, *Democracy Across Borders: From Demos to Demoi* (Cambridge, MA: MIT Press, 2007), 114.
38. Ibid.
39. Nancy Fraser, *Scales of Justice* (New York: Columbia University Press, 2010), 96–97.
40. See David Harvey, *A Brief History of Neoliberalism* (Cambridge, UK: Cambridge University Press, 2005).
41. Ingo Schmidt, "Introduction: Social Democracy and Uneven Development: Theoretical Reflections on the Three Worlds of Social Democracy," *The Three Worlds of Social Democracy*, Ingo Schmidt, ed. (London: Pluto Press, 2016), 20.
42. Alex Callinicos, "The Internationalist Case against the European Union, *International Socialism Journal*, no. 148 (October 2015); http://isj.org.uk/the-internationalist-case-against-the-european-union/ (accessed July 12, 2017).
43. For a broader discussion see Jurgen Habermas, *The Crisis of the European Union: A Response* (Cambridge, UK: Polity, 2012); Perry Anderson, *The New Old World* (London: Verso, 2009).
44. David Harvey, *The New Imperialism* (New York: Oxford University Press, 2003), 45.
45. Frank Lovett, "The Republican Critique of Liberalism," *The Cambridge Companion to Liberalism*, Steven Wall, ed. (Cambridge, UK: Cambridge University Press, 2015), 383–84.
46. Phillip Pettit, *On the People's Terms: A Republican Theory and Model of Democracy* (Cambridge, UK: Cambridge University Press, 2012), 32.
47. Ibid., 38.
48. Ibid., 39.
49. Ibid., 297–98.
50. Ibid., 207.

Chapter 3

The Real Contradiction between Inequality and Democracy

Struggles for democratic equality always contest this underlying structure of control over life-resources and major social and political institutions, whatever language they use to explain and justify themselves. From the halls of the International Monetary Fund, to liberal think tanks, to academic economics and political science, worries over the damage inequality is causing to liberal democracy are legion, but rarely, as we will see, do they examine the problem at this depth level. Mainstream liberal critiques of inequality focus on inequalities of income and the racial and gendered dimensions that exacerbate them. The extent of income inequality today also makes it impossible to avoid discussions of class and the dynamics of income distribution in capitalist society. Hence, mainstream alarm at widening income inequality has opened the door to a discussion of the structural inequalities of liberal-democratic capitalism. However, no sooner do mainstream economists open this door than they slam it shut, out of fear that inequality be exposed as endemic to capitalism, built into its historical class-race-sex structure of control over life-resources, and therefore inimical to the social conditions democracy demands.

My analysis and criticism will be developed in three sections. In the first I will examine the liberal and social democratic critique of income inequality. In the second, I will argue that inequality is not accidental but rooted in the class-race-gender structure of control over life-resources that capitalism has historically depended on. In the third section I will explain the real contradiction between inequality and democracy and the type of equality a fully democratic society requires.

INCOME INEQUALITY AND
CONTEMPORARY CAPITALISM

In November 2017 the bank Credit Suisse released a report showing that fully 50 percent of the world's wealth was controlled by 1 percent of the population.[1] Control over wealth is what allows the richest segment of the population to control the economic and political institutions of a country. Thomas Piketty defines wealth as "the total market value of everything owned by the residents or governments of a given country at a given point in time, provided that it can be traded on some market."[2] If wealth is distributed unequally, income inequality will follow. The international structure of wealth inequality is replicated within countries, with even the wealthiest liberal-democratic capitalist regimes—those that puff themselves up most about their egalitarian and democratic bona fides—characterized by massive and widening inequalities of income and wealth since the 1970s. In the United States, the top 10 percent of the population controls 70 percent of the wealth, and the top 1 percent controls just over 30 percent.[3] That same 1 percent of the population earned roughly 10 percent of the total national income in 1980; today they have doubled their share to 20 percent. The bottom 50 percent is the mirror image; they have seen their share shrink from 20 percent to roughly 10 percent. As we will see, this reversal is the consequence of economic dynamics and political power and policy. In the United Kingdom, the figures are roughly the same. The top 1 percent increased their share of the national income from roughly 10 percent in 1980 to about 17 percent today. Even in a country like Canada, whose international reputation for equality somehow survives despite observable realities, the same pattern emerges: The top 1 percent have increased their share of the total national income from about 9 percent to about 13 percent today.[4] The total income controlled by the 1 percent is lower than in the United States or the United Kingdom, but the trend line is the same, providing very strong evidence that we are not dealing with local contingencies but a global political economic pattern for which a systematic explanation must be found.

While these highly aggregated figures reveal a global pattern, they do not tell the whole story of income inequality. Wealth and income inequality are magnified when one takes into account the sex, gender, and racial dimensions of class structure. Where there is a history of structural patriarchal and racial oppression, the groups at the bottom of the hierarchy also do the lowest paid and most insecure work. Consequently, they are the poorest. In the United States that means black and Latino women are the poorest group in the country.[5] Black women would have to work an extra seven months into 2017 to earn the average male wage earned in 2016.[6] Overall, the inequality between black and white Americans is striking. "There has been no significant closing of the gap between African Americans (and Hispanics) in the last 30 years," notes Joseph Stiglitz. "In 2011, the median income for black families was . . . just 58 percent of the median income for white families. Turning from income to wealth, we see gaping inequality too. By 2009, the median wealth of whites was 20 times that of blacks. The Great Recession of 2007 (through 2009) was particularly hard on African Americans: they saw their median wealth fall 53 percent [largely as a consequence of losing their homes through foreclosure]."[7] African Americans were far more likely to be the victims of predatory "subprime" mortgage rates, and thus far more likely to lose their homes when the artificially low rates reset to unaffordable levels.

These raw economic numbers hardly capture the full scale of racialized inequality. In all dimensions of life, from income and wealth to political power to cultural perceptions, African Americans are structurally disadvantaged vis-à-vis their white co-citizens. The full picture is perhaps best captured by prison statistics. F. Michael Higginbotham notes that "nationally, blacks are imprisoned at more than five times the rate of whites, thus resulting in the loss of certain civil rights and employment, since opportunities in many states, such as voting rights, are denied to those with felony records."[8] Higher unemployment and ghettoization feed racist stereotypes, which increase public suspicion of African Americans, which is used to justify increasingly militarized policing. Intensified policing leads to higher arrest rates, more convictions and imprisonment, which then fuels the cycle of powerlessness and oppression because of the loss of employment opportunities and civil rights noted by Higginbotham. One does not need to pile numbers on top of more numbers to understand the reality of our world: There are wide and growing inequalities, magnified by race and gender, and they appear to be self-perpetuating. Hence the two key questions from the standpoint of democratic development: "Why are liberal-democratic capitalist societies unequal and growing more so?" and "What are the consequences of this structure of inequality for existing democratic institutions and practices?"

If we judge liberal societies by their stated values, the extent of inequality is surprising. As we saw in the previous chapter, equality is *the* central value of liberal political philosophy. To be fair, it is true that different groups have fought to gain the equal protection of existing rights as well as to expand the schedule of effective rights as a means to improve their quality of life. The gains have been real. Domestically, the struggles of working class people in their concrete sexual and racial identities in conjunction (although not always coordinated conjunction) with women and racialized groups fighting the specific inflections of sexist and racist discrimination did produce more equal income distributions in the middle part of the twentieth century in Europe and North America. Moreover, they expanded the political and cultural space for the free expression and participation of workers and oppressed groups. Internationally, anticolonial struggles ended white political rule over Africa, Latin America, and Asia—a tremendous democratic achievement at the political level. Only the most unthinking dogmatist could argue that since none of these struggles has led to the revolutionary overthrow of capitalism, these changes have made no concrete difference to people's lives. However, the other side of the same argument is that while they have profoundly transformed the legal, political, and cultural landscape, both domestically and internationally, and while they have changed to some extent the *composition* of the ruling class, they have not overthrown its power or the reified power of capital.

Liberalism has a difficult time seeing down to these global dynamics and structural inequalities of power because it proceeds, in all the permutations examined in the last chapter, from the assumption that all people are morally equal. That assumption is a historical novelty; most traditional societies were structured as hierarchical organic wholes in which one's place was assumed to be determined by one's nature, and rights and responsibilities radically differed depending on one's place in the hierarchy. Hence, liberal moral equality is itself a tremendous political victory. It was won only through revolutionary struggle— against the power of aristocracy and monarchy in the English, American, and French Revolutions, and then against European racism and colonialism in the San Domingo Revolution in the 1790s and the anti-colonial struggle across the globe in the twentieth century. Over more than two centuries of struggle, the principle that there is a hierarchy of moral natures that determines and justifies social position has been defeated, philosophically if not always in practice. The democratic principle is that all people are morally equal, from which it follows that everyone has the basic intellectual and practical capacities to govern themselves, collectively and individually. Once that principle has been constitutionally enshrined, it appears that material inequalities should be resolvable by making social practice adequate to constitutional principle. However, if material inequality is caused by economic forces that those same constitutions allow to operate free from direct political governance, then constitutional principles will prove inadequate as a basis to resolve material inequality. Since liberalism tends to prioritize constitutional structures as the solution to the problem of inequality, it is not conceptually set up to see and acknowledge systemic forces that produce material inequalities as a matter of normal social functioning. Inequality appears as a treatable disease, a temporary deviation, and not a chronic illness that must be addressed by fundamental changes to liberal-democratic capitalist society.

The best place to start the analysis of the liberal understanding of income and wealth inequality is the first serious empirical economic effort to understand equality as an inbuilt tendency of capitalist development. Classical political economists like Smith and Ricardo accepted the principle that people were morally equal, but also that capitalism was and would always be marked be serious material inequalities between classes. Market competition was valued for its productivity. Productivity reduces costs, including the costs of labor. Hence, they thought the free competition they supported would keep wages low (and, therefore, workers poor).[9] The observable state of working people in England in the nineteenth century, classically captured by Engels in *The Condition of the Working Class of England*, was the normal and natural state, according to classical political economy.[10]

More optimistic trends emerged in postwar America. In the red, white, and blue glow of the "free world," a new generation of American economists closed the books on the dismal science. Led by Simon Kuznets, the economists of the long boom argued that capitalism led naturally to technological development, which widely diffused marketable skills, which raised wages and reduced inequality. Capitalist development, historically considered, generated an inverted U-shaped curve. Inequality increased early on, leveled out, and then gradually declined. "One might thus assume," he argued, "a long swing in the inequality characterizing the secular income structure: widening in the early phase of economic growth when the transition from pre-industrial to the industrial civilization was most rapid, becoming stabilized for a while, then narrowing in later phases."[11] While he was using a fairly thin data set, his work was pioneering and resonated with the optimistic spirit of postwar America. People thought he had discovered an economic law of capitalist economic growth: Equality did not require affirmative action or union struggle; unfettered economic growth alone would create it.

Until the 1970s, Kuznets appeared to be correct. Unprecedented economic expansion and productivity growth did reduce income and wealth inequality. In the 1950s, one could reasonably assume it would continue. But things changed in the early 1970s. A severe economic crisis led to what was formerly assumed to be impossible: stagnant growth and inflation (stagflation). Keynesianism was discarded as the favored economic theory, and in its place what we today call the neoliberal austerity agenda began to take shape. The result of these political and economic changes was the inversion of the inverted-U; inequality began to rise, and it continues to do so.

The economic and political dynamics of inequality have forced a new generation of economists, led by Thomas Piketty, to rethink Kuznets's assumptions and data. The trend he discovered was real, but his subsequent claim that equality naturally emerged out of an archaic period of inequality was exposed as false. According to Piketty, slower economic and demographic growth, combined with a suite of monetary, fiscal, and tax policies designed to serve the interests of the ruling class, are the economic and political causes of the growth of income and wealth inequality.[12]

The magical Kuznets curve theory was formulated in large part for the wrong reasons, and its empirical underpinnings were extremely fragile. The sharp reduction in income inequality that we observed in almost all of the rich countries between 1914 and 1945 was due above all to the world wars and the violent political and economic shocks they entailed. . . . It had little to do with the tranquil process of intersectoral mobility described by Kuznets.[13]

Piketty's longer view concludes that greater equality was caused by shrinking fortunes during the Great Depression and war years, and rising wages in the long boom that followed World War II. Rising wages were not automatic but involved union-led struggle.

Then, beginning in the 1970s, a reaction against working class militancy began. The so-called "neoliberal" phase of capitalism tried to solve the problem of economic stagnation by attacking working class organizations, cutting back on public spending, weakening social safety nets, rolling back regulations, changing tax codes to further favor the rich, removing restrictions on the mobility of capital, and imposing the values of the capitalist market: cutthroat individualism, winner-take-all competition, and money as the primary good of life, across all social institutions. These are the policies that have caused the dramatic turn toward widening inequalities, between the Global North and South and within OECD (Organisation for Economic Cooperation and Development) countries.[14] In every major capitalist country, labor's share of the national income has fallen and capital's has risen. That means those who can live off their investments are gaining at the expense of those who must sell their labor, whose income has been stagnating or falling.[15]

In Piketty's influential analysis, the politics of upward redistribution are embedded in and motivated by what he calls two "fundamental laws" of capitalism. The first law states that capital's share of the national income is determined by multiplying the rate of return on capital by the capital income ratio.[16] The second fundamental law is that the capital-to-income ratio is equal to the savings rate divided by the growth rate.[17] As should be evident right away, these are not so much laws as mathematical formulas. That is, they do not provide a causal explanation of the economic forces that determine capital's share of the national income or what the capital-to-income ratio is, but just formulas that tell us how to calculate it.[18] The causal explanation lies elsewhere, in the political struggle over resources, institutions, and wealth. Nevertheless, Piketty's formulation is important because it does reveal an underlying structural ground to inequality in capitalism. Where growth rates are low (and they have been for most of the last forty years, relative to the postwar boom), capital enjoys a systematic advantage over labor. If the rate of return on capital is higher than the growth rate ($r>g$), those with sufficient capital can earn higher returns simply by saving and investing in securities rather than in the real economy.[19] The rich get richer, but without making the sorts of investments that generate pressure toward higher wages (the main ideological justification for wealth inequality). "The most important factor in the long run is low growth, especially demographic growth, which, together with a high rate of savings, automatically gives rise to a structural increase in the long run capital/income ratio."[20] The virtuous circle of Keynesian economics (the ruling class expands its wealth by making profitable investments that expand employment and raise wages) is broken and replaced by a vicious circle where ruling class wealth grows by *withdrawing* wealth from the real economy and investing it in speculative but profitable pursuits.

Piketty has proved such an influential and controversial figure because he has claimed, from the side of liberal egalitarianism and not Marxism, that there are structural forces at work in capitalism that tend toward inequality unless deliberately checked. This claim is heresy to orthodoxy's position that since the long-term tendency of economic development is toward equality, there is no need for working class struggle. At the same time, Piketty has also made it clear that although there are structural grounds for the growth of inequality, its rise is not automatic. The economic power of the capitalist class translates into political power.

The undemocratic implications of the ruling class's political struggle to create the policy conditions most favorable to its narrow economic interests has been most obvious in the United States. Nobel Prize–winning economist Joseph Stiglitz has been one of its most perceptive liberal critics. While Stiglitz has some technical economic disagreements with Piketty, he agrees there has been a shift away from productive investment to rent-seeking and speculation. Political power tracks economic power, which in turn derives from private and exclusive control over the resources and goods everyone needs to survive and develop. Hence, as inequality of wealth grows, so too does inequality of political power. The increasing political power of the ruling class has affected both international and domestic economic policy.

Internationally, Stiglitz demonstrates that the ruling class has used its power to elect governments that have rewritten trade policy to serve corporate interests. "The rules of economic globalization are . . . designed to benefit the rich: they encourage competition amongst countries *for* business, which drives down taxes on corporations, weakens health and environmental protections, and undermines what used to be viewed as "core" labor rights, which include the right to collective bargaining."[21] Domestically, those same governments have supported tax policies that undermine almost a century of progressive income tax systems and fiscal policies that prioritize controlling inflation (maintaining the value of money in the interests of those who live off their investments, not labor) over economic growth (which creates pressures toward higher wages). "The 1 percent has captured and distorted the budget debate—using an understandable concern about overspending to provide cover for a program of downsizing the government, an action that would weaken the economy today, lower growth in the future, and most importantly, . . . increase inequality. It has even used the . . . budget battle to argue for reduced progressivity in our tax system and a cutback in the country's already limited programs of social protection."[22] Internationally and domestically, the working majority loses more and more power to the ruling class. While the rot is perhaps deepest in America, the democratic side of liberal-capitalist democracy is everywhere reduced more and more to an empty slogan.

Democratic decline is so pervasive and precipitous that neither Piketty nor Stiglitz can avoid the term most anathema to usually hopeful liberals: class war.[23] Societies in which the interests of the rich constantly prevail, because they control political power by virtue of their control over resources and wealth, are not democracies. As Piketty has the courage to say, they are plutocratic oligarchies.[24] His meticulous charting of the actual dynamics of wealth and income inequality leaves little doubt about the truth of his key political conclusion: "The political secession of the largest fortunes is already well under way."[25] The wealthiest people do not depend on public hospitals, education, or transit; do not live next to their working class co-citizens; do not depend on paid employment; have politicians of all parties at their offices begging donations; and in return get what they demand, no matter which official party is in power. They determine policy and law for the whole; the majority of people are the increasingly angry objects of political power, not substantively equal participants in any democratic project of self-determination.

The obvious fission of the body politic has liberals across the world worried, but nowhere more so than in the United States, where the hollowing out of the democratic side of liberal-democratic capitalism has gone the furthest. Sanford Lakoff, following the line of thinking

initiated by Stiglitz, provides a systematic list of the threats that income
and wealth inequality poses to (American) democracy.

> Extreme economic inequality weakens the political process by undermin-
> ing the ties of citizenship—the sense of common interest, the recognition
> of a duty to participate, and the willingness to respect electoral out-
> comes. . . . Already in the US, a major study has concluded that affluent
> people have considerable clout, while the preferences of people in the
> bottom third of the income distribution have *no* apparent impact on the
> behavior of elected officials.[26]

One should add: no apparent *positive* impact. When oppressed people
gather to express their demands (i.e., attempt to democratically determine
a different future for themselves), they are now regularly met with ever
more militarized police units deployed to intimidate and disperse them.

Even if one wants to argue that "common interest," "solidarity," and
"democratic participation" were *always* ideological slogans masking the
class interests of white propertied men, one should still be concerned
about the widening income and wealth gap between the 1 percent and
everyone else. The fact that these slogans can be used ideologically
does not mean they are not real democratic values. Too often, radical critics conflate existing democracy and its severe limitations with
democracy as such. Jodi Dean, for example, scolds leftists for "calling
for democracy," because it "fails to emphasize the division necessary
for politics, divisions that should lead us to organize against the interest of corporations . . . on behalf of collective arrangements designed
to distribute benefits and opportunities more equally."[27] The problem is
not the values, but that the natural and social conditions for their realization in the lives of people have been attacked. The common interest
is the shared interest in need-governed access to the natural conditions
of life-maintenance and the political, economic, and cultural conditions
of life-development. Solidarity is rooted in the recognition across different concrete identities and histories of oppression and exploitation
that all oppressed groups experience systematic deprivation of some
subset of the resources, goods, relationships, and institutions required
for the full development of social self-conscious agency and meaningful and valuable projects of self-realization. It becomes real in social
movements that always emerge in response to concrete experiences of
deprivation, exclusion, and oppression.

If social critics allow the term "democracy" to be captured by real democracy's actual opponents, they lose the most effective political value with which to oppose the plutocratic oligarchy our society is increasingly becoming. The liberal critique of income and wealth inequality is immensely important because it is in effect a warning from inside the burning house that a potentially all-consuming fire has broken out. But they point to the flames, not to the source of combustion. To understand the fire, we need to understand where and what started it. That search takes us deeper into the dynamics of capitalism than wealth and income, and further back into its history than the beginning of the neoliberal period.

LIFE-RESOURCES, POLITICAL POWER, AND DEMOCRACY

The "Gloria to the Rule of Law" is the most soaring of all hymns sung during Capitalist High Mass. The rule of law, we are daily reminded, separates the free from the unfree, civilized from barbarian. It legitimates whatever is done under its name as fair and just. If corporate remuneration has soared in the United Kingdom to 386 times the income of the average living wage, that is just, because they have earned it fair and square.[28] Yet if one puzzles over the math a bit and asks: Can one person's work really be worth *386 times* as much as another in terms of their real contribution to social life and well-being, one starts to suspect that something other than a fair tallying of life-value is at work. A larger person needs more of the cake, but no one needs to devour every pastry in the city. If some gluttons are able to do so, then perhaps there is more to the game than the rules people are allowed to read.

The question for democrats is: How did that which we currently take to be legal come to be? When we peel back the layers of history (which neither Piketty nor Stiglitz does with sufficient depth), we discover a transition point between one set of laws and customs and new social forces that demanded new sets of laws and customs. We come to a struggle, therefore, over the fundamental resources upon which life depends, and from which all wealth and income *ultimately* derive. In the transitional period between feudalism and capitalism, or between the variety of collectivist social and economic systems of the indigenous peoples of Africa and North and South America and colonial capitalism, this struggle took the form of a struggle over ownership and control over the land on the one hand and workers' and women's bodies on the other.

In England, where the process began and achieved its earliest systematic victories, what Marx calls the "primitive accumulation of capital" took the form of land clearances and enclosures of customarily common land. The movement could not drape itself in the dignity of law because it was, according to both statute and custom, illegal. So the only alternative to removing the people who had been there for centuries was to physically liquidate them:

> Hence the historical movement which changes the producers into wage-workers appears, on the one hand, as their emancipation from serfdom and from the fetters of the guilds, and this side alone exists for our bourgeois historians. But, on the other hand, these new freedmen became sellers of themselves only after they had been robbed of all their own means of production, and all of the guarantees of existence afforded by the old feudal arrangements. And the history of this, their expropriation, is written in the annals of mankind in letters of blood and fire.[29]

The working class was not found, it was created through the most violent and life-destructive means.

In South America it took the form of dispossession of the indigenous peoples and the export of their gold and silver back to Europe. The export of these precious metals helped spur capitalist development. In Africa it took the form of the export of human beings as slaves to the gold mines, sugar plantations, and cotton fields of the Caribbean and North and South America. Colonialism and the slave trade were integral to the early development of capitalism, which also means that proletarianization and racial domination are inseparable in the history of capitalist development.

> Given its constitution in and through colonialism, slavery, and extermination of indigenous peoples, capitalist class formation has always been inseparable from the social organization of race and racism. Specific populations—Africans, Asians, the Irish, and the indigenous peoples of the Americas—were subjected to ruthless, even murderous regimes of pillage and brutality, consistently justified by doctrines of racial inferiority.[30]

The struggle was over control of their hands, needed to do the labor, and the earth their feet stood upon, the object of the labor from which capitalist fortunes would be made. From the rolling hills of Yorkshire to Africa, from the Strait of Gibraltar to the Cape of Good Hope, from the tip of Ellesmere Island to Tierra del Fuego, peasants and indigenous people were harassed, displaced, enslaved, and exterminated. For the victims of colonialism, expropriation was, quite simply, death and total destruction of their means and ways of life.

> Making the . . . shift in analysis . . . to the colonial-relation [allows us to see] the inherent injustice of colonial rule . . . *on its own terms and in its own right* . . . it becomes far more difficult to justify in antiquated developmental terms. . . . The assimilation of non-capitalist, non-Western, Indigenous modes of life based on the racist assumption that this assimilation will somehow magically redeem itself by bringing the fruits of capitalist modernity into the supposedly "backward" world of the colonized.[31]

The shared reality of English peasants and indigenous peoples was the systematic loss of control over the land, and thus their natural means of life support. Their social and cultural patterns of life and their collective values were undermined by the loss of control over the material conditions of existence. As Enrique Dussel has searingly demonstrated, the "goodness" of liberal-capitalist development has historically depended on silencing the scream of the exploited and oppressed.[32]

These material conditions of existence include the reproductive capacities of women's bodies. Hence, just as capitalist class formation is inseparable from the processes of expropriation of the direct producers from the land—processes that in the colonies generated the discourses and structures of institutionalized racism—so too it required a struggle over new ways of controlling women's bodies and organizing the care and nurture of new life. As colonization created the context for new theories of racial superiority, so too the privatization of childbirth and caring in the nuclear family created the context for new theories of women's nature, new modalities of patriarchal power, and new interpretations of "normal" forms of desire, intimacy, and sexual relationships.

> All societies have to organize the labor involved in maintaining and renewing the population—Marxist feminists term this social reproduction and we focus on this theoretical concept because the work of social

reproduction is fundamental to human survival. Social reproduction includes caring labor but also includes how sexuality is organized—not only because of biological reproduction but because intimacy and desire are mobilized in and through family household.[33]

The through-line that links enclosure, colonization, control over women's bodies, and intimate sexual life is: In order to control society, a ruling group must control the natural and social bases of life support, which include the female bodies that give birth to the next generation of humans and the sexual practices through which pregnancy is caused. From those material foundations it can control the institutions that propose and pass the laws and policies, and disseminate the "normal" values through which people interpret their lives. This deep structure of control is the real inequality, of which inequality of wealth and income is only a sign. Overcoming it is the real and only path toward democratic collective self-determination.

Piketty, Stiglitz, and others concerned with the decline of liberal-democracy see the sign but think the cause is contingent on policy choices, not the deep structure that subordinates the satisfaction of human needs to the conversion of labor and raw materials to money for private appropriation. Thus Stiglitz, writing about the rising power of financial markets, says that "the surrender to the dictates of the financial markets . . . applies . . . to any country that has to raise money from capital markets. If the country doesn't do what the financial markets like, they threaten to downgrade the ratings, to pull out the money, to raise interest rates. The financial markets get what they want."[34] Stiglitiz notes the capitulation, but not the reason governments capitulated. They have capitulated because they see their job as ensuring conditions for economic growth in capitalist terms. Without strong working-class opposition, political policy thus serves whatever demands the most powerful economic forces make. Finance capital is the most powerful economic voice today, and government does what it says.

It has not always been this way. In earlier phases of colonial capitalism, extractive industries got what they wanted. Colonial governments got what they wanted. *The power of capital has gotten what it wanted, by and large and for the most part, since capitalism consolidated itself as the dominant global system.* What McMurtry calls the "cancer stage of capitalism," in which profit is increasingly made from the privatization of once-public resources and speculative investment, which makes no contribution to the maintenance and development of human life at all, is still just one phase of a two-centuries-long history of the ruling class employing human beings as means to the creation of money-value.[35] They have exploited whatever racial and sex differences they could find or invent to legitimate and intensify this exploitation. The current neoliberal suite of policies that Piketty and Stiglitz rightly object to is not the cause of this problem but its effect. Likewise, the growing income and wealth gaps they rightly decry as unjust are not the cause of the erosion of democracy; they are the effect of the always already undemocratic nature of capitalist society.

How else could one explain the centuries-old, readily observable phenomenon of across-the-board oppression and exploitation than by its appeal to an underlying structure of subordination of the needs and value of human life—in all the concrete identities through which it is expressed, experienced, and lived—to the power of money-value and the class that lives by its accumulation? Concrete histories of oppression are experienced as discrete forms of deprivation by the subjects involved, but they all share in common the fact—which democratic critique must bring out in each case—of being dominated by deprivation of access to the goods, resources, and institutions people need to live freely and participate in collective life as equals. As Damien Cahill and Martijn Koning rightly argue, people who posit "neoliberalism" as a causal explanation for the current crisis often miss the deeper, sociostructural conditions that produced neoliberalism in the first place. These arguments tend "to be insufficiently concerned with the systemic dynamics of the capitalist economy and the common pressures that it imposes."[36] While they do not have Stiglitz or Piketty in particular in mind, this main thrust of their argument exposes the crucial limitation of their position.

On the surface, capitalist society functions according to legally regulated, free competition between businesses for consumer dollars. Beneath the surface of free competition lies the compulsion of needing to work for a living. This compulsion drives most people—even whole countries—to do what they *must* to find or create work. Were resources publicly owned and cooperatively managed, their fruits used to satisfy needs, and laws enforced that ensured access to them, this social compulsion to sell oneself to labor markets could not operate. But where life-serving resources are owned and controlled by private corporations, and where basic life-goods like water, food, clothing, and shelter are priced commodities, the lives of all who depend on jobs for money are going to be dependent, other things being equal, on those labor markets. Access to labor markets is determined not only by the state of market forces (the level of demand for labor) but also by sexist and racist ideologies about who is best "fit" for different types of work, who deserves what level of pay, etc. Hence, the general compulsive force generated by capitalist competition is supplemented by racist and sexist social structures and beliefs to ensure that race and sex hierarchies are reproduced within the working class, exacerbating inequalities even as, politically, liberal society affirms the equal dignity and rights of all.

The compulsive force of competition between private businesses is also the cause of the crises that periodically seize capitalist society, most recently in 2007–2008. Here, again, there is a superficial view that sees economic crisis as accidental. Yet while crises are indeed moments where living standards can dramatically decline, inequalities can sharpen, and the gains of past struggles be wiped out with the excuse that they have become unaffordable or impediments to economic recovery, democratic activists must not forget that crises are endemic to capitalist competition. Capital must grow or die. In order to grow, it must produce more and more commodities and sell them at a profit. There is pressure to continually increase supply, even beyond existing levels of demand. Hence capitalism is prone to periodic convulsions caused by overproduction. "In their scramble for profits . . . capitalists will over-invest (or over-accumulate); yet, in doing so they undermine profitability within the economy as a whole. It is not a psychological flaw that drives capitalism into crisis, therefore, but the very dynamics of an economy based on production for the market to maximize profit."[37] Since the health of the economy depends on profitability, and everyone who works for a living—the vast majority of people—depends on the economy, this *structural inequality of power* between those who work for a living (who cannot easily survive crisis) and those who live on their capital (who can) explains the structural contradiction between capitalism and democracy. "People live in the present," Immanuel Wallerstein told the US Social Forum in Detroit in 2010. Because "everybody has to eat today . . . everybody has to sleep today, everybody has to do all these ordinary things today," they will—in the absence of a credible alternative—normally comply with the demands of the forces that control their ability to eat.[38] The people can decide anything they want; if the capitalists decide that the people's needs and demands are impediments to profit, they will override the democratic decision. One can agree or disagree with capitalism as a productive system, but it is impossible, if words have any meaningful connection to lived experience, to claim that it is democratic.

Marxism has long been derided as antidemocratic, and there is no doubt that twentieth-century attempts to build revolutionary socialist societies led to totalitarian disasters. Nevertheless, at its theoretical core, as both a critique of capitalism and a set of principles for a new society, no other theory identified so clearly the structurally undemocratic nature of capitalism and the limited ability of liberal rights to correct this problem. Read charitably and not ideologically, Marx exposes the fact that minority control of that which everyone needs to survive and flourish is incompatible with democratic self-determination. That point is almost tautological. What inflames Marx's critics is the further claim that equal rights to participate in a political system that is constitutionally debarred from interfering with private property in those resources necessary for life is not a sufficient corrective for the undemocratic implications of basic property relations. His most systematic examination of liberal rights, the early essay "On the Jewish Question," does not conclude that liberal rights are undemocratic, but rather that the democratic potential of entitlements to participate in the political process and formal guarantees of due process, freedom of speech, conscience, and religion is limited, if not totally destroyed, by the fact that control over resources confers de facto social power over everyone's life, which is legitimated by de jure private property rights.[39] When he later returns to strictly political themes, in essays like "The Eighteenth Brumaire of Louis Napoleon," and "The Civil War in France," Marx proves himself a keen analyst of the complexities of actual political struggle and a champion of popular democratic power from below.[40] That which most dismays him about "bourgeois political democracy" is still an obvious problem today: It is a contest between parties and personalities, none of whom dare expose the real structure of inequality that undermines the ability of the majority of people to *effectively* participate in democratic self-governance. That which most excited him about the Paris Commune was not that it was an example of the "dictatorship of the proletariat" liquidating the class enemy, but that it showed that ordinary people really could run their own lives.

The Paris Commune was a representative democracy, but one that, even if only ephemerally and locally, overcame the structural impediments to self-determination that undermine liberal representative democracies. If Marx's critique of liberalism is paradigmatic for my own conception of democracy, it is as much because of what he retains of liberalism as what he rejects. What he rejects is not so much the need for formal constitutional rules to structure and limit political power as the underlying social structure that contradicts the democratic value of constitutional order. Recall from chapter 1 that Marx understood democracy through the lens of popular *self-constitution*, as expressed in collective practices like a constituent assembly, where people come together as a collective to decide the rules they will live by. As Georgios Daremas rightly argues,

> Any theory of democracy must conceptualize a rational state in which people's sovereignty is or can be self-consciously actualized. Marx's critique of both Hegel's state and the modern constitutional state castigates the disembodied character of existing "democracy" as pure formalism where the "democratic element" participates only "in abstraction" in an "abstract political state" divorced from the universal affairs of the actual society. The first step to remedy this schism is the actualization of political democracy via the consolidation of genuine popular representation.[41]

What worries Marx is the way in which property forms can act as a prior constraint on this self-constituting power.

The whole point of Marx's argument, therefore, is to illuminate the path down from the abstraction of the state into the depths of the "universal affairs" (i.e., the control over and values governing the use of life-sustaining and life-developing resources). There can be no real democratic self-determination until collective control and need-governed access to those resources is secured through democratic struggle. A democratic constitution would enshrine and protect those material gains. If liberals should rejoin that neither Marx nor later Marxists have figured out a workable overall social model that combines collective ownership, substantive democracy, *and* the constitutional limits on political power necessary to check totalitarian power, I would completely agree. That fact does not mean the required synthesis is impossible, and I will propose the outlines of such a synthesis in the final chapter. At this point, let us move to consider the real costs of the separation of formally democratic political power from the "universal affairs" of society.

INEQUALITY AS A LIFE OR DEATH ISSUE

Marx was famously critical of equality of rights. In "The Critique of the Gotha Program" he argued that rights abstract from the real differences between people. A free, democratic society must ultimately recognize these real differences rather than abstract from them. Nevertheless, equality of rights was an important plateau in the struggle for a society that required contribution on the basis of individual talent and rewarded it on the basis of individual needs.[42] As McMurtry argues, "equality is an appealing goal, but it is dismissed as 'crude leveling' by Marx. . . . The problem is that it is a reverse panacea to the private money-sequencing that multiplies inequality. The real issue is that people's lives are deprived of life-goods without which their human capacities are stunted."[43] The liberal critique of inequality of income illustrates Marx's and McMurtry's point clearly. It does not question the equation of good lives with the accumulation of money, or the reduction of the value of things and people to their price. Disparities of income in themselves are not the problem—the deleterious impact on the quality of people's lives is.

Pioneering work in the social determinants of health has revealed that inequality has statistically measurable negative impacts on health. The social determinants of health are, in general, "the cause of the causes" of morbidity and death.[44] Instead of focusing on disease as caused by pathogenic invasion, they call attention to the ways in which bodies are affected by the social environment. "Health" refers holistically to the quality of our lives, to our ability to realize our goals in meaningful and valuable projects. Income, exposure to pollution, education, the quality of work, access to cultural institutions, leisure, and, in general, the degree of control over one's life (which is determined by the other factors) all affect morbidity and mortality.

Few have done more to advance work on the social determinants of health and connect them to a critique of inequality than Sir Michael Marmot. In every country where the research has been undertaken, he has found that the lower down on the income scale one finds oneself, the less power over one's life one has, the worse one's health outcomes are. The rich live in cleaner environments, go to better schools, lead generally less stressful lives, have access to better health care, have richer cultural experiences, and, above all, have greater control over their lives and lifetime. Consequently, they are better able to satisfy their needs and realize their goals and capacities. He has discovered that health tracks what he calls the "social gradient." "All the way, from the top to bottom of society, the lower you are, the worse your health. The gradient includes all of us below the topmost 1 percent."[45] Our lives are our whole being. If they are damaged, nothing can compensate. Money is no good to a corpse. Hence, if the goal of democratic social organization is to ensure the best lives possible, Marmot's findings cannot be ignored.

They are ignored, unsurprisingly, by neoclassical economists blindly committed to measuring the value of life by a monetary metric. Unlike their egalitarian counterparts, who see monetary inequality as a violation of liberal egalitarianism, their neoclassical counterparts see inequality as a sign of the superior value of the lives of the rich. From their perspective, the only way to value anything is to see how much someone is willing to pay for it. Since the rich are willing to pay more for health care, they value their lives more than others who are willing to pay less, and so, judged by the only objective measure we have (price), the lives of the rich are worth more than the lives of the poor. It would therefore be economically irrational for the state to spend scarce health care dollars on the poor, since that would mean, in their view, spending more on lives that are less valuable. "Their model says that the societal value of life is greater, i) the higher the lifetime income, ii) the less illness people have, iii) the closer in age people are at the onset of illness. If you use [these economists'] valuation of life to make allocation decisions, you spend the money where it will yield the greatest result, measured in dollars. It is inefficient to care for the poor, the sick, the young."[46] One thus gets a health care system not unlike that of the United States, which keeps the very old, very white, and very rich alive at the expense of everyone else.[47] The vast majority of people, even in the age of the Affordable Care Act, cannot afford the top-quality health care on sale to the wealthy. The justification provided by the marginalist economists cloaks itself in the mantle of scientificity but is really a return to an aristocratic worldview in which those at the top of the class structure are assumed to deserve their social position because of superior moral worth. The degeneration of social science toward naked ideological excuse for the existing hierarchies of wealth and power tracks the decline of political life from liberal democracy to plutocratic oligarchy.

No one can mistake this plutocratic ethos for a democratic value once it is laid bare. It is a testament to the power of ideology that it is not laid bare clearly or often enough to spark a mass democratic opposition. But how would a democratic society value life? We have defined democracy as a collectively self-determining society. Its fundamental social condition is need-governed access to the fundamental natural and social conditions of life support and development for each and all, attained through self-organization and self-government across key social institutions, and not top-down bureaucratic management. The subjective dimension of democracy demands that citizens care about one another, as equally needy and capable humans and individuals with their own identity and goals. Allocative decisions would be made on the basis of the principle that all human life is of equal moral value, but actual distributions would have to take into account concrete differences. Women have different concrete health care needs than men, full equality in a multilingual state like Canada would require protection for minority languages, and so on. The overarching goal is to build a society in which (a) everyone has the effective power to speak and articulate their own interests, (b) everyone understands that they share fundamental interests with others, (c) that failure to satisfy these interests (their fundamental needs) is the social cause of irreparable harm to the quality of life, and (d) in which no one has anything to fear from an organized ruling class that controls what everyone needs to survive because that class does not exist. Such a society could not tolerate gross inequalities in the distribution of life goods.

Not only would allowing some to suffer be completely inconsistent with its ruling value principles, the organized political voice and power of people who currently occupy a subaltern position would always be powerful enough to stop it. That is, a society that contains differences of gender, race, ethnicity, and so on can only be self-determining if those differences are not marks of inferiority and oppression. They are sources of different perspectives and concrete shapes of universal needs, which have to be fully and freely articulated and *satisfied*. If any group's needs were not satisfied, the society would not be fully self-determining, because a society that contains different identities can only be self-determining if collectively binding decisions result from deliberations in which each group and individual affected has real political voice. Thus, assuming the general acceptance of the democratic ethos of solidarity and equal satisfaction of the shared life-interest of each and all, the expressed voice of groups who currently occupy a subaltern position would be sufficient to realign principle and practice wherever they deviate.

Of course the society I describe is an ideal horizon toward which democratic struggles tend. How far it can be realized in practice is an open historical question. The goal serves as a critical foil against which any actual democratic society can measure itself. In the current world, it exposes the real contradiction between inequality and democracy. Inequality of power over life conditions means objectively worse lives for those with less power. Rather than the virtuous circle of democracy (shared commitment to need-satisfaction frees people's talents and voices, which creates strong citizens, who participate in the public life of the society and ensure that resources continue to be used to satisfy needs and enable life-capacities), today's capitalism suffers from a vicious circle of inequality, disempowerment, lack of voice, entrenched political power of the rich, and deeper inequality. At the same time, the memory and reality of past democratic struggles have not been extinguished. There remains the social and political space to theorize and identify the problems and organize against them. Liberal-capitalism and democracy are in tension, as we discovered in chapter 2, but there are real democratic institutions that can be the basis for new struggles.

Unfortunately, these same political institutions can be captured by the ruling class and exploited for their own purposes. The most dangerous form of capture, from the perspective of future democratic development, occurs when a demagogue articulates people's legitimate anger at their own powerlessness into fuel for an authoritarian political machine. Inequality of power over life conditions has created tens of millions of people who are more or less disenfranchised and feel intense resentment. Right-wing populism has exploited the feelings of powerlessness that widening inequality has generated. These people come together as a collective political subject, but their democratic energies are turned not against the real causes of their powerlessness but against demonized scapegoats. I will argue in the next chapter that while superficially democratic, right-wing populism is the main political threat to democracy as self-determination today.

NOTES

1. Credit Suisse Research Institute, *Global Wealth Report 2017*; http://publications.credit-suisse.com/tasks/render/file/index.cfm?fileid=12DFFD63-07D1-EC63-A3D5F67356880EF3 (accessed December 14, 2017).

2. Thomas Piketty, *Capital in the Twenty-first Century* (Cambridge, MA: Harvard University Press, 2014), 48.

3. Ibid., 349.

4. All figures are from the *World Income Database*, compiled and maintained by Thomas Piketty and Emmanuel Saez; http://wid.world/ (accessed December 14, 2017). Since there is an ever-growing mountain of real-time income and wealth inequality data readily available, I will use statistics sparingly and focus on the theoretical explanations of widening inequality and its negative political consequences for democracy.

5. In the United Kingdom the same general structure of racialized inequality exists. A recent study found that South Asian and black families earned on average between 8,900 and 5,600 pounds less per year than white households. See Adam Corlett, *Diverse Outcomes: Living Standards by Ethnicity* (London: Resolution Foundation, 2017); http://www.resolutionfoundation.org/app/uploads/2017/08/Diverse-outcomes.pdf (accessed December 14, 2017). Similar racialized structures of inequality exist in Canada, but the bottom of the income hierarchy is occupied by indigenous women and children living on reserves. Sixty percent (!) of indigenous children living on reserves are in poverty. (By comparison, 18 percent of nonindigenous children live in poverty in Canada, which places the country twenty-seventh out of thirty-four OECD countries.) See David MacDonald and Daniel Wilson, *Shameful Neglect: Indigenous Child Poverty in Canada* (Canadian Centre for Policy Alternatives, 2016); https://www.policyalternatives.ca/sites/default/files/upload/publications/NationalOffice/2016/05/Indigenous_Child Poverty.pdf (accessed December 13, 2017).

6. Valerie Wilson, Janelle Jones, Kayla Blado, and Elise Gould, "Black Women Have to Work 7 Months into 2017 to Be Paid the Same as White Men in 2016," *Economic Policy Institute* (July 28, 2017); http://www.epi.org/blog/black-women-have-to-work-7-months-into-2017-to-be-paid-the-same-as-white-men-in-2016/ (accessed December 14, 2017).

7. Joseph Stiglitz, *The Great Divide: Unequal Societies and What We Can Do about Them* (New York: W. W. Norton, 2015), 140–41.

8. F. Michael Higginbotham, *Ghosts of Jim Crow: Ending Racism in Post-Racial America* (New York: New York University Press, 2013), 157.

9. The most extreme version of this argument was advanced by Thomas Malthus. Thomas Malthus, *An Essay on the Principle of Population* (Amherst, NY: Prometheus Books, 1998).

10. Friedrich Engels, *The Condition of the Working Class in England* (Frogmore, UK: Panther Books, 1969).

11. Simon Kuznets, "Economic Growth and Income Inequality," *The American Economic Review*, vol. 45, no. 1 (March 1955), 18.

12. Some American economists predict that the age of rapid economic growth is permanently over. Robert C. Gordon concludes his study of American growth with the conclusion that computing technology is unlikely to have the same growth promoting effects as earlier inventions like electricity and the automobile. See Robert C. Gordon, *The Rise and Fall of American Growth* (Princeton, NJ: Princeton University Press, 2016).

13. Piketty, *Capital in the Twenty-first Century*, 15.

14. For a more fine-grained analysis and critique of these policies, see Jason Hickle, *The Great Divide: A Brief Guide to Global Inequality and its Solutions* (London: Penguin Books, 2018).

15. Piketty, *Capital in the Twenty-first Century*, 48.

16. Ibid., 52.

17. Ibid., 166.

18. He has been criticized by Daron Acemoglu and James A. Robinson for calling these formulas laws. See Daron Acemoglu and James A. Robinson, "The Rise and Decline of General Laws of Capitalism," *Journal of Economic Perspectives*, vol. 29, no. 1 (Winter 2015), 3–28. He has also been criticized, more generally, by David Harvey for misunderstanding the nature of capital. See David Harvey, "Afterthoughts on Piketty's Capital," davidharvey.org; http://davidharvey.org/2014/05/afterthoughts-pikettys-capital/ (accessed December 19, 2017). Whatever the merits of these critiques, they do not undermine the general picture Piketty paints of contemporary capitalism as structurally and politically geared toward ever-widening inequalities.

19. Piketty, *Capital in the Twenty-first Century*, 179.

20. Ibid., 173.

21. Stiglitz, *The Great Divide*, 92–93.

22. Joseph Stiglitz, *The Price of Inequality* (New York: Norton, 2013), 296–7. These tendencies have only been exacerbated since 2013, when the second edition of the book was published. Trump's so-called tax reform's reductions in tax rates for middle income earners are ideological cover for a massive attack on progressivity; most of the planned reductions for middle income earners will expire by 2027. See Paul Krugman, "The Greatest Tax Scam in History," *New York Times,* November 27, 2017; https://www.nytimes.com/2017/11/27/opinion/senate-tax-bill-scam.html (accessed December 19, 2017).

23. Piketty, *Capital in the Twenty-first Century*, 246; Stiglitz, *The Price of Inequality*, 225, 279.

24. Piketty, *Capital in the Twenty-first Century*, 463.

25. Ibid., 464.

26. Sanford Lakoff, "Inequality as a Danger to Democracy: Reflections on Piketty's Warning," *Political Science Quarterly*, vol. 130, no. 3 (2015), 434–35.

27. Jodi Dean, *Democracy and Other Neo-liberal Fantasies: Communicative Capitalism and Left Politics* (Durham, NC: Duke University Press, 2009), 76. Wendy Brown makes similarly problematic claims. See Wendy Brown, *Undoing the Demos* (New York: Zone Books, 2015).

28. Katie Allen, "FTSE CEOs Earn 386 times more than workers on national living wage," *The Guardian*, March 22, 2017; https://www.theguardian.com/business/2017/mar/22/uk-ceos-national-living-wage-equality-trust-pay-gap (accessed December 20, 2017).

29. Karl Marx, *Capital*, vol. 1 (Moscow: Progress Publishers, 1986), 669.

30. David McNally, *Global Slump: The Economics and Politics of Crisis and Resistance* (Oakland, CA: PM Press, 2011), 120.

31. Glen Sean Coulthard, *Red Skin, White Masks: Rejecting the Colonial Politics of Recognition* (Minneapolis: University of Minnesota Press, 2014), 11.

32. Enrique Dussel, *Ethics of Liberation in the Age of Globalization and Exclusion* (Durham, NC: Duke University Press, 2013).

33. Johanna Brenner, "21st Century Socialist Feminism," *Socialist Studies*, vol. 10, no. 1 (Summer 2014), 33. For a detailed examination of the construction of heterosexual normalcy in the colonial context, see Maria Lugones, "Heterosexualism and the Modern Colonial/Gender System," *Hypatia*, vol. 22, no. 1 (2007), 186–209, and Alan Sears, "Body Politics: The Social Reproduction of Sexualities," *Social Reproduction Theory*, Tithi Bhattacharya, ed. (London: Pluto, 2017), 171–91.

34. Stiglitz, *The Price of Inequality*, 174.

35. John McMurtry, *The Cancer Stage of Capitalism: From Crisis to Cure*, second edition (London: Pluto Press, 2013).

36. Damien Cahill and Martijn Koning, "Neoliberalism: A Useful Concept?" *The Bullet*, December 1, 2017; https://socialistproject.ca/2017/12/b1518/ (accessed December 20, 2017).

37. McNally, *Global Slump*, 67.

38. Quoted in Grace Lee Boggs (with Scott Kurashige), *The Next American Revolution: Sustainable Activism for the Twenty-First Century* (Berkeley: University of California Press, 2012), 197.

39. Karl Marx, "On the Jewish Question," *Collected Works*, vol. 3 (Moscow: Progress Publishers, 1975), esp. 164–67.

40. Karl Marx, "The Eighteenth Brumaire of Louis Napoleon," *The Marx-Engels Reader*, Robert C. Tucker, ed. (New York, W. W. Norton, 1978),

594–618; Karl Marx, "The Civil War in France," *The Marx-Engels Reader,* Robert C. Tucker, ed. (New York, W. W. Norton, 1978), 618–53. The most detailed textual-historical study of Marx and Engels's actual positions on liberal-democratic norms and their actual practice vis-à-vis democratic self-organization of the working class is August H. Nimtz Jr., *Marx and Engels: Their Contribution to the Democratic Breakthrough* (Albany, NY: State University of New York Press, 2000).

41. Georgios Daremas, "Marx's Theory of Democracy in his Critique of Hegel's Theory of the State," *Karl Marx and Contemporary Philosophy,* Andrew Chitty and Martin McIvor, eds. (London: Palgrave MacMillan, 2009), 91.

42. Karl Marx, "The Critique of the Gotha Program," *The Marx-Engels Reader*, Robert C. Tucker, ed. (New York: W. W. Norton, 1978), 530–31. Despite the clarity of Marx's critique, some interpreters continue to read a liberal understanding of equality into his work. Norman Arthur Fischer, for example, claims that Marx's critique of private property is based on the belief that it violates certain negative liberties for working people. I cannot enter into the debate fully here, but I think there is abundant textual evidence in Marx, from the beginning to the end of his career, that proves Fischer's reading is simply wrong. Norman Arthur Fischer, *Marxist Ethics within Western Political Theory* (London: Palgrave MacMillan, 2015), 168.

43. McMurtry, *The Cancer Stage of Capitalism*, 300.

44. Michael Marmot, *The Health Gap: The Challenge of an Unequal World* (London: Bloomsbury Press, 2015), 45.

45. Ibid., 15.

46. Ibid., 86–87.

47. On average, as of 2015, white Americans could expect to live 3.4 years longer than black Americans. See Department of Health and Human Services, *Health, United States, 2015: With Special Feature on Racial and Ethnic Health Inequalities* (2017); https://www.cdc.gov/nchs/data/hus/hus15.pdf (accessed December 27, 2017).

Chapter 4

Right-Wing Populism as a Threat to Democracy

Democratic self-determination demands that everyone be able to mean-ingfully participate in the creation of law and public policy, that these laws and policies serve the shared life-interest in sustainable need-satisfaction, and that citizens consciously commit themselves to establishing the social conditions in which each can develop and flourish as self-creative com-munities and individuals. As it stands, while the majority of people might enjoy formal equality of rights, their lives are shorter, sicker, and more precarious—the very opposite of what a fully democratic society requires. Hence, instead of collective self-determination, purportedly democratic societies are ruled by private economic interests that prevail over all other interests, bend the platforms of all mainstream political parties to serve them, and capture major social institutions.

However, being poor and precarious does not undermine one's abil-ity to think and draw comparisons. Workers, whose real wages have been stagnant for forty years, can see that others are getting richer. Young workers struggling to hang on to part-time or contract jobs can see others go off to elite universities. The obvious disparities can cause frustration, resentment, and anger. Since political organization and mobilization is permitted in liberal-democratic societies, this resent-ment and anger can motivate political action. Marx hoped it would eventually unify the working class into a global revolutionary move-ment—an all too hopeful prediction that underestimated the complexity of political organization. In reality, political forces across the spectrum, from revolutionary socialists to fascists, compete to channel work-ing class anger. Most recently, right-wing populist movements have successfully captured enough of this anger to ensconce themselves in power.

At root, I will argue that driving this anger in that section of the working class attracted to right-wing populism are unmet fundamental natural and social needs. However, it is important to stress at the outset that the constituency for right-wing populism is not exclusively white working class people. In the United States, Trump attracted the typical wealthy white supporters of the Republican party and achieved victory by convincing a relatively small number of white working class voters in key midwestern states who had voted for Obama to vote for him. In the United Kingdom, while some working class voters were attracted by the anti-immigrant rhetoric of the Leave side, it attracted its deepest support from middle class voters and longtime Euro-skeptics in the Conservative Party.[1] That said, I will focus on working class support for right-wing populism not because white workers are primarily responsible for the phenomenon, but because those elements of the working class that do support it are impeding the consolidation of a new democratic movement from below. Their legitimate demands are being exploited by dangerous antidemocratic forces from above. The racist, anti-immigrant, and authoritarian tendencies of right-wing populists are the main *political* threat to existing democratic institutions, as well as a more democratic future.

The inequality of power that causes working class anger has also reinvigorated social democratic politics. Bernie Sanders in America and Jeremy Corbyn in the United Kingdom captured the imaginations of millions of young people, who flocked anew to the Democrats and the Labour Party. I will discuss the role of reinvigorated social democratic parties to the future of the democratic project in the final chapter. Here I want to concentrate on the antidemocratic danger of right wing populism. Thus, while my analysis rejects the view that right-wing populism has attracted a majority of the population of European and North American countries disillusioned by democracy, it acknowledges that it is currently in power in the most powerful nation and is shaping the politics of arguably the second most powerful liberal-capitalist democracy, the United Kingdom. This chapter will thus concentrate on the politics that allowed them to gain power in the United States and the United Kingdom (Brexit)—as well as Italy, Poland, Hungary, Austria, and most recently in the largest Canadian province, Ontario—and not the narrow margins by which they have won.

The growth of right-wing populism has set off alarm bells among defenders of liberal-democratic orthodoxy. Sanford Lakoff, whose concerns about the undemocratic implications of rising inequality we discussed in the previous chapter, draws parallels to the volatile situation in the 1920s and 1930s, when economic catastrophe catalyzed fascist movements in Europe.[2] Liz Fekete's detailed analysis of the reemergence of neo-fascist movements at the extreme right of the populist upsurge prove that Sanford is not indulging in hyperbole.[3] Others, like Foa and Mounk, claim that the growth of these movements portends the deconsolidation of democracy. They point to the ethnic uniformity of the mass base of the movements as evidence of deep racism, and they worry that mistrust of the mainstream media implies the splitting of the universe of truth into politicized camps where only partisan advantage matters. It would be foolish to dismiss these concerns. Right-wing populism does pose a number of threats to those elements of contemporary society that are democratic. The nationalist government of Poland has moved to undermine the independence of the judiciary, and right-wing populist movements everywhere strengthen the executive branch of government against the legislative branch. At the outer limits, strengthening executive power can lead to rule by decree that silences the broader range of voices represented in parliamentary bodies. Nationalist rhetoric obscures the reality of ethnic pluralism and encourages xenophobia, hostility, and violence against immigrants and minorities. The iconography of right-wing populism tends toward heroic portrayals of the military and police as guardians and saviors of the nation. Police and army worship binds the population more closely to the security and surveillance state that has done so much to erode civil and political liberties everywhere since 9/11. On the margins of the movement, like whitewater on the crest of a wave, far-right elements who are openly fascist in their aims are encouraged. But as dangerously undemocratic as all these elements of right-wing populist movements are, arguably the biggest threat they pose to the future of democracy may be the cult of personality they generate around a leader to the detriment of self-organization for systematic change from below.[4] There are no saviors in politics. Democratic development depends on organization and collective action.

Even though right-wing populism poses a serious threat to democracy, both the limited democracy of existing liberal-capitalist societies and a more deeply democratic future, it would be wrong to dismiss the mass base of right-wing populist movements as incorrigible, uneducated racists bent on destroying liberal-democracy. For the fact is, as chapter 3 established, that liberal civilization has failed working people of all colors and genders. Although there is much oppositional ferment, this bubbling has not yet coalesced into coherent programmatic alternatives to undemocratic capitalism, and this fact allows right-wing populists to channel the energies that could be channeled in more radically transformative, democratic directions. The only solution is to keep arguing with those supporters that the material interests they think will be served by Trump and his ilk will not be served. No movement that wants a more democratic future can afford to dismiss working class supporters of Trump or other right-wing populists as "a basket of deplorables."[5] Opponents must spend less time moralizing and more time convincing right-wing populism's supporters that a better world is possible. Democratic defenders must convince marginalized people of all sorts that their own understanding of their unmet needs forms the basis of their struggle, and that they need to develop their own collective agency rather than look for racialized scapegoats. They have to learn where real power lies, and imagine new ways of taking that power back. Unchallenged, right-wing populist movements represent a serious threat to the democratic elements of liberal-democratic capitalism. Properly understood, they pose a challenge to the status quo that creates an opportunity for rebuilding a democratic left capable of satisfying the unmet needs that motivate populism's supporters. Right-wing populism thus has a paradoxical relationship with democratic struggles. A crucial element of its supporters suffer from systematic deprivation of the goods they need to fully participate in the collective determination of their society's development, but this democratically legitimate demand for access and voice is being exploited by demagogic leaders with undemocratic goals.

I will develop my argument in three sections. In the first I will return to Foa and Mounk's hypothesis of "democratic deconsolidation." While acknowledging the legitimacy of their concern, I will reject their conclusion in favor of an alternative hypothesis. Support for right-wing populist movements does not mean people are rejecting democracy but, rather, are rejecting the mainstream politicians who have consistently failed them. The second section will focus on the history and distinguishing characteristics of right-wing populist movements. I will support my claims that right-wing populism has a paradoxical relationship with democracy with the example of the movement that elected Donald Trump. In the final section I will return to the problem first posed in chapter 1: What is really in everyone's interests? My answer is that the satisfaction of the core human needs discussed in chapter 1 is really in everyone's interests. It is necessary and politically possible to bring supporters of right-wing populist movements around to seeing that what they want from their populist leader they can only get from organizing themselves against the structures of class power and privilege.

DEMOCRATIC DECONSOLIDATION?

Foa and Mounk feared that the success of right-wing populist movements in Eastern Europe, the United Kingdom, and the United States was evidence of weakening support for democracy and the growth of authoritarian tendencies. "These changes," they write, "are worrying in and of themselves. What is all the more striking is that they are reflected in actual political behavior. In recent years, parties and candidates that blame an allegedly corrupt political establishment for most problems, seek to concentrate power in the executive, and challenge key norms of democratic politics have achieved unprecedented success in a large number of liberal-democracies."[6] Even more alarming is the possibility that these shifts of opinion and preference are not temporary but evidence of a systematic "deconsolidation" of liberal-democracy.

Consolidation theory argues that once democratic polities become stable, they prove so superior to other forms of social organization that their institutions become permanent. "Consolidated democracies," they write, "are stable, because their citizens have come to believe that democratic forms of government possess unique legitimacy and that authoritarian alternatives are unacceptable. . . . What happens to the stability of wealthy liberal-democracies when many of their citizens no longer believe their system of government is especially legitimate?"[7] The answer is that they enter into a period of political crisis where formerly fringe parties like the United Kingdom Independence Party or political jokes like Donald Trump gain voice and power. Whether that voice or power is evidence of a widespread and systematic rejection of democracy is another question altogether. There is no doubt that the trends that worry Foa and Mounk are real. What is less certain is whether their interpretation of the value of liberal-democracy and their conclusion that right-wing populism is essentially antidemocratic are correct.

Let us first note that for many citizens of wealthy liberal-democracies, life is already lived under an authoritarian cloud of policing and poverty. For First Nations youth in the cities of western Canada, police violence is a constant threat. If you are one of the millions of African American men in prison in the United States, daily life is already a militarized routine.[8] If you are a young woman in need of an abortion in a state that has effectively banned it, or an impoverished unemployed addict in the formerly bustling manufacturing cities of the US Midwest, the idea of a *wealthy* liberal-democratic society would be a fiction or a distant memory. It is true that these groups do not form the constituency for right-wing populism. The point here is that what Foa and Mounk call democracy is not close to fully democratic. Rejection of liberal-capitalist society is not necessarily rejection of "democracy." Hence the first problem with Foa and Mounk's analysis is that they do not consider the possibility that when people reject liberal-capitalist society, they might do so because, from their perspective, it is not democratic.

Expressions of disaffection with *the way things are* does not necessarily mean disaffection with democracy as such. Foa and Mounk write as though "corrupt elites" are a figment of people's imagination, whereas the trends toward increasing inequality studied in the previous chapter prove that they are all too real. When working class voters choose a right-wing populist candidate, they are expressing disappointment with other parties and asserting a demand for self-determination *against* structures of power and the institutions responsible for the social problems they face.

The problem is that by choosing the right-wing populist path, they end up investing power in an authoritarian movement that will further disempower them. The distinguishing mark of democratic power, remember, is that, because it emerges from the deliberative association of people themselves, it is not an oppressive external force. That holds only as long as people work as a collective to steer major social institutions through deliberations that include all concerned to ensure that the fundamental needs of each are satisfied. When citizens explicitly decide for themselves the laws and policies they will obey—within an over-arching commitment to the satisfaction of the core needs of each and all, in sustainable ways—they determine their collective life-horizons. Right-wing populists *promise* to restore "power to the people," but in practice they reinforce rather than challenge the undemocratic structures and forces of capitalist society.

Nevertheless, voting for a right-wing populist party because it promises to restore voice to people who feel their concerns have been ignored is not necessarily a vote against democracy. Any society is undemocratic to the extent that it fails to satisfy the natural and social conditions of self-determination. Liberal-democracies can be undemocratic if they operate according to reified system dynamics that fail to satisfy citizens' core human needs and are led by politicians who, wittingly or not, do the bidding of the socioeconomic groups that benefit most from those dynamics. Rejecting liberal-democratic norms because they do not work in the way they are advertised is not, therefore, *necessarily* a sign of democratic deconsolidation. It could also be a democratic expression of widespread frustration against norms and institutions that claim to be democratic but are not.

Let us examine this problem in more detail. The consolidation thesis assumes that democracy is some finally settled structure and not a *practice* and *collective activity*. If we examine the history of democracy from the English Civil War on, we can see the problem with this view. Democracy has always been a set of struggles between opposed visions of what it should look like. Liberals have struggled to stabilize democracy by domesticating democratic power as settled rights to be adjudicated by experts in the courts when alleged violations occur. Social movements, by contrast, have repeatedly arisen in response to systematically unmet needs and demanded actual power to participate as equals in the steering of public life. The solution of one structural problem expands the scope of democratic agency but simultaneously exposes new problems. The history of democracy is thus not a history that moves from dynamism to institutional stasis, but a dialectic of stabilization and popular unsettling in response to unmet needs. When this dialectic is pushed in a democratic direction, needs are better satisfied and the scope and depth of democratic agency expands. When anti-democratic forces push back, needs go unmet and democratic agency contracts and weakens. The current moment is paradoxical. Some of the political energy behind right-wing populist movements is democratic and is motivated by unmet needs, but it is being displaced onto deeply undemocratic movements and leaders who have effectively scapegoated immigrants and refugees as the cause of economic and social problems generated at a structural level. The solution is not to decry the people expressing the energy, but to argue with them politically that the search for a single champion who will solve all problems from above never works out in the interests of "the people."

This paradox takes the form of a political crisis and instability, but it does not follow that the instability must be solved according to the terms offered by right-wing populist leaders. Trump, for example, has not only energized his base but also revivified the American Left, which must now face the challenge of convincing Trump's working class base that he is not going to solve the problems they think he is going to solve.[9] However the struggle turns out, this degree of popular mobilization can hardly be dismissed as undemocratic. Polished professional party politicians who have for a century claimed to embody democracy while serving the socioeconomic interests of the ruling class are being challenged precisely because they have not represented or advanced the people's interests in securing the conditions for their own self-determination. Now, there are left and right, democratic and self-undermining ways to challenge the party machines and phony tribunes, but my point at this stage of the argument is simply to contest Foa and Mounk's conclusion that we are drifting toward authoritarian shoals. Of course we might be, but only if opponents of right-wing populism in America and Europe squander the opening for mobilization and political education that a crisis opens up.

POPULISM AND RIGHT-WING POPULISM

Before a final decision can be rendered on the paradoxical relationship between right-wing populism and democratic development, we need to think more carefully about the nature of populism in general and right-wing populism in particular. The most general feature of all populist movements is that they pretend not to appeal to sectional interests or identities like class or race, claiming to speak for "the people" in general. All populist movements thus draw upon the liberal-democratic and republican idea of popular sovereignty, but the extension of the concept "the people" differs significantly depending upon the actual politics of the particular movement. Left-wing populist movements try to construct popular fronts that include the exploited and oppressed—the majority of the citizen body—against the ruling class, while right-wing populist movements focus on a subset of the exploited, playing up their resentments against even more marginalized groups while targeting a nebulous "elite." The wide variability of the extension of the concept "the people" explains why, in his important examination of populism, Ernesto Laclau calls it an "empty signifier."[10] He means that it does not designate a natural kind, but rather refers to whatever subset of the totality of the citizen body can be mobilized around a set of demands presented as universally important. These demands will always be grounded in unmet needs, but right-wing populism dispenses with demonstrable causal explanations of poverty and powerlessness in favor of invigorating rhetoric that energizes but does not explain or solve problems. Nevertheless, that does not mean that the members of right-wing populist movements do not value democracy; it means the movements are ineffective means of solving the problems their impoverished supporters expect them to solve.

According to Laclau, the emergence of populist movements has three preconditions: "the formation of an internal antagonistic frontier separating 'the people' from power, an equivalential articulation of demands making the emergence of 'the people' possible, . . . and the unification of these demands . . . into a stable system of signification."[11] The key to the movement is to make a set of particular demands universal. No political demands are universally motivating just because they express unmet needs—needs go unmet all the time; they are not always motivating. A populist movement explodes when a set of those unmet needs is effectively activated as motivation for political struggle in the name of "the people" (i.e., the members of the movement). The demands become effectively universal when they become part of the platform of a movement with widespread (but never total) support.

Right-wing populism is a threat to democracy because it constructs "the people" against a demonized other, whom only a strong leader can vanquish. The other—always a different race, ethnicity, or nationality—masks deeper structural causes and class interests that are the real barrier to more inclusive and comprehensive satisfaction of people's needs. Left-wing populist movements, as I noted, can also invest too much hope and power in a leader, but they differ from right-wing populist movements in important ways. The most important is that left-wing movements tend to be inclusive of a variety of exploited and oppressed groups: workers, trade unionists, women, racialized minorities. Of course there can be tensions between these groups, between class and identity politics, for example, but the art of democratic politics is precisely to overcome these tensions by revealing the common needs that underlie social differences. Right-wing populists try to dissolve differences into a shared ethnic or national identity in opposition to universal needs shared beneath and across ethnic or national identities. They construct "the people" around an ethnic or racial identity set against other identities as the enemy: (white) Americans against Muslims and Mexicans; true Englishmen against Eastern European immigrants; law-abiding Filipinos against drug addicts. In left-wing populism, the enemy is defined by its structural position in the hierarchy of wealth and power. In right-wing populism, the wealth and power of a generic "elite" is denounced, but the cause of people's problems is typically deflected onto the demonized other, who is accused of soaking up benefits that would otherwise go the "deserving" group that forms the base of the movement.

John Judis explains the difference clearly:

> Left-wing populism champions the people against an elite or an establishment. There is a vertical politics of the bottom and middle against the top. Right-wing populists champion the people against an elite, that they accuse of coddling a third group, which can consist of, for instance, immigrants, Islamists, or African American militants. Left-wing populism is dyadic. Right-wing populism is triadic. It looks upward, but also down upon an out group.[12]

The out group is universally racialized and denounced as unproductive scroungers and greedy consumers of undeserved public benefits. In the classic case of the United States, the demonized outgroup almost always includes African Americans, but it has taken on a staggering variety of other identities in addition: American Indians, Jews, Muslims, the Irish, Catholics, Chinese, Japanese, Latinos—any immigrant group that can be portrayed as non-white and un-American.

The racialized dimension of right-wing populism is a primary reason for its paradoxical relationship with democracy. The unmet needs of the base and the political energy they expend mobilizing are democratic. As Judis again notes, "Populist campaigns and policies . . . often function as warning signs of a political crisis . . . ; they have won success . . . when people see prevailing political norms—put forward . . . as being at odds with their own hopes, fears, and concerns."[13] However, in the case of right-wing populism, the leaders divert this democratic energy toward exclusionary, undemocratic ends, racializing the conflict and setting subaltern groups against one another rather than socializing the conflict and building an inclusive movement of the exploited and oppressed. Racializing the conflict is undemocratic because democratic demands are those that seek to fulfill unmet core needs and satisfy the conditions for self-determination *for everyone whose needs are not met.* While the content that satisfies the needs might vary between different identities, their status as needs—natural and social conditions for life and self-determination—does not. Hence there is a real equivalence (as I will explain in more detail in the next section) between the unmet needs of workers of all races and genders and the concrete needs of women and racialized groups and other oppressed minorities that *ought to* form the basis for a common platform. The right-wing construction of "the people" drives a wedge between a deserving oppressed minority (the productive white American man, prototypically) and the demonized others, thus limiting the scope of the movement, sowing division where there needs to be unity, and empowering demagogic leaders rather than the people themselves.

It also tends to strengthen the state in wholly undemocratic ways. Berlet and Lyons's superb study of two hundred years of American populism concludes that a "right-wing populist movement . . . is a repressive populist movement motivated or defined centrally by a backlash against liberation movements, social reform, or revolution; . . . its goals are fueled in a central way by forces of the left and its political gains."[14] The backlash typically takes the form of a perceived correction in the proper use of state power. The Left is denounced for forcing the state to fund programs for the undeserving. Support for the right-wing alternative is built around returning the state to its proper function: repression of social movements, generalized law and order, and a strong military to defend against external enemies. Trump displays all the hallmarks of a repressive, right-wing populist leader. Using Obama as his foil, he has marshaled a large minority of working class whites to line up with ruling class Republicans in support of his anti-immigrant, reactionary nationalist agenda.

Trump defied the Republican establishment and the pollsters with his victory, and his narcissism and boorishness continue to antagonize and shock his opponents.[15] Nevertheless, it is not true, as Bret Stephens argued in the *New York Times*, that "a vote for Trump was a vote for vulgarity."[16] The evidence suggests, rather, that a vote for Trump was either a vote for a tax cut (among traditional wealthy supporters of the Republican Party) or a vote for jobs (among that section of white and working class voters that chose him). Unfortunately, the vote for jobs was also expressed as a vote against immigrants, who many Trump supporters wrongly perceive as stealing work from Americans. Whatever the outcome of Trump's presidency, the movement that supported him during his candidacy and first year in office is a textbook case of a right-wing populist movement, and it clearly illustrates the paradoxical relationship of such movements to democracy.

In order to fully appreciate the significance of Trump, we need to set his politics in historical context. As I noted above, all right-wing American populist movements have used a racialized other as a foil against which they have constructed the antagonism around which they have built. In Trump's case, the racialized other was a tripartite set of enemies: Latin American immigrants, Islamic terrorists, and black inner-city criminals. All are non-white, and all were portrayed as deeply threatening to the interests of productive Americans. Despite the relentless televised outrage of liberal commentators, this trope is nothing new. Compare the following three quotations:

> Government should come from us. Now it comes at us with a propaganda machine in Washington that Hitler's propaganda chief, Goebbels, would have just envied. We've got to put the country back in control of the owners. And in plain Texas talk, it's time to take out the trash and clean out the barn, or it's going to be too late.[17]

> You don't force Americans making ten dollars an hour to compete with Mexican workers who have to work for a dollar an hour. . . . A country that loses control of its borders isn't really a country anymore.[18]

> We're now one step closer to liberating our citizens from this Obamacare nightmare, and delivering great health care for the American people. We're gonna do that too. And now tonight I'm back in the center of the American heartland, far away from the Washington swamp to spend time

with thousands of true American patriots. [Chants of "Drain the swamp."] We have spent the entire week celebrating with the hardworking men and women who are helping us make America great again. I'm here this evening to cut through the fake news filter and to speak straight to the American people. [Chants of "Drain the swamp" from the arena.][19]

The first quotation is from a Ross Perot speech in 1992, the second from Pat Buchanan in 1996, and the third from a Trump rally speech in 2017. The only difference between Perot's third-party bid for the White House, Buchanan's bid for the Republican nomination, and Trump is that Trump won where they lost. In terms of actual politics, there is no difference. But we can go even farther back in American history. Herbert Marcuse was writing about Nixon, but his argument applies word for word to the 2016 election: "In free elections with universal suffrage, the people have elected (not for the first time!) a warfare government, engaged for long years in a war which is but a series of crimes against humanity, a government of the representatives of the big corporations . . . propped up by a Congress that has reduced itself to a yes-machine, . . . a government that was elected with a considerable labor vote."[20] Or farther still, to the first major populist movement led by Andrew Jackson in the 1820s. Like Trump, he mobilized a large minority of poor and working whites, using anti-elitist rhetoric and playing on racial anxieties to build his support. As Chip Berlet and Matthew Lyons note, Jacksonians combined an "inclusive ideology of White egalitarianism" with "a hard racism of exclusion, terror, and oppression against people of color," which "spoke to lower class whites who feared an upper class alliance with people of color against them."[21] What this historical context shows is that Americans have repeatedly turned to right-wing populists as saviors from a society that has consistently failed to satisfy the interests of any subaltern group.

Nevertheless, despite the reality of underlying shared interests, the ideology of white supremacy has allowed right-wing populist movements to racialize the working class, turning it into *white* anger at blacks and other people of color. Higginbotham is talking about the Civil War, but it could apply to any period in American history:

By affirming their superior legal and social status over blacks, racist politics encourage poor whites to bond with the merchant class on the basis of race, instead of bonding with poor blacks on the basis of their socioeconomic status. This strategy served the economic interests of upper class whites by uniting poor whites around a single cause—their racial superiority to blacks.[22]

Thus, racism has always been at the heart of American right-wing populism. There can be no flinching from criticizing it full on—as immoral violence on the one hand and self-undermining undemocratic political stupidity on the other. At the same time, critics also have to try to work down to the social causes of racism, and work to overcome racism as an attitude and disposition by eliminating the social mechanisms that produce it.

Dismissing Trump voters (or the supporters of any right-wing populist movement) as "deplorables," or accusing them of voting for a vulgar spectacle for their own amusement, makes the mistake of confusing a surface show for real causes. Thinking that they all suffer from the Dunning-Kruger effect (being so incompetent that you do not know you are incompetent) is disgraceful, snobbish obfuscation of the political and economic suffering that millions of his voters live.[23] Right-wing populists exploit anxieties, it is true, but they also speak to needs in a politically effective way (i.e., in a way that actually mobilizes support). One sees essentially the same dynamics at work in the other great failure of liberal establishment politics: the Brexit referendum. As Richard Seymour has shown, key elements of both Trump voters and working class supporters of Brexit were people who feel themselves on a downward class trajectory, and they quite reasonably are struggling to stop it. "Those of whatever class," Seymour writes, "who experience a personal social decline related to a whole class decline are most likely to express attitudes of resentful nationalism."[24] That is not to say that traditional nationalists among longtime Tory supporters who have not experienced any decline in their wealth or status were not crucial to the Brexit vote.[25] It is to say that resentful nationalism, like hard racism, divides workers against themselves and saps their movements of the size and strength they need to fight negatively against austerity and positively for more deeply democratized social and economic institutions. At the same time, workers who voted for Trump or Brexit have real concerns that have been ignored for decades. Right-wing populists will not go away just because opponents find them obnoxious; they must be defeated politically. Success in that project cannot be achieved unless activists understand what drives supporters of right-wing populist movements and argue and engage with them in a way that acknowledges their interests.

In the case of Trump, the evidence suggests that the factors that tipped the election in his favor were his ability to speak to working class whites in a way that gave enough of them confidence that he would solve the socioeconomic crisis they have been suffering under. An analysis of exit poll data shows that the biggest gap between Trump and Clinton was among white men without college degrees. A Pew research analysis of the data found that "College graduates backed Clinton by a 9-point margin, while those without a college degree backed Trump 52 to 44. This is by far the widest gap in support among college graduates and non–college graduates in exit polls back to 1980."[26] This group of workers tends to be in competition with immigrant labor for unskilled jobs, a fact that helps explain the effectiveness of Trump's anti-immigrant rhetoric.[27] This margin of victory over Clinton among white men who lack a college education was enough to give him the razor-thin victories in the midwestern states that gave him the Electoral College victory. Trump himself understood this fact. In the leaked transcripts of his phone conversation with the Mexican president Enrique Peña Nieto, he admitted that the border wall was political fodder for his base, but his real agenda and appeal among his supporters was the promise of jobs.[28]

It may also be the case that Trump's candidacy was helped by his promise of a more isolationist foreign policy. In a careful statistical analysis of voting outcomes in key battleground states, Douglas Kriner and Francis Shen conclude that those districts that had suffered proportionally higher casualties in America's twenty-first-century wars leaned toward Trump.

> The data analysis presented in this working paper finds that in the 2016 election Trump spoke to this part of America. Even controlling in a statistical model for many other alternative explanations, we find that there is a significant and meaningful relationship between a community's rate of military sacrifice and support for Trump. Indeed, our results suggest that if three states key to Trump's victory—Pennsylvania, Michigan, and Wisconsin—had suffered even a modestly lower casualty rate, all three could have flipped from red to blue.[29]

Statistical correlations are not deductive proofs of the conclusion, but this paper adds support to my claim that support for Trump and right-wing populist movements generally is not an irrational mania but a response to unmet social needs. The sources of the support are democratic, but they are channeled in undemocratic directions.

Rechanneling the energy in a democratic direction will require serious engagement and sharp political argument. What we have seen from mainstream opposition to Trump is less serious analysis and more of what Laclau calls the denigration of the masses. "Populism has not only been demoted," he argues, but also "denigrated." "Its dismissal has been the part of the discursive construction of a certain normality, of an ascetic political universe from which its dangerous logics had to be excluded."[30] He was writing in 2005, but the argument helps make sense of the vitriolic denunciations of not only Trump himself, not only the white supremacist faction of his supporters, but all of his supporters. The democratic establishment and respectable press in the United States all give the impression of treating Trump voters as oafs who should stay out of politics and listen to their betters—exactly the type of elite disdain that drives some workers into the maw of right-wing populism. Resolving the democratic paradox of right-wing populism requires that we start from the conclusion of chapter 1: Democratic struggles develop out of unmet fundamental human needs (i.e., those needs that must be satisfied if people are to be able to participate as equals in the collective project of self-determination). Once opponents reground in the needs that drive the support for the movement, they establish common ground, and from this common ground an inclusive movement for democratic development is possible. As at least one example, opposition to the repeal of Obamacare, proves that this argument is not platitude but underlies effective practice. To conclude this chapter I will explain how understanding the historical connection between unmet needs and democratic struggle is central to overcoming the threat of right-wing populism and building an inclusive movement for democratic development.

UNMET NEEDS AND DEMOCRATIC SOLIDARITY

Berlet and Lyons abstract a set of conclusions about why people have been attracted to right-wing populist movements. These include issues readily evident in the case of Trump: "anxiety over social, cultural, and political change, fear of losing privilege and status; . . . a sense of disempowerment in the face of massive bureaucratic institutions; . . . economic hardship and dislocation, correlated to globalization, disillusionment with mainstream political choices, [and] the weakness or nonexistence of left-wing alternatives that speak effectively to many people's concerns."[31] Three things are worth noting. First, right-wing populism has historically specific and not identity-essentialist conditions. Poor white people are not all indelibly racist, but they can be swayed in that direction in periods of socioeconomic crisis where left and inclusive alternatives are absent. Second, although poor whites are not indelibly racist, they do exist in a society in which systematic white supremacy is real, and from which they derive status benefits: *I may be badly off*, they think, *but at least I am not black*. This structural status privilege is at the root of the anxiety that right-wing populists exploit in periods of crisis. Finally, right-wing populism can win only where left-wing alternatives lose. There were fascist movements in America in the 1930s, but they never built a mass base because there was an active and powerful union movement and broad support for Roosevelt's New Deal welfare state reforms. The scale and scope of the anti–Vietnam War movement, radical feminism, and Black Power in the 1960s overcame those elements of the white working class opposed to them and profoundly transformed the cultural landscape.

If most working class supporters of right-wing populist movements are driven by status anxiety and economic insecurity, then they can be partners in political argument and dialogue. Both factors are normal human existential responses to social uncertainty. Our identities are formed in the life-spaces in which we grow up. They are never fixed entirely, but they do not change simply in response to abstract argument. Identity-changing politics has to have an experiential dimension. The political relevance of this point is that it helps explain the rapid-fire growth of right-wing populist movements and the reason democratic opposition has to find counter-experiences and not just abstract moralistic arguments if it is to be affective. If one grows up in a certain environment, a patriarchal family or a segregated community, and this structure is suddenly toppled, this experience will prove unsettling for most people who enjoyed status privilege in the hierarchy. As Berlet and Lyons noted, right-wing populism tends to be a backlash movement against social change. Hence, in an environment in which there is no history of racial integration, say, and no organized and credible left to defend the idea of racial equality, where all the political forces on the ground in the community experiencing the loss of status are conservative, a right-wing populist movement can build very quickly. The same is true of economic dislocation. Those on a downward class trajectory, to use Seymour's term—whose unions have been destroyed and hear only lectures from the mainstream left, the Democratic Party in the United States, or the pre-Corbyn, Blairite Labour Party in the United Kingdom, about how they need to adapt to the new economy—are ripe fruit for the picking by demagogues.

If opponents of populist leaders are revolted by members of the right-wing populist movement, they ignore the very fluidity of identity and character formation that any struggle for political changes presupposes. If one believes that politics can change the world, then one must presuppose that politics can change people too (since the social world is composed of people who act and interact on the basis of beliefs). No one is born into a political identity; it develops through experience and engagement. Different ways of seeing the world can change beliefs and identities. The task of opponents of the racism and authoritarianism of right-wing populist movements is to frame the issues currently driving people into the arms of demagogues in ways that help them see the structural and class factors at the root of economic insecurity and inequality and win them, through argument and changed experiences, to a more democratic alternative.

It is important to emphasize the experiential dimension of change. People do not cease to be racists, for example, because they hear a lecture about how wrong racism is. They are only going to change if they have a changed experience of the group they have always experienced as racially subaltern. As Higginbotham's critique of the lingering effects of Jim Crow segregation laws concludes, it is the ongoing structured separation of whites and blacks in America in schools and housing, in wealth and economic power, that sustains the racial paradigm of white superiority. As a black law professor, he understands full well the importance of legal and structural change, but perhaps the most important conclusion he reaches is that racism only ever fully breaks down where its experiential basis—segregation and public relegation of blacks to inferior positions—is overcome. "All change," he concludes, "begins with understanding and dialogue."[32] Obviously, change does not end there, but without a changed experience of the individual members of demonized groups, an inclusive democratic movement cannot be built.

If democratic opponents of right-wing populism treat *reactions* to social experience as fixed personality *structures*, they ensure that they will never gain a hearing among the not already converted. Dismissing people as deplorable, vulgar, or suffering from mental illness only serves to reinforce the view championed by the Right that the Left is a bunch of intellectual snobs disconnected from the concerns of ordinary people—sneering and humorless politically correct elites who worry more about language than unemployment and the purity of their diet more than rural poverty. The charge is a caricature, of course, and absurd when made by the political allies of the real elite—the 1 percent who continue to appropriate more and more of collectively produced wealth for themselves—but objective absurdity in politics can still be powerfully effective if it resonates rhetorically and emotionally. Fortunately, there are other forces among opponents of right-wing populism who understand the importance of experience and communicative engagement in the construction of a democratic movement.

By definition, a coherent democratic movement cannot exclude any subaltern group from its ranks. As we have seen, democratic movements begin when a group articulates the harm its unmet needs cause as political demands for structural change. If there were somewhere an ethnically and racially uniform society that contained only one sex, one gender, and one sexuality, then "the people" of that society would be correspondingly uniform. No such society exists or is possible. There are immigrants, minorities, men, women, and trans people everywhere, even if repressive societies try to erase the differences. Groups are oppressed when they experience systematic deprivation of their fundamental needs. When they fight against that structure of deprivation, they are in essence making the democratic demand for self-determination. *All groups in struggle against structures of need-deprivation are engaged in the same democratic struggle, and the goal that must be realized is unification around this principle.* However, the truth that a coherent democratic movement cannot coherently exclude any subaltern group from its ranks does not mean that all democratic movements begin as inclusive popular fronts.

That which applies to right-wing populist movements applies to movements for social democratization as well. They typically begin from a shared experience of deprivation specific to membership in one group rather than another. Women have organized against their shared experience of exclusion from political rights and sexual subordination in a patriarchal society; blacks against racial discrimination and violence; and workers for job security, higher pay, and workplace democracy. Obviously, people do not exist in each of these silos separately. There are white male workers and black women workers and black male bosses. All human beings are integral unities of different elements. But political mobilization tends to start from one aspect of a person's complex identity—whichever feels most burdened and deprived in a given sociohistorical context. The key to building democratic movements is to uncover the shared ground of transformative struggle (unmet needs) and build solidarity across differences on this basis. What has come to be called "intersectionality" is rooted in the shared needs that define all human beings.[33] When all oppressed groups come to identify the systemic causes of their particular deprivation in a social system which (a) allows for private control of universally needed resources, (b) exploits any and all existing forms of hierarchy and oppression to strengthen this control and reduce the cost of labor, and (c) continually finds ways to deflect attention of one group from this system to other groups as scapegoats, the chances for solidarity increase.

Let me spell out my argument with the example of the successful movement to resist the repeal of Obamacare. Repealing Obamacare was a key campaign pledge of Trump, but a funny thing happened on the way to achieving it—many Trump supporters realized they depended on Obamacare, and this realization created an opening for effective opposition. The achievement is all the more striking because, as we have already noted, Trump marshaled a backlash movement against Obama, and Obamacare was the defining achievement of Obama's presidency. That people could be moved so quickly on this issue testifies to the affective political power of unmet needs to move people quickly to democratic political perspectives. Once even Trump supporters recognized that they have bodies that are or could get sick, and realized that the Republican proposals would leave them worse off and probably without health insurance, some willingly joined the boisterous movement against repeal. They besieged meetings with Republican senators, joined sit-ins on Capitol Hill, and swayed just enough Republican senators to vote against repeal. There is no guarantee that their victory will be permanent. Most important for present purposes is the way that organizers refocused attention—away from whom one voted for and Trump's personality and toward what is really at stake in health care systems: meeting the needs of vulnerable embodied beings who get sick regardless of their political position. As a recent analysis of the success of Trump's health care opponents notes: "Republicans had no good answers for constituents, who confronted them with stories about how Obamacare had helped them with their own problems. The clips rocketed around Facebook, changing the public focus from insurance to human suffering."[34] The last point is crucial. We all experience the world from our own perspective. The light of the world is refracted by the lenses of identity—experiencing life in America as a black man is different than experiencing it as a white woman. However, the differences are not self-enclosed universes but are all built up out of common ground: dependence of the body, however gendered or "colored," on nature, on social relationships, on education, on having a political say. Democratic politics works down to this common ground of need and builds solidarity among different groups from that basis.

The fact that there is a common core of needs does not mean that democratic politics can assume they will be automatically recognized by different oppressed groups. Politics is work, and there is no substitute for patient argument, moving rhetoric, and clever tactics. In this regard, Laclau is correct to insist on the necessity and contingency of politics to successful solidaristic mobilization. However, he is wrong to argue that there is nothing but "the play of differences" in politics and "no ground which would a priori privilege some elements of the whole over others."[35] The problem with Laclau's argument is the implied identity between objectivity and the a priori. From my life-value perspective, the objective natural and social grounds of human life and freedom are not given a priori, but they remain objective; that is, if absent, definite knowable harms follow. It is not an a priori fact, but a consequence of the way our bodies have evolved, that brain development is harmed by lack of protein. This is a verifiable empirical fact (objective) but not a truth by definition (a priori). Laclau elides the difference between the material dynamics of nature and history and the logical structure of propositions and arguments. To insist on objective grounds of life and freedom is not to dispense with the need for argument, but rather to point the way toward a basis that can effectively mobilize different groups that share unmet needs but might not recognize that crucial fact. Of course political argument is necessary, but it has to be about something definite if it is to be effective; and historically, what democratic politics is *ultimately* about is systematically unmet needs.

We find the common ground of struggle not in a priori definitions of "human nature" but in the naturally evolved and socially elaborated needs of real human beings. Those needs differ in terms of content: A devout Hindu will not satisfy her needs for protein with beef; an orthodox Jew will not consume pork. But protein is not beef or pork; beef and pork are only different forms of protein. We need protein, not beef or pork. To find the common need, we move from the particular species to the generic form, and then work out institutional means to ensure that everyone can access the general need-satisfying substance or institution in the concrete shape they in particular require, so far as this attention to individual detail is materially possible. What we do know from history is that where there is democratic struggle, there are always unmet needs that prevent individual members of oppressed and exploited groups from full participation and self-creation. We also know from history that the mere fact of unmet needs among a diversity of groups is not a sufficient condition for the emergence of democratic movement held together by bonds of solidarity across differences. Here Laclau is correct: Politics is necessary; solidarity is a construction, not a mechanical reflection of objective conditions. Still, there *are* objective conditions, and reticence about focusing on them (unmet needs) has limited the effectiveness of much contemporary democratic theory, which must always be judged on its practical efficacy, not its philosophical virtuosity.

In the next chapter I will examine recent radical democratic theory and contemporary experiments in radical democratic practice. On the theoretical side, I will examine radical agonistic democracy and the critique of objectivity and essentialism that motivates it. On the practical side, I will examine the recent career of "horizontalist" politics as this has played out in the Arab Spring, Occupy, and the more general phenomenon of online activism. In both cases there are important lessons for Democrats to learn. Theoretically, agonistic democracy exposes the democratic limitations of what passes for politics in liberal-democratic societies today. Practically, horizontalist movements stress the importance of grassroots activism and alert us to the dangers of centralization and bureaucratic domination of transformative struggles. At the same time, both ultimately run aground against the same rock: the overarching need of democratic struggles for coherent direction, grounded in the solidarity built from explicit recognition of shared unmet needs, and expressed as fixed demands that each constituent group can support in a disciplined way.

NOTES

1. Gurminder K. Bhambra provides a detailed demographic analysis of Trump and Brexit voters and challenges the mainstream media and academic interpretations of the success of right-wing populism. See Gurminder K. Bhambra, "Brexit, Trump, and 'Methodological Whiteness': On the Misrecognition of Race and Class," *British Journal of Sociology*, vol. 68, no. S1 (2017), S214–32.

2. Samuel Lakoff, "Inequality as a Threat to Democracy: Reflections on Piketty's Warning," *Political Science Quarterly*, vol. 130, no. 3 (Fall 2015), 433.

3. Liz Fekete, *Europe's Fault Lines: Racism and the Rise of the Right* (London: Verso, 2018), 31–94.

4. This problem can also compromise the democratic potential of left-wing populist movements. Chavismo in Venezuela is a case in point. Although there were always structural problems with the "Bolivarian Revolution," and while the attempt to build twenty-first-century socialism was always threatened by a hostile United States in alliance with local elites, the movement also suffered once Hugo Chavez died. Democratic movements, which by their nature are multigenerational and open-ended, cannot rely on single individuals for their vitality and coherence. For a discussion of the contradictions of Chavismo, see Yannis Stavrakakis et al., "Contemporary Left-wing Populism in Latin America: Leadership, Horizontalism, and Postdemocracy in Chávez's Venezuela," *Latin American Politics and Society*, vol. 58, no. 3, 51–76.

5. As Hilary Clinton did, to her detriment. Katie Reilly, "Read Hillary Clinton's 'Basket of Deplorables' Remarks about Donald Trump's Supporters," *Time* (September 10, 2016); http://time.com/4486502/hillary-clinton-basket-of-deplorables-transcript/ (accessed August 25, 2017).

6. Robert Stefan Foa and Yascha Mounk, "The Signs of Deconsolidation," *Journal of Democracy*, vol. 28, no. 1 (January 2017), 8.

7. Ibid., 9.

8. In 2017 there were 2.3 million Americans in prison, 40 percent of whom were African American. Peter Wagner and Bernadette Rabuy, "Mass Incarceration: The Whole Pie 2017," *Prison Policy Initiative* (March 14, 2017); https://www.prisonpolicy.org/reports/pie2017.html (accessed August 28, 2017).

9. For an overview of the extent of left mobilization inside and outside the Democratic Party, see Seth Adler, "By Party or Formation," *The Bullet*

(July 27, 2018); https://socialistproject.ca/2018/06/by-party-or-by-formation/ (accessed July 16, 2018).

10. Ernesto Laclau, *On Populist Reason* (London: Verso, 2007), 154.

11. Ibid., 74.

12. John B. Judis, *The Populist Explosion: How the Great Recession Transformed American and European Politics* (New York: Columbia Global Reports, 2016), 14–15.

13. Ibid., 16–17.

14. Chip Berlet and Matthew M. Lyons, *Right Wing Populism in America: Too Close for Comfort* (New York: Guilford Press, 2000), 5.

15. They have also tried to paint his victory as the result of Russian interference in the 2016 election. The Mueller investigation is ongoing as I write, but what we can say definitively is that Russia did not infiltrate more than fifty million people into America to vote for Donald Trump, and it is impossible to trace any causal line from Russian propaganda efforts to any particular vote or set of votes. It would also be remiss in a book on the problems of existing democracy to not note that for all the hymns being sung to the "sacred rights" of Americans to vote, American governments have regularly overthrown democratically elected governments when they conflicted with American imperial policy. Since 1947 they have overthrown or tried to destabilize seventy-two different governments, most recently in the Ukraine in 2014. If one wants to understand why Russia might have tried to influence the 2016 election, one needs look no further than CIA and State Department involvement in Ukraine. See Lindsey A. O'Rourke, "The US Government Tried to Change Other Countries' Governments 72 Times during the Cold War," *Washington Post* (December 23, 2016); https://www.washingtonpost.com/news/monkey-cage/wp/2016/12/23/the-cia-says-russia-hacked-the-u-s-election-here-are-6-things-to-learn-from-cold-war-attempts-to-change- regimes/?noredirect=on&utm_term=.00a1ba21c77f (accessed July 17, 2018).

16. Bret Stephens, "Presidency without Guardrails," *New York Times International Weekly*, included in the *Toronto Star* (August 5–6, 2017), 15.

17. Quoted in Judis, *The Populist Explosion*, 48.

18. Ibid., 52.

19. Alana Abramson, "'I Can be More Presidential Than Any President': Read Trump's Ohio Rally Speech," *Time* (July 26, 2017); http://time.com/4874161/donald-trump-transcript-youngstown-ohio/ (accessed August 30, 2017).

20. Herbert Marcuse, "The Historical Fate of Bourgeois Democracy," *Herbert Marcuse: Towards a Critical Theory of Society: Collected Papers Volume 2*, Douglas Kellner, ed. (New York: Routledge, 2001), 168.

21. Berlet and Lyons, *Right Wing Populism in America*, 42.

22. F. Michael Higginbotham, *Ghosts of Jim Crow: Ending Racism in Post-Racial America* (New York: New York University Press, 2013), 48.

23. Chauncey DeVega, "Idiocracy Now: Donald Trump and the Dunning-Kruger Effect—When Stupid People Don't Know They Are Stupid," *Salon* (September 30, 2016); http://www.salon.com/2016/09/30/idiocracy-now-donald-trump-and-the-dunning-kruger-effect-when-stupid-people-dont-know-they-are-stupid/ (accessed August 30, 2017).

24. Richard Seymour, "Ukip and the Crisis of Britain," *Socialist Register 2016: The Politics of the Right* (London: Merlin Press, 2016), 35.

25. See Liz Fekete, *Europe's Fault Lines: Racism and the Rise of the Right* (London: Verso, 2018), 117.

26. Alec Tyson and Shiva Maniam, "Behind Trump's Victory: Divisions by Race, Gender, Education" (Pew Research Center, November 9, 2016); http://www.pewresearch.org/fact-tank/2016/11/09/behind-trumps-victory-divisions-by-race-gender-education/ (accessed August 30, 2017).

27. Robert J. Gordon, *The Rise and Fall of American Growth: The US Standard of Living Since the Civil War* (Princeton, NJ: Princeton University Press, 2016), 614–15.

28. Greg Miller, Julie Vitkovskaya, and Reuben Fischer-Baum, "'This Deal Will Make Me Look Terrible': Full Transcript of Trump's Calls with Australia and Mexico," *Washington Post*, August 3, 2017; https://www.washingtonpost.com/graphics/2017/politics/australia-mexico-transcripts/?utm_term=.cadded59c572 (accessed August 30, 2017).

29. Douglas Kriner and Francis Shen, "Battlefield Casualties and Ballot Box Defeat: Did the Bush-Obama Wars Cost Clinton the White House?" *Social Sciences Research Network*, 2; https://papers.ssrn.com/sol3/papers.cfm?abstract_id=2989040&download=yes (accessed August 31, 2017).

30. Laclau, *On Populist Reason*, 19.

31. Berlet and Lyons, *Right-Wing Populism in America*, 346.

32. Higginbotham, *Ghosts of Jim Crow*, 202.

33. The term derives from a paper by legal scholar Kimberlé Crenshaw. See Kimberlé Crenshaw, "Demarginalizing the Intersection of Race and Sex: A Black Feminist Critique of Anti-Discrimination Doctrine, Feminist Theory, and Anti-Racist Politics," *University of Chicago Legal Forum*, vol. 139, no. 1 (1989), 139–67. I will discuss the issues relevant to my understanding of democracy and the construction of an internally unified democratic movement in chapter 6.

34. Daniel Dale, "Against the Odds," *Toronto Star* (Sunday, August 6, 2017), A4.

35. Laclau, *On Populist Reason*, 69.

Chapter 5

Radical Democracy

Agonistic Theory and Horizontalist Practice

The previous chapters have explored the underlying normative limitations and practical problems faced by liberal democracies. The conception of people as abstract individual rights holders, the right to private property in universally required resources, the exploitation of natural resources for private profit and not need-satisfaction, and the exclusion of democratic deliberation from economic life add up to a world in which people are harmed because they are deprived of that which they need and therefore lack the social power they ought to wield in a democratic society. Democratic struggles emerge against those structures of need-deprivation and powerlessness.

Such has been my argument. Not every democratic theorist agrees with its underlying principles, especially the interlinked claims that human beings share a core set of natural-social needs and that democracy depends on institutionalizing values and practices that ensure their equal satisfaction. Indeed, the most influential contemporary *radical* democratic criticisms of liberal-democracy *reject* the existence of universal needs and instead maintain that democracy depends on recognizing and protecting a plurality of forms of life. In the view of these thinkers, whose lineage can be traced to the failure of the 1968 student-worker uprisings in France, struggles for democracy have not been advanced by "human beings" fighting for their needs but by racialized minorities, women, gays and lesbians, and other minority identities fighting to open public space to include their distinct and singular forms of life. Along the way, they have rejected hierarchical and centralized political structures like parties and experimented with leaderless and directly democratic forms of organization and resistance.

This chapter will interrogate the role that pluralism, agonistic political debate, and horizontalism play in contemporary radical democratic theory. In the first section, I will look at the development of radical democratic theories as they have developed from 1968 to the present. My primary focus will be on French political philosophy from Claude Lefort to Chantal Mouffe, because it provides the sharpest divergence from my claim that democratic struggles have historically emerged from unmet, shared human needs. According to Mark Wenman's careful analysis, radical agonistic democracy is defined by three values: constitutive pluralism, a tragic sense that democracy can never be completed, and the view that ongoing (nonviolent) conflict is politically essential to democracy, all of which call into question the soundness of my position.[1] While this theory yields important insights about the need for democratic societies to respect differences, I will argue that it ultimately presupposes the very common interests it denies. The creation of any particular identity depends on the satisfaction of the shared needs I have identified. Moreover, the democratic value of the struggle to protect certain identities depends on their being able to show that they have been illegitimately excluded. Illegitimate exclusion, I will argue, must invoke universal values that the radical democrats cannot coherently deny, but are at odds with their explicit rejection of universal values and material interests.

In the second section I will focus on horizontalist democratic practices. Both the theory of radical agonistic democracy and horizontalist practice value difference dispersion and loose coalition over movements and parties unified by a shared understanding of fundamental human needs. While the horizontalists affirm the existence of shared life-interests, they make the mistake of thinking that it is opposed to vertical, hierarchical, and representative political organization, when in fact advancing the struggle to better satisfy this life-interest demands organized political parties that can fight for and win state power.

DEMOCRACY AND DIFFERENCE

The development of radical agonistic democracy marks a break with the link (which my own argument accepts) between the struggle for democracy and the struggle for socialism. Rejection of this link on the radical left begins with the failure of the 1968 uprising in France. A group of activist intellectuals emerging out of that struggle began to rethink the institutional forms a radical democracy might take, and they were led, in consequence, to reevaluate the democratic value of institutions like rights they had formerly dismissed as "bourgeois." The most important of these reevaluations was conducted by Claude Lefort. He had been a communist militant but had broken away to form his own small group, Socialisme ou Barbarie, which also counted Jean-François Lyotard among its members.[2] What is significant about its history is Lefort's conclusion that the struggles of the 1960s were a practical refutation of Marx's theory of political crisis. What appeared initially to be a coalescence of struggles into a unified revolutionary movement was in reality a much looser coalition of struggle of different groups with heterogenous demands. That is not to say those demands shared nothing in common, but what they shared was not an objective class interest but the desire to live openly and free in an inclusive public space.

Whereas Marxism was continuous with the great themes of Enlightenment humanism, Lefort claims that the new struggles rejected "the text . . . written in capital letters. . . . Humanity, Progress, Nature, Life."[3] Democratic politics develop from the particular experiences of differently oppressed and demonized groups. It is not a demand to take over the state to make it serve the shared interests of "the people," but stems from "a domain the state cannot occupy . . . constantly aroused by the need for the aspirations of minorities in particular sectors of the population to be socially recognized."[4] Democratic struggles are struggles of minorities to protect their identities. They expose universality and unity as repressive state functions and assert the radical freedom that allows groups to be different from one another, incommensurable under any overarching value system.

An effective illustration of this problem is the current struggle around migrant rights. Right-wing populists argue that "the people" comprises only legal citizens of the nation-state and rejects any claims that migrants make on state resources in consequence. From the point of view of the migrants and their supporters, this construction of the people is too narrow; regardless of legal membership, migrants exert a compelling demand to belong to the nation in which they make a claim of asylum. They are an outside force that exposes the unity of the state and any definition of democracy that is rooted in it as violent, exclusionary, and illegitimate. From a perspective like Lefort's, democratization means cracking open the exclusionary unity and creating a more complex form of inclusive social relationship. While Lefort is correct to see existing forms of civic closure as still exclusionary and violent, I will argue that they are so not just because they draw a line between citizens and noncitizens, but because the way that line is drawn means that those on the wrong side of the line are left without even their basic human needs being met.[5] The issue is not inclusion and exclusion of differences as such, but satisfaction or nonsatisfaction of the needs essential to a human life. Practical reconfigurations of social institutions that better respond to these needs thus, from my perspective, create a more coherently inclusive and democratic social unity.

From Lefort's perspective, by contrast, "the One" is always the enemy of democracy. The State, the Party, the Leader, objective interests, and universal values or goals are all equally problematic. "The One" is the enemy of democracy because society is, and must be, pluralistic. Any and all attempts to reduce difference to "the One" are totalitarian.

> I am trying to catch a glimpse of one dimension of social space which is generally obscured . . . because of a phantasized attraction to the One. . . . Whoever dreams of an abolition of power secretly cherishes the reference to the One and the . . . Same: He envisages a society that would accord spontaneously with itself, a multiplicity of activities which would be transparent to one another and which would unfold in a homogenous time and space, a way of producing, living together, connecting, associating, thinking, feeling, teaching, that would express a single way of being.[6]

There is no singularly good way of life. Spontaneity produces difference and democracy—the rule of an internally diverse people—and preserves it. Totalitarianism denies it and tries to repress or manage difference out of existence. The final hope of Marxism, to eliminate power and politics in favor of habitual compliance with the elementary rules of sociality, as Lenin put the point, is the dream not of a democrat but an authoritarian.[7] Like Foucault, Lefort rejects as impossible a society beyond power and opposition.

Lefort's critique of totalitarianism is understandable in light of his experience of the official communist movement. While he remained critical of the merely formal liberal interpretation of rights, he broke from the dominant Marxist critique according to which rights are nothing but political forms that paper over and legitimate exploitation and alienation. For Lefort, on the contrary, rights are vital to protect civil society as a space for diversity and difference:

> at the heart of civil society, in the name of an indefinite need for a mutual recognition of liberties, a mutual protection of the ability to exercise them . . . one may discern a movement antagonistic to that which is propelling state power. . . . This brings us to the second feature of the struggles inspired by the notion of rights: emerging or developing in various centers, sometimes as a result of temporary conflicts, those struggles do not tend to fuse together.[8]

The very generality of rights allows them to be vehicles for heterogeneous struggles. But if "the people" is really groups of people with heterogenous goals and interests, then a self-governing society must respect and preserve these differences. This new logic of democratization will prove central to contemporary radical, agonistic democracy. The connective thread is the idea that democracy is not the institutionalization of objectively shared interests but the exercise of rights to protect social differences from domination and suppression. Jacques Rancière is crucial to the subsequent development of the connection between democracy and pluralism. For Rancière, the story of democracy, from Greece to the twentieth century, is the story of subaltern peoples typically judged inferior and incapable of speaking of fighting for the space in which they can speak as equals. Hence all democratic struggle is "antinatural." Aristocracy has always been based on the principle of natural fitness to rule: Only a genetic or intellectual elite is fit to rule because only they have the natural capacities to understand what the community needs. If the democratic gambit is successful, then anyone can speak about any matter of public concern, and the naturalistic foundation of aristocracy collapses.

Thus, like Lefort, Rancière believes that central to democratic struggle is the use of rights to renegotiate public space. When they are successful, they expand the set of groups with a public existence.

> Democracy can never be identified with a juridico-political form. This does not mean it is indifferent to real forms. It means that the power of the people is always beneath and beyond social forms. Beneath, because these forms cannot function without referring . . . to that power of incompetents. . . . Beyond, because the very forms that inscribe power

are continually re-transcribed through the play itself of the governmental machine.[9]

Democracy is thus never coincident with "liberal-democracy" or "a people's democracy." It is always an unsettled institutional state because the very power of the people upon which it rests is a dynamic and socially transformative power. Democracy is always in a state of change because "the people" is diverse and new voices constantly emerge with new demands and the institutionalization of new demands changes the institutions. The key to a vital democracy is not to let it congeal around fixed institutions but to keep it open to new groups demanding the right and the space to speak.

Rancière uncovers an important historical truth. The rule of the people has always been regarded as scandalous by ruling classes because their ideologies flatter their group as uniquely fit to rule. If democracy works, it proves not only that the ruling class was not uniquely fit to rule but also that in matters of public affairs, anyone can develop the requisite knowledge and expertise to effectively participate. Political understanding is not the exclusive knowledge of the technocrat or scientist but can be acquired on the basis of lived experience and reflection. Hence, all citizens have a claim to be valued equally as people whose voice needs to be heard when public affairs are in play. The logical end point of democratic development is thus a society in which all institutions are governed through the collective deliberations of their members. The democratic principle is radically unsettling of all settled conventions. The work of democracy is never finished because there is always a hierarchy to overturn. "If there is a 'limitlessness' specific to democracy, [then] it lies not in the exponential multiplication of needs or desires emanating from individuals, but in the movement that ceaselessly displaces the limits of the public and the private, the political and the social."[10] But if politics is public and the social is private, and democratic struggle concerns publicizing and politicizing private social power, then to call this struggle ceaseless is to admit that democracy as a fully realized social system is impossible.

Democracy as "unfinished business" is the core theme of the work of arguably the most important agonistic radical democrat, Chantal Mouffe. Her version of radical, agonistic democracy inherits three ideas from the work of Lefort and Rancière: (1) the idea that democratic demands stem from different experiences of social identity and not a shared set of needs anchored in our biosocial nature; (2) the idea that democracy is an open-ended process and not a fixed form; and (3) the idea that the defining value of democracy is political contestation, not the satisfaction of the material conditions for collective self-determination and meaningful and valuable self-realization.

Like Lefort, Mouffe's interpretation of radical democracy developed out of a critique of the politics of the Marxist left. In her case the ideas first began to take shape in her infamous joint work with Ernesto Laclau, *Hegemony and Socialist Strategy*. Their argument was vehemently attacked by Marxists, but I am not going to revisit those debates. The pivotal claim for current purposes was that Marxist politics have repeatedly failed because they assumed that democratic politics was unified by class interests rooted in objective needs. Politics consisted in Marxist experts clarifying these needs for the working class, building appropriate alliances with other groups, and overthrowing capitalism. In her subsequent work she extended this critique to classical liberalism. While free of the revolutionary illusions of Marxism, liberals like John Rawls and Jürgen Habermas also pine for a world in which real political conflicts are overcome.

"The political" is Mouffe's term for the unique type of conflict that defines democratic society. Since she claims there is no such thing as "social objectivity not grounded in an original exclusion," conflict over what matters in society, what policy should be adopted, what law regarded as legitimate, is permanent.[11] As we will see, this rejection of underlying universal interests and values will leave her unable to *coherently* explain what decisions are consistent with democratic forms of power and exclusion and which not. For Mouffe, whichever proposal ultimately wins becomes a fact of life in that society by excluding a number of competing alternatives, which never simply disappear, but reconstitute themselves for another battle. The political is this ongoing play of differences over what should count as socially objective. It derives from the pluralism of society and ensures that it will never be resolved into any final unity of purposes, goals, and needs. "Pluralism" means, she says, "the end of the substantive idea of the good life (what Lefort called the dissolution of the markers of certainty)."[12] Like Lefort and Rancière, Mouffe thus regards democracy not as an institutional structure valued by citizens because it ensures the satisfaction of their needs and the free pursuit of their goals, but as a space of contestation valued precisely because it allows different groups of citizens to articulate their unique interests and identities and (nondestructively) fight for those interests against other competing interests. Democracy is the journey, not the destination (to which we can never, in any case, arrive).

Like Rancière, Mouffe is concerned with defending democracy as an open set of possibilities for the reconfiguration of public space. "I would like to emphasize that the aim of a counter-hegemonic intervention is not to unveil "true reality" or "real interests," but to rearticulate a given situation in a new configuration."[13] The legitimacy of any given state of society can be contested by oppositional (counter-hegemonic) movements. It is not that they give voice to the truth against ideological untruth but, rather, that they reconfigure social space to make room for expressions of identity that were formerly forbidden. The *political* problem is never to give voice to the objectively true against the ideologically false, but to increase the space available for the public manifestation of differences.

Given that for Mouffe there are no objective needs, there will never be an end to democratic politics. "There will always be antagonisms, struggles, and divisions of the social, and the need for institutions to deal with them will never disappear."[14] Democratic antagonisms are distinct from zero-sum struggles between enemies. Antagonists argue about how to regulate public space, but they do not try to destroy one another. People who advocate for more health care spending might, in a given context, clash with people who want more money for higher education. They try to win supporters to their side, but they do not argue that the other side should be sent to the gallows.

> For the agonistic perspective, the central category of democratic politics is the category of the "adversary," the opponent with whom one shares a common allegiance to the democratic principle of "liberty and equality for all," while disagreeing about their interpretation. Adversaries fight against each other because they want their interpretation of the principle to be hegemonic, but they do not put in question the legitimacy of their opponent's right to fight for the victory of their interpretation.[15]

Democratic antagonism is thus the opposite of revolutionary violence; it seems to turn enemies into adversaries, not corpses.[16]

At the same time, in Mouffe's view, not every opponent is an adversary. There are some political differences that must be defeated, not simply opposed, because they are a threat to the existence of democracy itself. Yet insofar as some groups can put themselves beyond the pale, Mouffe will be forced to concede, against her own view, that there are universal political values, and these presuppose universal material interests. Far-right racists in the United States and elsewhere are not just expressing a different interpretation of "liberty and equality for all" but are actively attacking and killing other human beings because they look different than they do, an objective harm if there ever was one. "A well-functioning democracy," Mouffe argues, "calls for a confrontation of democratic political positions. If this is missing, there is always the danger that this democratic confrontation will be replaced by a confrontation between non-negotiable moral values or essentialist forms of identification."[17] But what she needs to add is that the problem is not "non-negotiability" (presumably the protection of the lives of racial minorities should be nonnegotiable), but the real life implications of different policies. Those that better satisfy people's needs and empower them are democratic; those that degrade and destroy others for the sake of the power of the ruling class are not. Hence, the bigger issue concerns what the social, economic, and political *causes* of undemocratic forces are. As soon as we examine those causes, the problems in the agonistic account that I have alluded to become unavoidable.

Unlike the horizontalist practices I will examine in the next section, Mouffe insists that there will always need to be representative institutions to mediate political conflicts. The realm of the political goes beyond the state and its representative bodies, but it cannot do away with those bodies. Counter-hegemonic struggles demand institutional expression and security in the form of changed law and policy. This much I agree with. But what marks the essential difference between undemocratic and democratic forces? Is it really a problem of "essentialism" (i.e., a belief in fixed differences between different classes of things)? Indeed, does not a stress on a fundamental difference between democratic and undemocratic—a difference of a political *kind*—instantiate a type of politically important essentialism? That is, if we ought to tolerate democratic movements but struggle to eliminate undemocratic movements, does this not tell us that undemocratic movements are *essentially* different, and this difference authorizes different forms of struggle against them (making them illegal, for example, which would be wrong in relation to democratic opponents)?

This objection points us to a deeper problem with radical agonistic democracy. Its valorization of difference and pluralism as good *because they are opposed to* the One and the Same (as forces of repressive order) confuses two very different types of Oneness and Sameness. When a particular position assumes control over the state and defines opposed movements as "enemies of the people" (as we have seen all too often in history), they become totalitarian. They should rightly be opposed by democratic movements. However, the fundamental natural and social resources that all human beings require to live, collectively determine their lives, and realize their individual life-projects are also a form of One and the Same, but a form that is better understood as the universal enabling conditions for the production of valuable social differences. When totalitarian forces control these resources, they are in a position to demonize and oppress certain differences because the members of the demonized group are dependent on access to them. Were that dependency overcome, they could no longer be oppressed, because they would be in control of their lives. Where all groups collectively control and deliberatively resolve differences about how to use natural and social resources, *there* and only there do we have the conditions for *democratic pluralism.* Yet these conditions for democratic pluralism are grounded in shared, objective needs for definite social and natural resources, which is what radical agonistic democrats deny. The "equality" that Mouffe invokes must involve equality of access to fundamental need-satisfying goods or else prove incapable of promoting the real "liberty" she simultaneously demands.

Mouffe herself seems to recognize that there are universal material conditions of democratic pluralism when she examines the (now threatened) achievements of left-wing governments in South America. She attributes "the important democratic advances" made by these "progressive governments" to their use of "representative" institutions to "challenge neoliberal forces."[18] What she does not add—but which is the essential truth she only gestures toward—is that they challenged neoliberal forces by taking control over the natural resource wealth of the country—oil in Venezuela, tin in Bolivia—and using that wealth to fund non-market economic activity, social development, and neighborhood organization.[19] None of these movements doubted for a second that the poor and oppressed had real, objective, unmet needs: to establish collective control over the resources that could produce the wealth to satisfy the needs and empower the erstwhile downtrodden was the raison d'être of these "progressive governments."

Support for the life-value interpretation of the foundations of radical democracy is found in the latest work of an unlikely ally: Judith Butler. Butler has long been an influential critic of political universality and essentialism, but her recent essay on precarity has opened her thinking to the political importance of access to the basic conditions of life. The issue here is not that all important differences collapse to nothing in the face of the demands of existence. Rather, it is that no one can live freely who cannot live, and no one can live without access to fundamental need-satisfiers. "No self and no human can live without this connection to a biological network of life that exceeds the domain of the human animal."[20] Without this sustaining connection to the complex web of life, social and cultural differences are impossible. "Only as creatures who recognize the conditions of interdependency that ensure our persistence and flourishing can any of us struggle for the recognition of any of those important political goals."[21]

In a similar vein, William Connolly also understands that human life depends on regular, need-governed access to the natural world. The social and cultural differences we produce are not constituted solely through language and self-interpretation but also through the appropriation and transformation of scarce natural resources, and they have effects in the material world. Unless we attend to these effects, we risk undermining the natural foundations of social and cultural life. "Today, under conditions of neoliberal capitalism and the onslaught of massive climate change, what is needed above all . . . [is] militant drives to *slow down* and *retune* practices of production, consumption, and demands for material progress."[22] Democratic struggles for those goals—struggles to ensure that the totality of people in a given political unit determine their own lives—are thus, by definition, *common* struggles to reappropriate what has been appropriated by ruling groups as their exclusive property. However, both Butler and Connolly tend to focus on the personal dimensions of the struggle—on how each can explore different performative roles that might constitute starting points of broader resistance. While I do not want to discount role transformation as irrelevant, I think the revitalization of democratic struggle demands that we focus on the ways in which different groups can discover common ground in the most basic fact of democratic life: Need-deprivation causes harms that impede people from participating in social life as equals and impairs the extent to which they can freely realize their cognitive and creative abilities in valuable and valued ways.[23]

If what we want is a dynamic and pluralistic political culture, we have to ground it in objective needs and life-interests and fight for control of fundamental social institutions that produce, distribute, and regulate the use of natural and social resources. Defenders of "horizontalist" politics recognize the common bases of life and creativity more clearly than radical democrats, but they too end up demonizing the state and political parties because they are purportedly the enemies of difference and spontaneity. They thus make the same error as the radical democrats: failing to distinguish two very different types of sameness and unity.

HORIZONTALISM AND DEMOCRATIC POLITICS

Radical agonistic democracy valorizes the practice of democratic debate against any and all attempts to capture and normalize it. Hence its defining opposition between pluralism and difference (democratic activity) on the one hand and sameness and universality (normalizing structures) on the other. The goal is not an anarchistic association of self-organizing autonomous communities, but an institutional order that is constantly open to revisions demanded by newly politicized groups claiming their right to public space. While what Mouffe calls "the political" is essential to any genuine democratic society, differences, I argue, are not free floating but are enabled or impeded by the way in which social life as a whole is organized, especially how resources are controlled or utilized. If ruling groups can employ their control over basic life resources to determine access to employment, education, health care, and cultural resources, then they are in a position to decide, if not what differences exist, then at least how freely differences are able to express and realize themselves. The free expression of democratically important differences demands collective control over the resource base needed by all. The universal, or the common, is thus, in this sense, not the enemy of democratic differences but its necessary presupposition.

Natural and social common wealth is the starting point for the influential work of Michael Hardt and Antonio Negri. For Hardt and Negri the fundamental struggle today is between a placeless Empire bent on appropriating more and more of the world's wealth to itself and dispersed groups of people organized in online and real-world networks arranged in opposition to Empire's appetites.[24] Hardt and Negri draw on an older (and less well known in the English-speaking world) tradition of working class struggle in Italy known as autonomism.[25] The practice of autonomism was an early instance of what is today called a "horizontalist" democratic organization. Horizontalism argues against institutional mediations of democratic spontaneity and instead maintains that only self-organizing local movements directly grounded in life-sustaining "common wealth" can be democratic. I will begin by examining Hardt and Negri's arguments in favor of what they call "absolute" democracy and then conclude with a sympathetic but critical account of recent examples of horizontalism in (mass political) action: the Arab Spring and Occupy.

Negri was a major actor in Autonomia Operaia, the autonomist Italian workers movement, and his work with Hardt reflects that experience. Their joint work is also clearly influenced by another autonomist theorist, Paolo Virno. Like Lefort, Virno was a veteran of working class struggle who was forced by the failure of its revolutionary forms to rethink the relationship between Marxism and democracy. Also like Lefort, Virno came to see older forms of political universality and unity as the fundamental problem. Virno adds that the belief that the state had to be overthrown by a unified people under the leadership of the working class overlooked how changing technology, patterns of work, and class composition were creating the possibility of freedom without revolution and democracy without conquest of the state.

On the one hand, the social basis of working class unity, the concentration of labor in massive factories, was dissolving in the 1980s and 1990s. On the other hand, new forms of work afforded more opportunity for workers' ideas to be realized independently. Time and space outside the control of capital was the other face of precarity, and Virno sought to theorize this time and space as a liberated zone within capitalism that workers and newly radicalizing subjects could seize. If the old Left relied upon a mythical "People," a diversity that acts as a single entity, the new Left (as in Lefort) would abandon that myth in favor of a dispersion of identities *sidestepping* the state and major economic institutions in favor of living freely right now, utilizing the potential for non-alienated labor that symbolic production in the information economy made possible. Virno calls the sum of these dispersed identities "the multitude," and distinguishes them from the People of the old Left:

> The multitude . . . is the result of a centripetal movement: from the One to the Many. But which One is it that forms the starting point from which the Many differentiate themselves? . . . the People. . . . The multitude does not converge to a *volonte generale* . . . because it already has access to a general intellect. The public intellect . . . which appears in a Post-Fordist world . . . can constitute a . . . non-state public sphere.[26]

This non-state public sphere is defined by the range of practices associated with increasingly immaterial labor.[27] Immaterial labor does not depend on access to a physical means of production but rather symbolic knowledge, which, according to Virno, is more difficult to centrally control. There are good reasons to suspect whether this belief is true, as I will argue below.

The "general intellect" is Virno's term for the dispersion of productive knowledge throughout society in a "post-Fordist" world that makes immaterial labor possible. "Fordism" was Antonio Gramsci's term for the phase of capitalism based on assembly-line production; "Post-Fordism" was the first name given to what we now call the information economy. The means of symbolic production today, as well as the knowledge of how to use them, are not the private property of major corporations. Virno was prescient in seeing the potential of new communication technologies just now coming to fruition. The "public intellect" allows creative workers to produce free from the constraints of corporate capital. If a musician cannot get a recording contract from a major label, she can record and disseminate her own music through a relatively cheap, self-built website. Services of all sorts can be advertised, and political and cultural affinity groups can form, all without central oversight or direction. The "non-state" public sphere takes shape as a complex, multifaceted, self-organizing, and self-governing virtual world.

Democratization, for Virno, is not a process whereby initially dispersed groups learn to recognize a common life-interest that binds them in solidarity to one another, but a process where groups maintain their difference and network with one another on an as-needed basis. Having been forcibly freed from old forms of Fordist labor, small groups of creative people should, Virno argues, fight to stay outside the factory and independent of the state and simply pursue their own agendas with the tools (the general intellect) they have been given by structural economic changes. In effect, Virno enjoins new workers to occupy the space vacated by capital and invent new forms of non-alienated labor and self-organization. The real democrats are those who "defect" from official society. "Nothing is less passive than the act of fleeing. Defection modifies the conditions in which the struggle takes place. In short, *exit* consists of unrestricted invention."[28] To be sure, structural economic changes have freed many workers *from* the oppressive routines of factory life, and also freed some (a smaller subset) workers *to* work autonomously and creatively. However, Virno's unfortunate metaphor to explain defection—the colonization of the American and Canadian West—reveals a deep-seated problem with the argument.

Virno sees the colonization of the West as the result of a refusal, on the part of eastern urban workers, of the drudgery of factory life. They accepted the offer of cheap land and moved to create their own reality in "unoccupied" territory. "Think . . . of the mass exodus from . . . the factory carried out by American workers in the middle of the nineteenth century. By venturing into the 'frontier' to colonize inexpensive land, they seized upon the opportunity to reverse their initial condition."[29] Perhaps from their perspective they saw the West as a land of "an exuberance of possibilities."[30] Unfortunately, the territory was not unoccupied, but the traditional lands of indigenous people whom the settlers, with the aid of the US Army (the Northwest Mounted Police in Canada), drove off or killed. I am sure that Virno is not a supporter of genocidal war against indigenous peoples. The problem is, one cannot understand that defection as an autonomous act of the working class. There was cheap land to "settle" only because the government made it available at that price to *entice* workers to go west. The availability and price of the land were both predicated on violent state action.

Exit is always going to fail because the space into which people can "defect" is made available (and thus, in a sense, negatively regulated) by the state and central authorities. As we will see later in this section, well-meaning but shockingly politically naive hackers and online militants like Julian Assange find out the hard way that there is no space really vacated by capital and the state, only spaces they regulate by fencing. Should anyone try to climb the fence, the full repressive powers of the state remain available. My point is not to say that there are no possibilities for self-organizing creative activity today, but only that these virtual spaces cannot substitute for new forms of vertically organized, deeply unified, and disciplined political movements and parties. Thinking we can shift democratic organization from the streets to cyberspace simply sidesteps the main and difficult problem of how to organize in sufficient numbers and with sufficient staying power to fundamentally change social institutions in ways that actually address the primary causes of social harm. In order to understand why such movements remain necessary, we need to examine the more contemporary version of Virno's "exit strategy" to see what it importantly adds, but also how it ultimately runs into the same roadblock.

Hardt and Negri begin from Virno's idea of "the multitude." For Virno, "multitude signifies plurality" and is thus a better vehicle for democracy.[31] Like Virno, Hardt and Negri see the multitude as a loose collection of different identities who pursue their own interests and come together only when those interests overlap, rather than because they become conscious of an universal objective interest. Hardt and Negri provide a more concrete account of what these relationships look like, given contemporary technological developments. Social media and communication technologies have made it possible for spontaneous networks to form and for those networks to reach collective decisions without centralized coordination. This space is creative and productive but also political, the embryo of a "nonrepresentative" democracy in which collective decisions emerge from open-ended online discussion and problem solving.

The important difference between Hardt and Negri and the radical democrats who derive from Lefort's critique of universality is that Hardt and Negri acknowledge that different identities have shared conditions of possibility: access to "the commons" without which life and creative activity are possible. Their version of the common embraces both natural resources and social institutions and products of collective labor.

> A democracy of the multitude is possible only because we all share and participate in the common. By "common" we mean, first of all, the common wealth of the material world . . . we consider common also and more significantly those results of social production that are necessary for social interaction . . . such as knowledge, languages, codes.[32]

Virno's "general intellect" can be seen as an essential part of "the common": the intelligence of individuals distributed through open networks that anyone can access almost cost-free.[33]

While Negri and Hardt agree with my general argument that plurality presupposes common interests in access to need-satisfying goods, relationships, and institutions, they draw significantly different political conclusions. Their goal is not to build an internally unified movement that seeks to wrest control of the commons from private capitalist control, but rather to work within existing networks of the electronic commons to build up an alternative political reality. They agree with Virno that the way forward is to defect—not to a material frontier beyond the reach of the state and capital, but into digital networked worlds. Their project draws inspiration from the open-source software movement. In this movement people arrive at solutions to problems through open-ended dialogue and discussion and disseminate the results of that collective work free of charge to anyone who needs it. The spontaneity of the activity and the non-commodified (common) nature of the products of work prefigure a democracy without borders or state institutions. They "understand the decision-making capacity of the multitude on analogy with the development of computer software and the innovations of the collaborative, open-source movement. . . . When source code is open so that anyone can see it . . . the better a program it becomes."[34] Likewise, rather than trusting party experts to solve every political problem, online networked citizens can collaborate and generate superior solutions on their own. While democracy does require collective engagement, and while technologies that facilitate engagement are to be welcomed, there are limits to the analogy between political and technological problems, as we will see. Unless citizens share a common ethical and political framework, political collaboration is impossible. The dispersion and fragmentation of interests the internet encourages is not obviously conducive to the formation of shared political and ethical frameworks. To build that unity, political and philosophical work is required.

Surprisingly, despite the fact that they start from the recognition of the indispensable role of the commons, their political goal is not overarching unity around a project to reclaim the common, but rather to build a separate reality outside the state and existing economy in which differences can freely proliferate. Quoting Rancière, they argue, "Politics is the sphere of activity of a common . . . that can only ever be contentious. The making of the multitude must arrive at the point of a *partage*, dividing and sharing the common. Making the multitude, and thus the event of insurrection, we should repeat, is not a process of fusion, as Jean-Paul Sartre suggests, but rather sets in motion a proliferation of singularities that are composed of lasting encounters in the common."³⁵ These singularities are like Lefort's "minorities" or Mouffe's democratic movements; they aim at securing their own interests and identities, but can cooperate when conditions highlight intersections. The complex movement, although not internally unified, is democratic because it accepts the equal value of the singularities and hopes to secure the conditions of their free exercise and proliferation.

The argument ends up in a contradiction. On the one hand, their acknowledgment that all groups depend on access to the common presupposes that there are universal needs and interests. On the other, they reject a politics of "fusion" and celebrate the wide dispersal and independence of social differences, each with its own needs and goals, living and creating in its own networks, and coalescing only as situations demand. In their most recent work they seem to acknowledge the need for leadership and focused political parties, but at the end of the day they re-fetishize the spontaneous wisdom of the assembled multitude.³⁶ They thus repeat the inconsistent wavering one finds in *Commonwealth.* There, on one page they call for "insurrection," while on the next they write as if existing networks are sufficient for a democratic society. Invoking Baruch Spinoza, they insist that "the path of joy is constantly to open new possibilities, to expand our field of imagination, our abilities to feel and be affected."³⁷ The problem is that if joy is an individual experience produced by expanding individual powers through multiplying connections and interactions, and the online network is the scene for these interactions, then staying in one's room and multiplying connections and interactions is as joyful as (or more joyful than) the sort of very unjoyful confrontations in material space over access to resources that their discussion of the importance of the common and the need for insurrection would suggest. This contradiction remains unmediated in their work.

The significance of the contradiction can be highlighted by contrasting their conclusions with another thinker who has also carefully studied online networks: Yochai Benkler. In one sense, Benkler agrees with Hardt and Negri: Online networks are liberatory. They have freed people's creativity and imagination from the constraints imposed by massive corporations and mass markets. Anyone with any talent can produce from home or a small shared creative space and seek out their own markets. He does not use the term "the multitude," but the basic idea is the same: The mythically unified "people" has dispersed into self-organizing creative communities that collaborate on self-chosen projects, all free from (as far as possible) the visible hand of the state and mass market pressure. For Benkler, however, networks are not revolutionary alternatives to liberal capitalism; they are the realization of its highest promises. Networks are the solution to the main internal threat to liberal-capitalist freedom: monopoly on markets and power.[38] "Liberal theories of justice," he argues, "can be categorized according to how they characterize the sources of equality in terms of luck, responsibility, and structure."[39] He concludes that "the networked information economy improves justice from the perspective of every single one of these theories of justice."[40] Networks free people to create by abolishing monopoly control over the conditions of creation. They portend a truly open society, culture, and economy. He draws on the work of Bruce Ackerman to make the link between the freedom to create and the freedom to participate in (self-created) markets.

> The basic prerequisites for participating in a market economy [are] access to a transactional framework, to basic information, and to an adequate educational endowment. To the extent that any of these basic utilities required to participate in the information economy are all available without sensitivity to price—that is, free to anyone—they are made available in a form that is substantially insulated from the happenstance of initial wealth endowment.[41]

Here is another version of Virno's exit strategy, but the doorway leads to capitalism fulfilling its promises of an economy based on free competition between different ideas and products, not to a radically democratic alternative.

Setting aside the issue of whether the freedom that networks promise is capitalist or anticapitalist, the deeper issue for our purposes is whether networks *democratize* society. Do they strengthen collective control over the institutions in which life-horizons are shaped, in ways that ensure all-around need-satisfaction? Do they empower historically oppressed groups to free themselves from the structural violence that has dominated their history? Do they enable individuals to realize their projects in ways that are individually fulfilling, valued and valuable to others, and ecologically sustainable? There is some evidence to support the conclusion that the expanded range and ease of communication, the reduction of costs to creators to produce and disseminate their work, and the possibilities of online political mobilization (think of the almost immediate global impact of #MeToo) have had democratizing effects. Nevertheless, from my perspective, crucial problems with the claim that networks are the road to a more democratic, participatory future are being overlooked.

Radical agonistic democracy and Hardt and Negri's "absolute democracy" share the principle that democracy is an essentially political system in which new space for the formerly voiceless is constantly engendered. Hence the attractiveness of online networks. They seem to reach into the unlit corners of civil society to enable ordinary people to become politically active. Jacob Appelbaum, in a conversation with Assange and others, puts the point clearly:

> It's not about a political vanguard, it's about channeling through the political system this new ability to express ourselves that we all have between our hands, to share our thoughts, to participate in the sharing of knowledge without being a member of a political party, of a media company, or of whatever centralized structure you needed in the past in order to be able to express yourself.[42]

Empowerment lies in access to information and the unfettered freedom to disseminate it: "There is a battle between the power of this information collected by insiders . . . versus the increased size of the commons with the internet as a common tool for humanity to speak to itself."[43] Assange and his collaborators have a superficial understanding of the basis of that power. Hardt and Negri are not superficial about the basis of that power, but they do not draw the appropriate political conclusions.

The basis of state power is not the control over information, but control over the entire institutional apparatus of society, which is in turn grounded in control over the fundamental resources from which everything is produced, including computers and the infrastructure that networks them. The state does not directly control these resources in capitalist countries. Instead, it protects the private appropriation and commodification of the commons. The main point is that decommodifying information, developing the power to spill state secrets, or mobilizing online campaigns is not sufficient to overcome the main impediment to democratic control over social life: the private control, protected ultimately by the state's monopoly on the means of violence, over the whole material bases of life and sociocultural institutions and creations.

This lesson was harshly taught by the magnificent but ultimately failed struggle for democracy in Egypt. In the West, breathless press reports gushed about the magical power of the internet to topple dictators and empower ordinary people. The social basis of the struggle was completely ignored. Alec Ross, a senior figure at the US Department of State, commented at the time that we did not see revolutionary heroes like Lech Walesa in Egypt because "the internet has distributed leadership."[44] For Ross and others, the real revolutionary force was technology, and it did away with the need for vertical organization and discipline. He and other Western commentators were wrong on both counts.

First, the political agency driving the revolution was not "the internet" but the poor and working class of Egypt. Commenting on the early days of the 2011 revolution, Samir Amin argued: "Contrary to what the mainstream media say, it was not a pro-West demonstration but an anti-imperialist demonstration. The demands were anti-imperialist and social, not socialist. Renationalization, not privatization. United States, out; United States' agreement with Egypt, out. Schools, hospitals, labor, et cetera, in."[45] The movement was motivated by lack of control over the social bases of life support, not only the absence of liberal-democratic institutions. The latter certainly played a motivating role, but the ultimate fate of the revolution—reimposition of the old regime in reaction against the Muslim Brotherhood's election victory—shows that political struggle is not enough. Political reforms cannot be secured if the state retains control over the ultimate means of life support.

This deeper struggle was lost to Western media commentators, for whom the struggle was not between poor and working class Egyptians and the Egyptian ruling class and army, but between the emancipatory force of technology and dictatorship. Although she was writing before the revolution, Jodi Dean's critique of "technological fetishism" exposes the problem of this sort of commentary. "Technology fetishism reduces the complexity of politics . . . to . . . one problem to be solved and one technological solution . . . democracy might be treated as a singular problem of information: people don't have the information they need to participate effectively. Bingo! Information technologies intervene to provide people with information."[46] Having information and being able to do something with the information that one has are different things. Assange released very important information about American war crimes in Iraq, but *he* paid the price, not the perpetrators, because just giving people information does not give them power. Power depends on mobilization, but not only mobilization. It also depends on being able to sustain a struggle, and that depends on having access to means of life the ruling class cannot simply cut off. While we need different organizational forms that respond to the current moment in history, we can still learn from earlier periods of mass working class struggle. Mass strikes, for example, were never just about withdrawing labor; they were about withdrawing commodified labor from the bosses but continuing to work for each other—freeing, if only for a moment, the means of life from ruling class control.

We did see some of that emerge in the mass strikes and demonstrations in Egypt. There was mutual material support for basic life-necessities, but well-organized political movements capable of coherently channeling these energies and resisting reaction were lacking. It is no accident that the Muslim Brotherhood, the longest and best politically—and vertically—organized movement won the elections. So while "the internet" did enable new political actors to mobilize at lightning speed, transformative change requires more patient forms of organization and development. Evgeny Morozov reveals the limits of networked politics as democratic force for change:

> Digital networks have simply provided the appearance of an infrastructure in which horizontal modes of governance could be enacted. But here, once again, these new possibilities may have imposed themselves as preferred solutions to every organizational challenge, even if the task at hand requires a more vertical, hierarchical structure. . . . This is precisely what . . . David Harvey means when he complains that "unfortunately . . . the idea of hierarchy is anathema to many segments of the oppositional left these days. A fetishism of . . . pure horizontality . . . all too often stands in the way of exploring appropriate and effective solutions."[47]

Horizontalism eschews leaders and makes decisions based on agreements that emerge from full and free debate and, in that regard, is democratic. However, the Arab Spring provides evidence that pure horizontalism is not the best approach to the conquest of state power. Occupy—the North American and European movement inspired by the Egyptian occupation of Tahrir Square, the symbolic heart of the Egyptian revolution, provides evidence that horizontalism cannot create and maintain an alternative democratic space outside of state power and institutions. Contrary to John Holloway, democratic movements *cannot* change the world without taking power, and we know this because when the existing rulers are left in power, the problems a movement like Occupy tried to solve are left to fester or get worse. Defenders of horizontalism believe the world can be changed without taking power because they believe in the power of human beings to organize and determine their own lives. Indeed, this belief is the moral wellspring of democratic movements going back to ancient Greece. In Marina Sitrin's influential formulation, horizontalism "rejects political parties from the right and the left," because it rejects "homogeneity and ingrained ideas."[48] It does so because it believes in the capacities of "everyday" people to govern their own lives through "autonomous forms of decision making."[49] Horizontalism thus combines the radical agonistic democratic valorization of difference and pluralism with Virno, Hardt, and Negri's valorization of exit and withdrawal from existing state institutions.

The message that ordinary people could reclaim their lives without the mediation of established political parties resounded in the Occupy camps. Joe Freisen, an Occupier in the New York City camp, articulated this perspective clearly in an interview with Chris Hedges: "I have no interest in participating in the political process. It's bureaucratic, it's vertical, it's exclusive. The principles I'm pushing and many people here are pushing . . . are horizontal in terms of decision making, transparency, openness, inclusiveness, accessibility."[50] Again, no democratic society can exist without horizontal deliberative practices. Still, a stable, functioning democratic society—also one that is fair, that ensures all voices are heard—has to institutionalize and formalize these practices, and that requires vertical organization and control over state institutions.

What happens when democratic movements eschew formal organization, institutionalization, and vertical organization? They cannot make decisions and become easy targets for state power. Rather than ensure inclusiveness and accessibility, lack of formal procedures lead to constant *conflicts* about whose interests were being heard and how differences of political position were to be treated.[51] Lack of instituted rules made these conflicts impossible to resolve. Moreover, since the movement did not aim to reappropriate collectively produced wealth from private, exclusive control, they had to rely on volunteer labor and donations to survive. Unless democratic movements can sustain themselves through the organized labor of their members, they are not sustainable in the long-term. For all these reasons, Occupy became, in fairly short order, cacophony rather than argument; splits rather than unity. Once this disorder was generalized, state power decided that enough was enough; the police did not really have to break a sweat to clear the camps.

Unfortunately, democracy cannot be realized as a set of alternative practices outside of state and other major social institutions. Robin Dunford's focus is peasant movements in the Global South, but the critique he launches against the belief that political movements will spontaneously cohere is apropos of my argument. Noting that movements like the Landless Workers Movement in Brazil combine horizontal alternative communities with direct engagement with state power, Dunford argues that these movements do not "emerge 'rhizomatically' and spontaneously cohere together." Rather, "they involve arts of government that organize forces by developing the knowledge, skills, and identities that enable grassroots alternatives to agri-industry and foster ongoing contestation."[52] In other words, these movements start by ensuring access to life-sustaining resources and also engage critically with state power. They are thus sustainable in a way that Occupy was not: They take over the land and put to life-valuable purposes the potential that was lying fallow, and they engage with the state to legally legitimize that which is morally asserted: the right of each and all the access to life-sustaining goods. I have shown that both agonistic radical democrats and horizontalist activists have misunderstood the way in which democracy depends on universal values and shared interests, and how these shared interests form a common basis around which unified, disciplined political movements and parties must be built. The future of democracy depends on activists grasping the practical implications of this lesson and building unified, disciplined movements and parties from that ground up.

NOTES

1. Mark Wenman, *Agonistic Democracy: Constitutive Power in the Era of Globalisation* (Cambridge, UK: Cambridge University Press, 2013), 28.

2. John B. Thompson, "Editor's Introduction," in Lefort, *The Political Forms of Modern Society: Bureaucracy, Democracy, Totalitarianism* (Cambridge, MA: MIT Press, 1986), 2.

3. Claude Lefort, *The Political Forms of Modern Society* (Cambridge, MA: MIT Press, 1986), 205.

4. Ibid., 264.

5. I do not intend this example as a solution of the extraordinarily complicated problem of migrant rights and the problems of exclusionary citizenship. I intend it only as an example to illustrate why thinkers like Lefort regard existing forms of unity as oppressive, but also why any solution to a problem like migrant rights presupposes the universal material interests that thinkers like Lefort reject.

6. Ibid., 270.

7. Vladimir Lenin, *The State and Revolution* (Moscow: Progress Publishers, 1975), 85.

8. Lefort, *The Political Forms of Modern Society*, 266.

9. Jacques Rancière, *Hatred of Democracy* (London: Verso, 2006), 54–55.

10. Ibid., 62.

11. Chantal Mouffe, *The Democratic Paradox* (London: Verso, 2000), 11.

12. Ibid., 18.

13. Chantal Mouffe, *Agonistics* (London: Verso, 2013), 76.

14. Ibid., 84.

15. Ibid., 7.

16. Mouffe's conception of democratic adversaries instantiates Balibar's idea of civility as a core democratic value. Balibar too rethought his way from Marxist revolutionary theory back to an embrace of the values of existing democratic institutions. Revolutionary violence straightforwardly failed to solve the problems of capitalism and created its own set of totalitarian monstrosities. The lesson that failure teaches is that opponents should be opposed, not destroyed. "I shall call a politics which regulates the conflict of identifications between the impossible . . . limits of a total and floating identification 'civility.' Civility excludes extremes of violence, so as to create a (public, private) space for politics (emancipation, transformation)" (Etienne Balibar, *Politics and the Other Scene* [London: Verso, 2011], 29). Civil, democratic politics is not conservative; its goal is (ongoing) social transformation, but by means of political mobilisation and persuasion, not the violent destruction of enemies, class or otherwise.

17. Mouffe, *Agonistics*, 7–8.

18. Ibid., 75–76.

19. For a detailed discussion of the Venezuelan movement in its most progressive moment, see Greg Wilpert, *Changing Venezuela by Taking Power* (London: Verso, 2007). I leave open the question of the long-term implications of relying on the extractive industries—in Venezuela, Bolivia, or anywhere else. I would argue that these problems cannot be solved by relatively poor countries acting in isolation. Dependence on fossil fuels or single resources like tin in Bolivia is a problem that can only be overcome through transnational cooperation. The practical challenges exceed what any book can meet.

20. Judith Butler, *Notes Toward a Performative Theory of Assembly* (Cambridge, MA: Harvard University Press, 2015), 43. What else is this connection than the "felt bond of being" that McMurtry calls the "life-ground of value"? See John McMurtry, *Unequal Freedoms* (Toronto: Garamond, 1998), 23.

21. Butler, *Notes Toward a Performative Theory of Assembly*, 45.

22. William Connolly, *The Fragility of Things* (Durham, NC: Duke University Press, 2013), 136.

23. Robin Dunford develops a nuanced critique of the political limitations of Connolly's ideas about role experimentation and self-organization. See Dunford, "Autonomous Peasant Struggles and Left Arts of Government," *Third World Quarterly*, vol. 36, no. 8 (2015), 1455–56.

24. See Michael Hardt and Antonio Negri, *Empire* (Cambridge, MA: Harvard University Press, 2000). Their analysis of Empire is really background historical material for their arguments about the theory and practice of democracy. Given the focus of this book, I will have to confine my attention to the latter.

25. I cannot do justice to the history of autonomism here. A good introduction and overview can be found in Sylvere Lotringer, ed., *Italy: Autonomia: Post-Political Politics* (New York: Semiotext(e), 1980).

26. Paolo Virno, *A Grammar of the Multitude* (Los Angeles: Semiotext(e), 2004), 42.

27. The problem of the extent to which immaterial labor has superseded the importance of material labor is important, but goes beyond the theme of this book. I note that the entire infrastructure of the "public intellect" that makes immaterial labor possible is material. Computers and computer networks are built of physical stuff that had to be dug from the ground and requires energy.

28. Virno, *A Grammar of the Multitude*, 70.

29. Ibid.

30. Ibid.

31. Ibid., 76.

32. Michael Hardt and Antonio Negri, *Commonwealth* (Cambridge, MA: Harvard University Press, 2009), viii.

33. Although, it should be pointed out that corporations have been hard at work finding ways to erect all manner of pay walls and monetary impediments to access.

34. Michael Hardt and Antonio Negri, *Multitude: War and Democracy in the Age of Empire* (New York: Penguin, 2004), 339.

35. Hardt and Negri, *Commonwealth*, 350.

36. See Michael Hardt and Antonio Negri, *Assembly* (New York: Oxford University Press, 2017), xv.

37. Hardt and Negri, *Commonwealth*, 379.

38. Yochai Benkler, *The Wealth of Networks* (New Haven, CT: Yale University Press, 2006), 464.
39. Ibid., 303.
40. Ibid., 305.
41. Ibid., 307.
42. Julien Assange, with Jacob Appelbaum, Andy Muller-Maghun, and Jérémie Zimmermann, *Cypherpunks: Freedom and the Future of the Internet* (New York: OR Books, 2012), 44.
43. Ibid., 15.
44. Quoted in Evgeny Morozov, *To Save Everything, Click Here* (New York: Public Affairs, 2013), 127.
45. Wang Hui, Wen Tiejun, and Lau Kin Chi, "The Movement in Egypt: Dialogue with Samir Amin," *Boundary 2*, vol. 39, no. 1 (2012), 176; https://read.dukeupress.edu/boundary-2/article-pdf/39/1/167/232164/b2391_09Hui_Fpp.pdf (accessed April 12, 2018).
46. Jodi Dean, *Democracy and Other Neoliberal Fantasies* (Durham, NC: Duke University Press, 2009), 38.
47. Morozov, *To Save Everything, Click Here*, 126–27.
48. Marina Sitrin, *Everyday Revolutions: Horizontalism and Autonomy in Argentina* (London: Zed Books, 2012), 65.
49. Ibid.
50. Quoted in Chris Hedges and Joe Sacco, *Days of Destruction, Days of Revolt* (Toronto: Knopf Canada, 2012), 250.
51. For an autobiographical critique from the perspective of an activist who learned from her own experience about the limits of horizontal organizing, see Jo Freeman, "The Tyranny of Structurelessness," https://www.jofreeman.com/joreen/tyranny.htm (accessed September 20, 2018).
52. Dunford, "Autonomous Peasant Struggles and Left Arts of Government," 1459.

Chapter 6

Shared Life-Interests and Democratic Self-Determination

I have argued that the struggle to realize the value of self-determination underlies the various forms that democracy has taken. The demand is articulated in different ways—sometimes as a struggle for rights, sometimes as a struggle for substantive equality, sometimes as a demand for new institutions, sometimes as a demand for new forms of social relationship. In all cases the struggles arise from people's experiences of social, political, economic, and cultural power as an oppressive, alien force exerted against their social self-conscious agency and interest in living full lives. Social self-conscious agency requires political voice, but much more besides. It requires health, education, the opportunity to realize our talents in ways that are personally fulfilling and socially valuable; it requires a life-supportive natural world, an inclusive cultural milieu, and time for self-development and open experience of the world. The struggle for democracy thus involves multiple demands, but what makes these demands democratic is that they all concern the satisfaction of the natural and social needs without which social self-conscious agency cannot develop. If social self-conscious agency cannot develop because the preponderant social power puts its own perpetuation ahead of the shared interests of all, then that society is not democratic.

Thinking of democracy as a form of social life and not just a political arrangement helps avoid three key problems that democratic theory has traditionally faced. First, we avoid an overly narrow understanding of democracy as identical with one historically and culturally specific set of institutions—for example, the institutions of liberal-democracy. When democracy is narrowly conceived in this way, it cannot learn from other forms of social life that may contain important lessons for democratic social organization but which, since they are not legally embodied in a constitution and may not respect private property, have been historically dismissed by liberals as undemocratic. Second, we become aware that a democratic society requires a democratic economy. The deep democratic truth of the Marxist tradition, whatever its practical failings might have been, is that people cannot be self-determining if they are dependent on reified market forces for their lives and livelihood. The problem here has two dimensions. First, our livelihoods can be cut off if economic conditions make it unprofitable to employ us. Second, we have no say in the organization of our work, in how much time we have to spend doing it, and whether it affords any opportunity for meaningful forms of self-realization. Since a majority of our active life is spent working, societies that allow work to remain outside the zone of collective self-determination are not democratic. Finally, we can see why democracy is not a neoliberal fantasy and why we are not in a "post-democratic age." The idea of democracy, like any value-term, can be appropriated by its enemies and used to support policies that are the opposite of what it demands. Decades of attacks on past democratic achievements have rendered many people passive spectators of a political process from which they feel alienated. The only solution to those problems is to discover new ways of mobilizing people. There is no other society that can replace democracy as the organizing goal of mass mobilization, since those mobilizations either better satisfy the conditions for self-determination or do not. If they do, then they are democratic, and part of the solution to the post-democratic malaise; if they do not, they are part of the problem.

Of course avoiding problems is not the same as finding a practical solution to the main challenges of our age. The main problem is how to build cohesive, unified movements that can recapture the political initiative from right-wing populists, begin the process of democratizing economic life, and ensure that social and cultural differences are able to fully articulate their experiences. This goal differs from the approach of the radical democrats and horizontalists examined in chapter 5. While some agreed there are shared foundations to democratic life and others implied that point without making it explicit, all valorized differences and autonomous organization over shared life-interests and centrally organized political movements and parties. Democratic activists have to be honest: Dispersed forms of struggle have not worked. Antidemocratic forces have captured all major social and political institutions, intensified the hold of market forces over almost all aspects of life, strengthened the security state to manage the conflicts that growing inequality causes, normalized the cultural power of abstract individualism and competition, demonized cooperation as anti-freedom, and spread xenophobia and indifference to preventable destruction and death across the Middle East and Global South. If all that evidence does not add up to proof that the future of democracy demands a different politics, then nothing will.

This new approach does not have to be invented ex nihilo. Its contours are outlined in the history of democratic struggle. Chantal Mouffe is spot on when she argues that "democratic values still play a significant role in the political imaginary of our societies," and that their "critical meaning can be reactivated to subvert the hegemonic order."[1] However, her understanding of pluralism fails to see the way in which, historically, democratic values have always presupposed shared objective needs and fought to ensure their satisfaction. Her Left populism demands a basis of unity, and unmet needs are the only coherent unifying basis around which different groups of oppressed and exploited people can come together.

At the same time, we cannot just repeat the struggles of the past. We have to interpret those lessons in our contemporary context and reshape the historically validated principles to suit our times. Major democratic advances have occurred through massive social struggles that succeeded in releasing resources from private and exclusive control, changed the laws to allow more universal access to major social institutions, and won greater power for formerly excluded voices. In all cases, different social identities had to fight together to win. Different groups took the lead on different fights. Women led the fight for women's suffrage; blacks for civil rights in the Jim Crow South. The consolidation of the victories depended on building a universal case for the particular demand. The universal case is not abstractly moralistic but a *concretely universal* demand for something that everyone requires in forms anchored in the particularities of actual histories and identities history. Everyone needs protein, as I explained in chapter 1; but some people get it through eating meat, others through eating beans. So too with all democratic demands. The democratic form is the same: what we need to become social self-conscious agents and work together to determine law and public policy. The content can differ depending on the specific histories of deprivation different groups have suffered. The key to the future of democracy is thus democratic solidarity: all groups recognizing the universal value, the human life-requirement, deep within particular demands. Recognizing the common in the particular helps build unified collective struggles for institutional changes in the way law and public policy are formulated and the values that major social institutions serve. Everyone benefits when any formerly excluded group is better able to satisfy its historically unmet needs. Democracy advances as a result.

That claim might seem platitudinous, but there is in fact empirical evidence to support it. We saw in chapter 3 that inquiries in the social determinants of health reveal that making society more equal improves health outcomes for the worst off, without in any way damaging the health of the better off. Kate Pickett and Richard Wilkinson have demonstrated similar results with regard to psychological well-being: The more inequality in a society, the more anxious and unhappier everyone is. "In this book we show that the quality of social relations in a society is built on material foundations . . . the scale of social inequality provides a powerful policy lever on the psychological well-being of all of us."[2] If we think of physical and mental health in a holistic way to describe our ability to develop all our cognitive, relational, and creative capacities, then Marmot, Pickett, and Wilkinson provide robust empirical evidence for my argument: Democracy is not just a political form but an overall structure of social life, which improves the real lives of everyone to the extent that it advances.

This chapter will flesh out the case for unified struggle as the general means of democratic advance and the specific condition of successful struggles for any particular democratic demand today. In the first section I will bring to light the common basis of different forms of oppression by examining intersectionality and social reproduction theory. Both are different ways of understanding the common aspects of oppression that make implicit or explicit reference to unmet needs, but both fail to fully appreciate the universal implications of this recognition. Once those universal implications have been unpacked, particular struggles like Black Lives Matter, workers' struggles in the Global South, or indigenous peoples' struggles to reclaim their traditional lands can be understood in their universal significance as democratic struggles. In the second section I will explain the principle of democratic solidarity. Unlike loose coalitions between self-organizing struggles, democratic solidarity demands the recognition of the real common source of oppression. Democratic solidarity requires that each group recognize the universal form of their own particular demands and see the solution to everyone's problems in fundamental institutional changes. In the third section I will conclude by arguing that the initiative can be wrested from right-wing populist and neoliberal forces by unified democracy movements fighting to protect and expand public investment and public institutions. The principle, if not always the practice, of public institutions has been radically democratic: distribution of needed goods independent of the ability to pay, funded by progressive taxation. An expanded public sphere is not the *end* of the democratic journey, as social democrats believe, but it is the best starting point for a new campaign. We know from history that they work. Rather than utopian promises that do not feed people or keep them warm, they are a reality, the fruit of past struggles, and thus a plateau from which assaults on higher peaks can be launched.

INTERSECTIONALITY, SOCIAL REPRODUCTION, AND THE LIFE-VALUE OF STRUGGLE AGAINST OPPRESSION

Unity in struggle between oppressed groups presupposes that they find or build some common ground. The firmer the common ground, the stronger the political unity. From the perspective of Mouffe and other radical agonistic democrats, common ground is constructed, not discovered. Let us accept that whether there is objective common ground to discover or not, the construction requires *materials*. What are the materials out of which democratic solidarity can be built? It will not do to infer an answer from ahistorical principles. A convincing political answer must be developed by listening to the voices of oppressed groups. I will argue that an examination of the self-understanding and struggles of oppressed groups reveals that unmet needs are the material from which solidarity is constructed. I will go further and claim that these needs are objective and that political argument is a process whereby different groups recognize that they all suffer from different forms of the same problem. However, even if one wants to resist that stronger conclusion, one must still admit that solidarity is either real or fictional, and if it is real, it must be built out of something; the words of the oppressed themselves tell us that their suffering is the consequence of unmet needs. In practical terms, the conclusion is the same either way: A unified democratic movement depends on different groups recognizing that they share something in common with other groups.

My argument will be stronger if it uncovers a role for unmet needs even in theories of oppression that seem most distant from its universal values. Since the 1980s, "intersectional" theories of oppression have been perhaps the most influential explanations of oppression. They start from the fact of multiple forms of oppression and examine the points where they intersect in real people. Intersectional theory treats different histories of oppression as systematically distinct but accidentally conjoined in concrete individuals. Sexism and racism have different histories and structures, but in black women those histories intersect to produce a sui generis form of oppression that is not reducible to either. The same would hold true for any other intersection.

This explanation of oppression was pioneered by Kimberlé Crenshaw, who was tackling a narrow legal problem: In the United States in the 1980s, one could sue for discrimination on the basis of race or sex, but not both together. This peculiarity of antidiscrimination law meant that black women found themselves with no legal recourse for their unique experiences of being discriminated against—not as blacks on the one hand and women on the other, but as black women. Her analysis of the legal dimension of the problem had general theoretical and political implications.

> Because the intersectional experience is greater than the sum of racism and sexism, any analysis that does not take intersectionality into account cannot sufficiently address the particular manner in which Black women are subordinated. Thus, for feminist theory and antiracist policy discourse to embrace the experiences and concerns of Black women, the entire framework that has been used as a basis for translating "women's experience" or "the Black experience" . . . must be rethought.[3]

Note that Crenshaw here claims that an intersection produces a whole greater than the sum of its parts. If that is so, then there must be some commensurable elements in the two forms of oppression that can combine to produce a third form of oppression, which is neither racial nor sexual but both together and more intense as a result. We will come back to what Crenshaw thinks this element is, but first we need to note a tension at the heart of the metaphor of the intersection.

Crenshaw developed the idea of intersectionality by thinking about traffic flows. Streets all have their own direction, and where they meet, traffic has to be regulated in order to flow smoothly. The intersection does not face in any direction, but is the space that all traffic must cross. In the crossing, accidents can happen. "Discrimination, like traffic through an intersection, may flow in one direction, or it may flow in another. If an accident happens . . . it can be caused by cars traveling from any number of directions. . . . Similarly, if a Black woman is harmed because she is in the intersection, her injury could result from sex discrimination or race discrimination."[4] This conclusion is not the same as the conclusion she set out to illustrate with the metaphor. She sought to illustrate the conclusion that the whole of multiple forms of oppression is greater than the sum of its parts, but the metaphor draws her back to the very problem her argument was trying to avoid: seeing racial and sexual oppression as separate.

The problem is with the metaphor and not the goal of thinking of multiple oppressions as unified in the experience of the real people who suffer from them. The metaphor stresses the separateness of histories of oppression and lends itself to more and more complex maps of streets (histories of oppression) with more and more complex intersections. The coherence and commensurability that was central to Crenshaw's political and theoretical aims become lost in a tangle of fragmented experiences and subjective claims for recognition of one's uniqueness. Asad Haider's very important critique of identity politics exposes the issue. "Intersectionality . . . generalizes the condition of the plaintiff: equating political practice with the demand for restitution of an injury, inviting the construction of baroque and unnavigable intersections consisting of a litany of different identities to which a given person might belong."[5] Haider is quick to emphasize (as I have too) that the *intent* of intersectionality was to discover and explain common ground. Unfortunately, it has devolved into a moralistic and liberal politics of commas. Political argument is reduced to individuals standing up and listing adjectives that apply to them (black, woman, lesbian, etc.), with no explanation of social causes and no politics aside from moralistic demands that other, "privileged" subjects ally with them. The democratic idea of solidarity in struggle for fundamental institutional change is lost.

In order to realize the actual goal that Crenshaw was trying to advance, the metaphor of intersections needs to be abandoned in favor of one that can grasp the ways in which different structural forms of oppression stem from a common social source. Social reproduction theory shares with Crenshaw the belief that there are multiple forms of oppression that are experienced in a singular way by real individuals. However, it explains these different structures as the product of a single social drive to reproduce society through the exploitation of labor. Oppressions have their own histories, but these histories cannot be separated from the way in which capitalism prioritizes the appropriation of surplus value produced by working people of different sexes, races, genders, and sexualities. McNally, sympathetically criticizing intersectional theories, replaces the mechanical metaphor of intersections with an organic metaphor of the interaction of bodily systems.

> There are properties that are specific to different parts of the whole. The eye has particular functional properties quite different from that of the hand. Racism has specific characteristics that allow us to distinguish it . . . from sexism. They afford a starting point from which thought unfolds the internal relations of parts to other parts and to the organic system as a whole. Racism, in other words, can be understood as a *partial totality* that must ultimately be grasped in relation to other partial totalities that make up the social whole in its process of becoming.[6]

One cannot understand the eye by dissecting it on an examining table. Its function must be understood in part from its structure, but *in connection* with the living whole of which it is an organic part. From any organic part we can move to the whole, and only when we grasp the whole in its dynamic interconnection *and unified functioning* can we understand any part. Thus, for social reproduction theory, the way in which productive and caring labor is exploited is the unifying core—the body, if you will—of which sexism and racism and other forms of oppression are partial wholes.

Social reproduction theory has the advantage of allowing us to grasp different systems of oppression as different forms of a single organizing social drive. It better realizes Crenshaw's original goal: grasping the ways in which the experiences of intersecting oppressions add up to a whole greater than the sum of its parts. The problem with social reproduction theory, however, is political. By focusing on the central role of labor, it concludes that the real problem is class and capitalism, and this conclusion will sound sectarian to people organizing on the basis of race and sex. The political conclusion is thus too particularistic and inconsistent with its universal theoretical aims. Its political goals, like those of intersectional theory, must be expressed in terms that are not particular to a given identity or structural location but pertain to every identity in different ways. It is true that workers share in concrete racial and sexual identities, but a unified political movement requires more than a complex account of the identities of real workers; it has to explain exploitation, as it explains oppression, as a function of deprivation of needs workers (whatever their identity) share with other oppressed groups. The underlying common ground is the human needs explained in chapter 1. All human beings must satisfy these universal life-requirements, and people are oppressed when, *and to the extent that, social structures, dynamics, and values prevent them from satisfying* some subset of those natural and social needs.

This conclusion is implicit in both intersectional and social reproduction theory, as well as workers' struggles, antiracist fightbacks, and indigenous peoples' movements. Crenshaw's analysis treats racism and sexism as distinct forms of oppression, but her argument critiques both (and, by extension, all forms of oppression) in the name of self-determination. "If any real efforts are to be made to free Black people of the constraints . . . that characterize racial subordination, then theories and strategies purporting to reflect the Black community's needs must include an analysis of sex and patriarchy. . . . The praxis of both should be centered on the life chances and life situations of people."[7] In other words, Crenshaw argues that different forms of oppression must be judged against a common basis: life chances and life situations. The struggle, whatever the precise contours of the oppressed situations, is thus for the same general goal: satisfaction of the conditions for self-determination, which are in turn the conditions for free individual self-realization.

What are those conditions? Here social reproduction theory provides the necessary detail. Tithi Bhattacharya, examining the struggles of working women in the Global South, explains that because capitalism affects all dimensions of life—conditions of work and access to health care, income levels and the quality and purpose of schools, the amount of free time available and the condition of the natural environment—workers' struggles are always about work *and* home, the point of production and the quality of life in the wider community. Studies of these struggles "bring to striking analytical prominence not only the places where the working class works, but also the spaces where workers sleep, play, go to school—in other words, live full sensual lives beyond the workplace."[8] These struggles are clearly struggles for the goods, relationships, resources, and institutions people need if they are to collectively determine their public lives and freely realize their individuating creative capacities. The details of the struggle will differ from country to country, but they are unified by the same goal that Crenshaw invoked. Sheila Rowbotham, looking at two centuries of women's struggles from a socialist feminist perspective, states that goal clearly: a society in which "social and economic development [is] geared to human needs through wider control over and access to economic and political power."[9] No form of oppression can be overcome save by the group coming to more fully control its conditions of existence and activity. Here is further evidence that at the basis of all forms of oppression are systematically unmet needs and that particular struggles against oppression point toward the political need for a unified democratic movement focused on control over major social institutions. Democratic control means ensuring that all major social institutions serve their proper function: satisfying one or more fundamental life-requirements so that people are able to fully participate as equals in public life and realize their creative capacities in their own lives.

This conclusion is buttressed further by the stated goals and values of perhaps the most vital antiracist movement today, Black Lives Matter. This claim might seem surprising. Black Lives Matter openly proclaims itself a movement of Black People, for Black People. It has resisted abstractly universalist claims that "all lives matter." In response to a criticism from police unions that Black Lives Matter was indirectly responsible for the murder of police officers, and that its name and slogan were divisive, the movement responded: "There will be no end to the cry of Black Lives Matter, and this movement will not take responsibility for crimes it did not commit. Period. I don't have to say that 'Blue Lives Matter,' because neither society nor 'the system' has ever suggested otherwise."[10] The case is completely different with black lives, which have been treated as expendable since the days of slavery. Nevertheless, the vigorous assertion "Black Lives Matter" is clearly not the assertion of a particular value against an oppressive universalism, but the assertion of a concrete universal—the value of black *lives* against the oppressive particularity of a racist culture in which white lives have mattered more. Valuing black lives does not *devalue* white life; it is the condition of all life being equally valued. The point is forcefully made in the Black Lives Matter statement of principles: "We work vigorously for freedom and justice for Black people, and, by extension, all people. . . . In affirming that Black Lives Matter, we need not qualify our position. To love and demand freedom for ourselves is a prerequisite to wanting the same for others."[11] While the struggle has emerged in response to the specific threats to black lives, it rests on the same universal foundations as all struggles against oppression. As such, it points beyond its immediate organizational form to the need for deeper social changes that require larger and internally unified democratic movements.

If we turn to the labor movement, we also once again find universal life-values beneath the apparent form of merely sectional demands. The labor movement around the world has been put on the defensive by neoliberal restructuring and austerity, and it is easy to dismiss struggles over wages as rear-guard actions of a labor aristocracy protecting its privilege against workers in much more precarious situations. Unfortunately, sometimes that criticism is true. However, the labor movement has also been in the forefront of struggles against austerity, successfully leading fights across North America to raise the minimum wage. It has also fought for environmental protection in the form of health and safety regulations, has tried to protect pensions and public services, and has led the fight for equal pay for work of equal value. The value of collective bargaining is not only its historic success in improving conditions of work. It is a concrete means by which workers can democratically shape their conditions of work. It prefigures more deeply democratic forms of economic life. The life-value of the labor movement, as I put it in an earlier analysis, was forcefully brought home in South Africa at the Working Class Summit held in August 2018.[12] It brought together 147 different unions and social movements to make the connections between the particular forms of harm each suffered as a consequence of capitalist exploitation, oppression, and alienation:

> The Working Class Summit not only endorsed the binding principles around which it will unite such as anti-racism, anti-sexism, anti-patriarchy and anti-xenophobia, but unanimously agreed that capitalism is the common cause of the misery experienced by the majority.
>
> There was unanimous agreement that the working class movement must be independent and adopt a bottom up approach to democracy. . . . The Working Class Summit agreed to build the working class power in every workplace, in every community and society in general to defeat the logic of capitalist accumulation that has not only pauperized workers across the continent but it has caused the widest inequality and deepest poverty ever recorded in the history of humankind.[13]

Once again, at the root of the struggle we find unmet life-needs and the overarching goal: the transformation of all social institutions so that they satisfy these needs and empower people to govern the common affairs collectively and shape their own lives freely.

Arguably the most explicit link between need-satisfaction as the material conditions of self-determination and democracy is made in the struggles of indigenous peoples to reclaim control over their traditional territories. In Canada, countrywide indigenous struggle has been rekindled under the banner of the Idle No More movement. It emerged in 2012 in response to a severe housing crisis on the Attawapiskat First Nation reserve in northwestern Ontario. Chief Theresa Spence flew to Ottawa and began a hunger strike while encamped on the Ottawa River beneath the Canadian Parliament.[14] Her actions sparked a nationwide movement demanding not only immediate investment in infrastructure on First Nations lands but also meaningful self-government and honoring the treaties that legally govern the relationship between Canada and the First Nations. Yellowknive's Dene theorist and activist Glen Sean Coulthard explains its key demands were to "improve aboriginal education and housing, fully implementing the UN Declaration of the Rights of Indigenous People, [and] the establishment of an implementation framework for First Nation Treaty Rights."[15] Together, the UN declaration and concrete enforcement of First Nation Treaty Rights would guarantee indigenous people in Canada control over their traditional lands and waters, and allow them to go forward to rebuild their communities according to their traditional principles of sustainable resource use and distribution according to need. Bruce Ferguson, an Algonquin activist, brings out the life-value core of indigenous principles of resources: "Our thinking traditionally . . . is take what you need, no more and then share it with your community."[16] The principle is of obvious universal validity; indeed, it must be the basis for any sustainable economic system, no matter the identity of the people who run it. If sustainability is a condition of a materially rational democracy, this principle of exploitation for use must underlie the economy of any democratic society.

Around the world, indigenous people are fighting the same legacy of colonial dispossession. Robin Dunford uncovers the shared principle uniting peasant and indigenous struggles across the Global South. "In multiple localities peasants have mobilized in movements . . . to directly occupy and produce on the land, seeking to reclaim territory they have lost and to regain the ability to engage in smallholder forms of production."[17] The struggles for land are not a supplement to struggles for democratic voice; they are themselves forms of democratic voice. In reestablishing the connection to the land that colonial exploitation severs, indigenous and peasant communities reclaim control over the basic material conditions of their lives, thus proving their subjecthood whether those who would treat them as mere objects of a capitalist "modernizing" process accept it or not. Their self-assertion against their oppressors helps to establish themselves as citizens who must be heard and whose interests must be taken into account by the nation. The struggles are local and particular, but the underlying value served is universal. Its democratic significance is brought out forcefully by Enrique Dussel:

> The *critical* discursive criterion of validity [implicit in the struggles of oppressed groups] consists, then, in the reference to the intersubjectivity of the victims who are excluded from the decisions that affect them (by alienating them at any level of their real existence) . . . there is *critical* validity when the community of the excluded victims, having recognized each other as distinct from the oppressive system, symmetrically participate in the agreements about what affects them.[18]

The link between democracy and the overcoming of the various forms of alienation between people and their life-conditions is clear. Democracy is not identical to representative institutions and constitutional guarantees of power but demands real collective control over need-satisfying resources, institutions, and relationships.

Wherever there are groups that are treated as mere objects of political and economic power, there is oppression. Where there is oppression, the society as a whole is not self-determining, but some groups' lives are determined by forces and powers over which they have no say. Hence democracy requires the realization of Dussel's critical discursive criterion of validity, and that in turn requires collective control over fundamental resources and major social institutions. It is through successful reclamation of control over those resources and institutions that those who are treated as mere objects of power prove they are subjects who must be heard. Even where struggles are separate and dispersed, they serve this universal value; but it cannot be fully realized, I will argue in the next section, if struggles remain dispersed. Hence the crucial practical question is: How to enable distinct groups engaged in separate struggles to recognize the universal life-interest in need-satisfaction that each of their struggles strives to satisfy?

DEMOCRATIC SOLIDARITY

In his aptly titled lament for the Left, *We Can Do Better*, David Camfield argues that democratic forces can overcome their recent history of defeats. He acknowledges the weakness of the labor movement, celebrates the creativity of social movements outside the labor movement, but concludes that future success will require new forms of political unity. Political skeptics might reasonably point to the intense polarization of liberal-capitalist societies and dismiss his calls for unity as just another balloon full of utopian hot air. Perhaps they will be proven correct. Yet Camfield is not naive, he does not believe the scales will suddenly fall from everyone's eyes because some platitude seizes their imaginations. There are common interests, but it takes political work for different groups to recognize them. People's self-understanding and their understanding of others changes through the experience of political work.

Social movements happen when large numbers act together to mount institutional challenges. They allow many people to realize that what they once thought of as private problems . . . are actually public issues that call for collective solutions. Taking part in the movement encourages people to question the status quo, to realize that injustice . . . [is] the result of social arrangements that can be changed.[19]

Social movements bring to light the power of ordinary people to change the conditions of their lives, but they also bring to light the power of some ordinary people to change their understanding of other ordinary people who are different in some respect.

Recall F. Michael Higginbotham's argument examined in chapter 4 that racism in the United States is sustained by the isolation of white from black America. Where people have no direct experience of the fullness of the lives of others, their one-sided assumptions are never challenged. When people are thrown together in struggle, they have a chance to see the whole person and not the stereotyped caricature. When the falseness of their experience is objectively challenged in this way, they can change their interpretation. Democratic movements emerge when different people recognize that they have a shared interest in making key institutional changes. This shared common interest is not "an abstraction inherent in each individual," as Marx dismissed Ludwig Feuerbach's conception of human beings, but real material needs for access to the resources and institutions they each discover that all need in order to live freely as social self-conscious subjects.[20]

The argument is not moralistic pleading for everyone to get along. People's own political behavior when confronted by common problems confirms my argument. Activists from Black Lives Matter went to Standing Rock, South Dakota, to support the Lakota in their struggle against the installation of an oil pipeline across their traditional territory.[21] The struggle against climate change, racialized oppression, colonialism, and police violence all coalesced. Black Lives Matter has also reenergized the union movement. The struggle against police violence, the struggle against poverty, and the struggle for secure employment all come together.[22] Or recall the example from chapter 4 of Trump supporters and opponents both rallying to save Obamacare. I could multiply examples, but I want to focus on the underlying conditions that allow for successful coalescence of struggle.

I take it as axiomatic that two people or groups who have absolutely nothing in common could not understand each other. Perhaps there are extraterrestrials that are so different from us that we could not recognize them as life forms, but even that seems unlikely. If they are in any sense alive, they would have to keep themselves alive. Therefore, even if they fed on very different energy sources (perhaps even us, if they do decide to visit!), as soon as we understood that need, we would understand their basic forms of behavior. We do not share a language with animals, but we can interpret their behavior because we can understand some of what they do, because we understand they are doing what they need to do to survive. If we can understand animals, and (hypothetically) extraterrestrials once we understand what they need, then there can be no doubt that different groups of human beings can understand each other. The process of mutual political understanding does require work, but it also requires an object on which the work is performed. The work involves argument, dialogue, listening, explaining, disagreeing, and, ultimately, broadening of perspective. The object of the work is the core human needs that everyone must satisfy if they are to survive and realize their creative and cognitive capacities. I understand others in a democratic, nonpatronizing way when I understand that their demands are the same demands I would make if I stood in their shoes, because the demand stems from fundamental natural and social needs.

I agree with thinkers like Mouffe that constructing unified political movements requires political work. There is nothing automatic about democratic solidarity. At the same time, I strenuously disagree with her claim that different identities do not share anything objective in common, but that all commonalities are discursive constructions. "What appears as the natural order is never the manifestation of a deeper objectivity that would be external to the practices that brought it into being."[23] Neither this claim nor the opposite is true. The truth is that there is a dialectical (and dialogical) connection between underlying objectivity and the concrete forms that practice shapes that objectivity into. It is mid-August as I write this chapter, and our tomatoes are ripening in the backyard garden. They would not be growing without the work of my partner and I, but they would also not grow had *tomato* seeds not been planted in nutritious soil that received adequate rain and sunlight. The genetic program in the seed, the soil, water, and sunlight are deeper material conditions for the growth of the tomatoes, but they alone do not mechanically create the fruit. The fruit depends equally on the labor we performed to plant, stake, and tend to their development. No objective fruit without the work, but no work *on the fruit* apart from its deeper material conditions.

Political work is analogous. If people decide to fight together, there must be an underlying reason. They all need access to a resource or an institution or, at the very least, recognize that a particular group in struggle needs access to what others already have, and that their not being able to access it is unjust and illegitimate because their deprivation harms them. Recognition of the illegitimate or unjustifiable harm that unmet needs causes is the basis from which democratic solidarity is built. I want to emphasize again that it must be *built* through the sorts of political work Mouffe defends. But the work will be for naught if there is no soil, no "deeper objectivity" upon which political argument works.

At the same time, the deeper objectivity of fundamental human needs is not an abstraction apart from the concrete identities of real people. People are not "human" in terms of their core needs and "black" or "women" in terms of their identities. Democratic struggles are the struggles of real people, acting on the basis of their real identity, for access to the goods, resources, and relationships they require to satisfy their fundamental needs. When successful, they overcome the historical forms of oppression, exploitation, and alienation from which the groups have suffered; ensure that their collective identities are no longer demonized; and ensure that their members are free to contribute to the health of the social whole by realizing their creative capacities in ways that are fulfilling and individuating. Democratic struggles are thus in a sense struggles for recognition and redistribution at once, but at the same time deeper than either.[24]

The "power of the people" is grounded in their collective control over universally required resources and institutions. Since "the people" is not a generic mass, its power is not generic either, but the real interconnected activity of the individual members of the different groups that compose it. Where groups are oppressed because of false constructions of their "nature," they will have to fight back together against the constraints these false constructions of their possibilities legitimate. In so doing, they contribute to the universal struggle for the satisfaction of the total conditions of self-determination (democracy as a form of social life). When other groups recognize the universal value of particular struggles, they can first support the movement and, second, work together toward a common agenda of institutional change. The principle that governs the democratic agenda is: All institutions must be governed by those whose lives they shape, for the sake of ensuring that they satisfy the human needs they have been developed to satisfy, and not the exclusive private goals of a ruling class.

Solidarity thus begins when people recognize that *human beings* express their lives in different ways. The legitimacy of the claim on resources that any group makes lies in their humanity, understood as the natural and social life-requirements they must satisfy if they are to live full and free lives. Once this humanity is recognized, people either respond to it by attending to the unmet needs of the other person or stand condemned of inhumanity in the face of obvious suffering. When ordinary Germans welcomed more than one million refugees and resisted racist fearmongering, they were saying, in effect, "We accept the different language you speak and the different religion you practice as essential to your humanity, and we welcome you in your differences as fellow human beings who have suffered greatly. We want to help alleviate your suffering and offer you a new home, where you can begin to participate as equals." Opponents of the decision to welcome the refugees refused to acknowledge the legitimacy of the suffering as the basis of a claim on the resources of German society. They constructed the cultural differences as ultimate, not as different expressions of humanity but of different human kinds. For the racist, we only have obligations to our kind. But the idea of ethnic kinds is illusory, both because all nation-states contain ethnic and other differences, but more importantly because there are no pure types of which individuals are programmed functions. There are languages and traditions of course, but no one is simply programmed by the language he or she speaks to accept a definite set of political-cultural values. We can all think for ourselves and are not programmed to feel proud of "our traditions" and less of different ones. It is true that people can be moved by racist constructions, but only responses that attend to the humanity of people expressed through their differences are compatible with democracy. The humanity to which we respond, and upon which democratic solidarity is built, is the shared needs each and all must satisfy to develop and express any of the abilities that make life valuable and valued.

PUBLIC INSTITUTIONS AND
DEMOCRATIC RENEWAL

It remains to sketch in general terms the practical goals around which democratic movements should be built. I will argue that the general focus of democratic struggles today should center on the defense and expansion of public institutions, public goods, and public regulation of markets and consumer behavior. These practical goals are neither platitudes without determinate content nor specific tactical demands. They translate the universal values that underlie democratic struggles into the language of institutional change, identifying the institutions that need to be changed and the general changes required to bring them into coherence with democratic values. Since all contemporary societies are structured by the same major institutions, these practical goals are generalizable across different societies.

However, since the historical development of those institutions differs, as do national histories of struggle and political organization, a list of practical goals (just like the defense of democratic values) cannot substitute for local political argument and organization. I will argue that the practical goals I will defend are justified on two interrelated grounds. First, they follow from my conception of democracy as self-determination. If that conception is both sound and superior to the competing conceptions I have examined and criticized, then the superiority of these practical goals follows from their coherence with this conception of democracy. Secondly, these practical goals have the advantage of being grounded in the historical achievements of past struggles. Unlike abstract platitudes or utopian ideas, we already know they can be achieved. However, the historical forms they have taken have not yet realized their full democratic value. They thus enable future democratic movements to continue the struggle, on the concrete basis of a given level of realization, to deepen their democratic implications. To the extent that the democratic value of public institutions is realized, people's lives are freed from domination by market forces and the ruling class. They are thus freer in the moment to live—and better able because they are less dependent on exploitative and oppressive forces that can destroy them—to struggle upward to the next plateau.

My defense of public institutions invites two challenges. The first is the familiar neoliberal critique of public institutions as wasteful, one-size-fits-all institutions that deprive consumers of free choice. If we equate free choice and democracy, then they are also undemocratic. None of these charges stick. While it is possible to organize public institutions poorly, evidence suggests that when they are thoughtfully organized, they are less wasteful and produce better outcomes, in terms of satisfying the needs they are supposed to satisfy, than market competition. Take the example of health care. While the American model of private health care provision does generate much technological innovation—and provides on-demand care for those who can pay—it is vastly more expensive to run than well-organized public systems, leaves millions without any access at all, and proves inferior to public systems on most health outcomes.[25] To take another example: The government of the Province of Ontario recently privatized its electricity system. The result was not greater efficiency but higher prices.[26] The same goes for the privatization of the national rail service in the United Kingdom. The vaunted efficiencies of "free competition" never appeared, but higher prices did.[27] While there might be less choice between physicians for the rich in the public rather than a private system, this fact is hardly undemocratic. Democracy means self-determination for the entire society, not untrammeled free choice for the wealthy. Any set of institutions can be better designed; public institutions are no exception. They are essential to democracy rather than its antithesis, because only public provision of fundamental need-satisfiers ensures the universal access democracy demands.

Public provision interferes with "free choice" in two other ways, both of which are fully consistent with the demands of democracy. First, it demands, at an initial stage, rigorously progressive taxation. It is impossible to imagine a situation in which a revolutionary movement emerges in the short term that is capable of seizing the means of production and establishing "worker control" over the entire society. Sloganeering along these lines will not build the needed movement. "Another world" might be possible, but if anyone wants to build a democratic movement to explore the outer limits of possibility, he or she better begin with what is actual. Public provision through progressive taxation is actual (even if under severe stress) and demonstrably works—when it is consistently applied. The conditions that allowed for it in the past (gross disparities of wealth and income combined with unmet social needs) exist in even stronger form now. If all countries adopt and enforce similar tax regimes, there is nowhere for capital to flee, and it will have no choice but to accept a higher taxation burden. There can no more be democracy in only one country than there could have been socialism in only one country. The goal cannot be accomplished immediately, and the ruling class of all countries can be expected to fight back. I have emphasized throughout that democracy is a struggle, and there are no historical guarantees.

The same response applies to the need for public regulation of market and consumer behavior. Public environmental regulations, whether they focus on what businesses produce (including pollution) or on what consumers buy, are fully consistent with democracy when they aim to ensure the long-term consistency of the economic system with the life-support function of the natural world, even if they interfere with some choices. The typical capitalist dodge—that the environment must be "balanced" with economic growth—is materially irrational. *Every* type of economy presupposes a life-sustaining natural world. Collectively decided limits on what can be produced, how it can be produced, and how much of it can be consumed are not totalitarian assaults on liberty, but collectively rational decisions to ensure the open-ended future for human life.

The second objection bears a superficial relationship to the neoliberal complaint that public institutions deprive citizens of free choice. Instead of free choice, the second complaint worries about the loss of autonomy that people suffer when they are reduced to "clients" of the welfare state, racialized and sexualized inequalities of access, and the way in which citizenship-based inclusivity excludes migrants and non-citizens.[28] All these criticisms are legitimate, but none touch upon the democratic value of the *principle* of public institutions: distribution on the basis of need, not ability to pay. Each of these problems involves a practical limitation of function that contradicts the principle. For example, if universities are bureaucratic monsters serving the economy and not the intellectual needs of students, the solution is not to privatize them or raise fees but to return them to their proper social function: producing and disseminating knowledge in the public interest. Any contradiction between the purpose and practice of public institutions can be similarly resolved by ensuring that they function to satisfy the needs they are designed to meet (hospitals to cure, schools to teach); that they are funded at optimal levels; and that they are governed by boards representative of, and accountable to, the communities they serve, not to bureaucrats or the government of the day.

We must not forget that public institutions might have been legislated from above, but the legislation was forced on governments by struggles (or the threat of struggles) from below. The postwar period saw working people win "important elements of the better life they were fighting for—trade union rights, increased job security, better pay, improved workplace and state benefits . . . new opportunities for education, pensions, . . . and social programs that provided some degree of protection from the ups and downs of life."[29] Even if the gains were cynically granted by the ruling class, they were (and are) gains. We miss the full democratic value of these institutions if we focus only on the way in which they benefitted people as individuals. Viewed socially, public institutions, public goods, and public regulations are a vast "civil commons"—a collective, multigenerational creation that is the manifest form of democratic commitment to the well-being, the freedom, of each and all. "The civil commons is the ultimately organizing idea of what is best in 'civil society,' 'the commons,' 'progressive movement,' 'the Left,' 'the community,' 'unions,' and 'cooperatives.' . . . The civil commons = any and all social constructs that enable universal access to life-goods."[30] The core pieces of a democratic civil commons—that which must be defended where it exists or built where it does not—include, first, environmental regulations serving the universal life-interest in a sustainable natural life-support system, natural spaces protected from economic exploitation, and public ownership of core natural resources (including indigenous control where the resources lie on or under traditional territory). Next, they involve public control over the production of energy and a realizable plan for a transition to clean, renewable sources. Public health care and education at all levels is required, as is the cost-free availability of information on public services in the languages that are spoken in different communities, publicly funded science and real open access to information, diverse and vital cultural institutions, and publicly accessible internet and bandwidth reserved for community use. There must be consistent efforts to ensure democratic integration of newcomers that respects their cultures while ensuring they are not ghettoized and exploited. The housing crisis in major urban areas around the world demonstrates the need for public housing that responds to the articulated needs of the homeless and precariously housed, and public regulation of housing markets to ensure affordable access. There must be robust public law governing familial life including, especially, laws against domestic violence and child abuse, and community alternatives to militarized policing. Laws that allow workers to organize and defend their rights, including the right to participate in the governance of firm, robust antidiscrimination and affirmative action policies, are essential. At the level of the economy as a whole, plans that gradually reduce mandatory hours of work, increase free time, and expand meaningful employment opportunities are crucial. A democratic economy will also require public banking that frees investment funds from the control of speculators and hedge funds. Taken together, this commons—under threat but not yet undermined—represents the legacy and the future of struggles for the natural and social conditions of self-determination: democracy.

Any impediment—racist, sexist, ableist, homophobic, and so on—that impedes anyone from accessing these needed life-goods is thus not only oppressively exclusionary but *undemocratic*. People cannot participate as equals in the determination of public affairs if they are systematically deprived of that which they need to become social self-conscious agents. The civil commons ensures access to those life-goods, and is thus the guarantor of democratic social life.

Just because it frees people from dependence on the market, the civil commons has been the target of an unrelenting forty-plus-year assault by revanchist neoliberals. The watchword of their attack is "individual liberty." But democrats cannot be hoodwinked by this rhetoric. "Liberty" asserted as a slogan in the absence of the material and institutional conditions of biological life and social self-development is a smoke-screen masking the rule of a minority class. It could care less about the civil commons because it appropriates most of the wealth others pro-duce and thus does not need public institutions. The exploited and the oppressed do, but they are left dependent on mindless and meaningless work—or ruthless welfare state bureaucracies imprisoning them in a web of surveillance designed to disempower and humiliate. Democratic struggles are not about adding to this authoritarian bureaucracy but supplanting it with collective control over needed resources and institu-tions, freeing people from dependence on labor markets and bureau-cratic hierarchies. Democratic struggles contest minority control over that which is common. Natural resources are common wealth because they were not created by human beings. Social wealth is not produced by the genius of the rich but by the work of everyone. The collective labor required to produce social wealth is the basis of the democratic claim on its use to satisfy the needs of all. Funding public goods through progressive taxation is thus not "The Government," some oppressive excrescence undermining individual initiative and responsibility, as neoliberal caricature assets. It is the opposite: a virtuous circle in which individuals contribute labor and financial resources (taxes) to the production of collective goods they could not produce for themselves and in turn receive back what they need to live and flourish as self-creative individuals. The civil commons is the connecting thread of democratic struggles across cultures and throughout history.

The only way to consistently advance the development of the civil commons is to win state power. The success of the right wing in rolling back democratic gains has depended entirely on its success in winning elections and using legitimate state power to change tax and fiscal policy and labor law to suit its purposes. As Nick Srnicek and Alex Williams show, this struggle for state power also involved cultural struggle for hegemony against the liberatory ideas of the New Left and social movements of the 1960s.[30] However, this cultural counterrevolution was conceived as instrumental to gaining state power. With the state comes control over other major social institutions and the revenue that funds them. It is naive to believe, with the horizontalists, that informal and autonomous networks acting outside state power can radically transform the world. It is also naive to believe, with Camfield and others committed to a traditional Marxist conception of revolution, that the state must be overthrown before real democratic advance is possible. Camfield's ideas about political struggle are correct, but he is wrong to argue that "states are not neutral servants of their citizens. State power is deployed for two key objectives. The first is to guarantee the power of those who rule [and] . . . the second is to keep the wheels of capitalism turning."[31] It is true that the parties that have typically ruled liberal-capitalist states have used state power to accomplish those objectives, but state institutions have also been shaped by democratic struggles against capitalism and oppression. The institutions themselves can be used for democratic or undemocratic purposes, pro- or anticapitalist policies. Venezuela under Chavez certainly did not use the state to keep the wheels of capitalism turning. The attempt to internally transform Venezuelan society in a socialist direction and empower the historically excluded might have failed, but it did not fail because constituent assemblies and parliaments are somehow intrinsically incapable of being used to pass socially transformative laws. It failed because it was relatively isolated and overly dependent on oil revenue. The same point could be made with regard to Syriza in Greece. The party ran up against the limits of a small state trying to act alone. The solution is not to pretend there is some revolutionary alternative that can be brought into being through marches and strikes that does not involve using existing institutions to transform the priorities of existing societies, but to build networks between nationally grounded democratic forces who can jointly cut off the escape routes of capital seeking to flee democratic governance.

Parties do need to be disciplined by social movements, but they remain crucial to the future of the democratic project. Control over parliaments means control over the power to make and enforce legitimate law. Democratic forces like Syriza can be faulted for getting cold feet once in power. Here Margaret Thatcher and Trump teach an important lesson: Be bold in office; do what you say you will do. The temptation to practical conservativism, to try to do no further harm rather than courageously fund an expanded sphere of public goods and services, is always strong. Social movements connected to the party but not under its direct control are thus crucial to ensure that democratic agendas are advanced. Hilary Wainwright is talking about the Labour Party under Jeremy Corbyn, but the argument's conclusion is generalizable: "We need, therefore, to envisage a party as a means of expanding and prefiguring in the present, the relations we envisage in the future between politics and everyday material and cultural life . . . its task becomes to build and realize citizens' capacities for self-government and social and economic transformation."[32] Revolution today does not mean insurrection behind a red flag, but winning state power and keeping it by proving, through argument and in practice, that public provision of fundamental life-necessities is superior to the market. It means using legislation and policy to set society on a path that leads ultimately toward democratic control over all life-resources; their sustainable use to ensure the development of life-capacities, not private profit; deliberative governance of the institutions that produce and distribute life-goods; and peaceful cooperation between nations and cultures. Together, these are the general natural and social conditions of collective self-determination. Individual freedom, in turn, can only be guaranteed in societies that collectively control their conditions of life, and is only worthwhile to the extent that its concrete forms contribute to the health of the social whole upon which all individuals depend.

NOTES

1. Chantal Mouffe, *For a Left Populism* (London: Verso, 2018), 40.

2. Kate Pikett and Richard Wilkinson, *The Spirit Level: Why Equality Is Better for Everyone* (Harmondsworth, UK: Penguin, 2010), 16–17.

3. Kimberlé Crenshaw, "Demarginalizing the Intersection of Sex and Race: A Black Feminist Critique of Anti-Discrimination Doctrine," *University of Chicago Legal Forum*, vol. 139 (1989), 140.

4. Ibid., 149.

5. Asad Haider, *Mistaken Identity: Race and Class in the Age of Trump* (London: Verso, 2018), 35.

6. David McNally, "Intersections and Dialectics: Critical Reconstructions in Social Reproduction Theory," *Social Reproduction Theory,* Tithi Bhattacharya, ed. (London: Pluto, 2017), 105.

7. Crenshaw, "Demarginalizing the Intersection of Sex and Race: A Black Feminist Critique of Anti-Discrimination Doctrine," 166.

8. Tithi Bhattacharya, "How Not to Skip Class: Social Reproduction and the Global Working Class," *Social Reproduction Theory,* Tithi Bhattacharya, ed. (London: Pluto, 2017), 91.

9. Shelia Rowbotham, "Women: Linking Lives with Democracy," *Rethinking Democracy: Socialist Register 2018*, Leo Panitch and Greg Albo, eds. (London: Merlin Press, 2018), 41.

10. Dewey M. Clayton, "Black Lives Matter and the Civil Rights Movement: A Comparative Analysis of Two Social Movements in the United States," *Journal of Black Studies* (2018) online publication; DOI: 10.1177/00211934718764099 (accessed March 12, 2018).

11. Black Lives Matter, "Guiding Principles." *Black Lives Matter*; https://blacklivesmatter.com/about/what-we-believe/ (accessed July 5, 2018).

12. See Jeff Noonan, "The Historical and Contemporary Life-Value of the Canadian Labour Movement, *Labour/Le Travail*, 71 (Spring 2013), 9–27.

13. South African Federation of Trade Unions, "Working Class Movement Must Be Independent," *The Bullet* (August 5, 2018); https://socialistproject.ca/2018/08/working-class-movement-must-be-independent/ (accessed August 5, 2018).

14. Glen Sean Coulthard, *Red Skin, White Masks* (Minneapolis: University of Minnesota Press, 2014), 121.

15. Ibid., 164.

16. Bruce Ferguson, "Re-Thinking Struggle: Starting from Story," *Social Inequality and the Spectre of Social Injustice: Alternate Routes*, vol. 29 (2018), 316.

17. Dunford, "Autonomous Peasant Struggles and the Arts of Left Governance," 1457.

18. Enrique Dussel, *The Ethics of Liberation in the Age of Globalization and Exclusion* (Durham, NC: Duke University Press, 2013), 345.

19. David Camfield, *We Can Do Better* (Halifax, NS: Fernwood Publishing, 2017), 117.

20. Karl Marx, "Theses on Feuerbach," *The German Ideology* (Moscow: Progress Publishers, 1976), 619.

21. Ferguson, "Re-Thinking Struggle: Starting from Story," 308.

22. Mike Elk, "Justice in the Factory: How Black Lives Matter Breathed New Life into the Union Movement," *The Guardian* (February 10, 2018); https://www.theguardian.com/us-news/2018/feb/10/black-lives-matter-labor-unions-factory-workers-unite (accessed February 13, 2018).

23. Mouffe, *For a Left Populism*, 88.

24. In a famous debate, Nancy Fraser and Axel Honneth argued over the question of whether democratic struggles are mostly over redistribution of resources (Fraser) or recognition of concrete identities (Honneth). My position is that they focus on both, but ultimately go deeper than either, toward the structures of exclusionary control over resources. See Nancy Fraser and Axel Honneth, *Redistribution or Recognition: A Political Philosophical Debate* (London: Verso, 2003).

25. Two empirical studies, one a direct comparison between the Canadian and US systems, the other between the United States and all OECD countries (all of which, aside from the United States, have some degree of public health care), bear out my claims. Gordon H. Guyatt, PJ Devereaux, Joel Lexchin, Samuel B. Stone, Armine Yalnizyan, David Himmelstein, Steffie Woolhandler, Qi Zhou, Laurie J. Goldsmith, Deborah J. Cook, Ted Haines, Christina Lacchetti, John N. Lavis, Terrence Sullivan, Ed Mills, Shelley Kraus, and Neera Bhatnagar, "A Systematic Review of Studies Comparing Health Outcomes in Canada and the United States," *Open Medicine* (April 17, 2007); https://www.ncbi.nlm.nih.gov/pmc/articles/PMC2801918/ (accessed August 9, 2018); Bradley Sawyer and Selena Gomez, "How does the quality of the US healthcare system compare to other countries? *Health System Tracker* (May 22, 2017); https://www.healthsystemtracker.org/chart-collection/quality-u-s-healthcare-system-compare-countries/#item-hospital-admissions-preventable-diseases-frequent-u-s-comparable-countries (accessed August 9, 2018).

26. Five Reasons the Privatization of Ontario Hydro Is a Really, Really, Bad Idea," *Press Progress* (October 29, 2015); https://pressprogress.ca/5_reasons_privatization_hydro_one_is_a_really_really_bad_idea/ (accessed September 20, 2018).

27. Andrew Bowman, "An Illusion of Success: The Consequences of British Rail Privatisation," *Accounting Forum*, 39 (2015), 51–63.

28. Alan Sears, *The Next New Left: A History of the Future* (Halifax, NS: Fernwood Publishing, 2014), 56–57.

29. John McMurtry, *The Cancer Stage of Capitalism: From Crisis to Cure* (London: Pluto, 2013), 237.

30. See Nick Srnicek and Alex Williams, *Re-inventing the Future: Post-Capitalism and a World without Work* (London: Verso, 2015), 51–67.

31. Camfield, *We Can Do Better*, 63. It is especially important in the struggle to free the democratic institutions of the state from capitalist control to fund an alternative international finance system. At present, dependence on the US dollar and access to US banks leaves any government vulnerable to US sanctions. Venezuela under Chavez understood this need and was among the founders of a Latin American alternative to the IMF and the World Bank. For a discussion see Stephen Lendman, "The Bank of the South: An Alternative to IMF and World Bank Dominance," *Global Research* (October 29, 2007); https://www.globalresearch.ca/the-bank-of-the-south-an-alternative-to-imf-and-world-bank-dominance/7207 (accessed August 20, 2018).

32. Hilary Wainwright, "Radicalising the Party-Movement Relationship: From Ralph Miliband to Jeremy Corbyn and Beyond," *Rethinking Revolution: Socialist Register 2017* (London: Merlin Press, 2017), 98.

Further Reading

I have tried to combine economy of words with comprehensiveness of reference in the argument. The texts listed below supplement the works upon which the main argument drew. Even after including them, a vast literature exists covering every dimension of the problems of democratic theory and practice remains. Nevertheless, collectively, the in-text references and these further readings will provide students directly with what they need to further their own thinking or lead them beyond to still other resources that will. If a topic is not mentioned here, I have decided the in-text references suffice.

CHAPTER 1

On the revolutionary history of modern democracy, see Christopher Hill, *The Century of Revolution 1603–1704* (New York: Scholar's Choice Press, 2015; E. P. Thompson, *The Making of the English Working Class* (Harmondsworth, UK: Penguin, 2013); Eric Foner, *The Story of American Freedom* (New York: Picador, 1999); Howard Zinn, *A People's History of the United States* (New York: Harper, 2015); George Lefebvre, *The French Revolution: From Its Origins to 1793* (New York: Routledge).

For more on the relationship between revolutionary socialism and democracy, see Ellen Meiksins Wood, *Capitalism Against Democracy* (New York: Cambridge, 1995); Hal Draper, "Marx on

Democratic Forms of Government," *Socialist Register 1974* (London: Merlin Press, 1974), 101–24.

On the relationship between feminist struggle and democracy, the original classic of liberal feminism is Mary Wollstonecraft, *A Vindication of the Rights of Women* (Harmondsworth, UK: Penguin, 2004). For more on the socialist feminist contribution see Sheila Rowbotham, *Women, Resistance, and Revolution: A History of Women and Revolution in the Modern World* (London: Verso, 2013).

On the role of struggles against colonialism, slavery, and racism, see W. E. B. Dubois, *Black Reconstruction in America* (New York: Oxford, 2014); Malcom X, *By Any Means Necessary* (New York: Pathfinder Books, 1992); C. L. R. James, *Black Jacobins* (Harmondsworth, UK: Penguin, 2001); Howard Adams, *Prison of Grass: Canada from a Native Point of View* (Markham, ON: Fifth House Publishers, 1989); Angela Y. Davis, *Women, Race, and Class* (New York: Ballantine Books, 1983). For a different interpretation of the relationship between need-satisfaction and democracy, see Lawrence Hamilton, *The Political Philosophy of Needs* (Cambridge, UK: Cambridge University Press, 2008).

CHAPTER 2

Other key texts in the classical liberal tradition include Thomas Hobbes, *Leviathan* (Indianapolis, IN: Hackett, 1994); Charles de Montesquieu, *The Spirit of the Laws* (Cambridge, UK: Cambridge University Press, 1989); John Locke, *A Letter on Toleration* (Indianapolis, IN: Hackett, 1983); Immanuel Kant, *Political Writings* (Cambridge, UK: Cambridge University Press, 1991); Jeremy Bentham, *Principles of Morals and Legislation* (Amherst, NY: Prometheus Books, 1988); Adam Smith, *The Wealth of Nations* (New York: The Modern Library, 1994); Friedrich von Hayek, *The Road to Serfdom* (Chicago: University of Chicago Press, 1994); Isaiah Berlin, *Four Essays on Liberty* (Oxford, UK: Oxford University Press, 1990).

The entwining of the history of classical liberalism and capitalism is explored in C. B. Macpherson, *The Political Theory of Possessive Individualism* (Oxford, UK: Oxford University Press, 1965); John Polanyi, *The Great Transformation: The Political and Economic Origins of*

Our Times (Boston: Beacon Press, 2001); Ralph Miliband, *The State in Capitalist Society* (London: Quartet Books, 1973); Michael Neu, *Just Liberal Violence: Sweatshops, Torture, War* (London: Rowman & Littlefield International, 2018).

Important developments in egalitarian liberal thought are elaborated in John Dewey, *Liberalism and Social Action* (Amherst NY: Prometheus Books, 1999); Ronald Dworkin, *Taking Rights Seriously* (Cambridge, MA: Harvard University Press, 1978); Stephen Darwall, ed., *Equal Freedom* (Ann Arbor, MI: University of Michigan Press, 1995); Alan Gewirth, *The Community of Rights* (Chicago: University of Chicago Press, 1998); Brian Barry, *Why Social Justice Matters* (Cambridge, UK: Polity Press, 2005); Will Kymlicka, *Multicultural Citizenship: A Liberal Theory of Minority Rights* (Oxford, UK: Oxford University Press, 2000).

For more on deliberative democracy, see Jurgen Habermas, *Between Facts and Norms* (Cambridge, MA: MIT Press, 1998); James Bohman and William Rehg, *Deliberative Democracy: Essays on Reason and Politics* (Cambridge, MA: MIT Press, 1997); Amy Guttman and Dennis Thompson, *Why Deliberative Democracy?* (Princeton, NJ: Princeton University Press, 2004); Zsuzsanna Chappell, *Deliberative Democracy: A Critical Introduction* (New York: Red Globe Press, 2012).

For further explorations of cosmopolitanism, see Thomas Pogge, *World Poverty and Human Rights* (Cambridge, UK: Polity Press, 2008); David Beetham, *Democracy and Human Rights* (Cambridge, UK: Polity Press, 1999); David Held, *Cosmopolitanism: Ideals and Realities* (Cambridge, UK: Polity Press, 2010); Garrett Wallace Brown and David Held, *The Cosmopolitan Reader* (Cambridge, UK: Polity Press, 2010).

On the history and contemporary importance of republicanism, see Niccolò Machiavelli, *Discourses* (Harmondsworth, UK: Penguin, 1984); Jean Jacques Rousseau, *The Social Contract* (Harmondsworth, UK: Penguin, 1968); Benjamin Barber, *Strong Democracy* (Berkeley, CA: University of California Press, 2004); Richard Bourke and Quentin Skinner, *Popular Sovereignty in Historical Perspective* (Cambridge, UK: Cambridge University Press, 2017); William Clare Roberts, *Marx's Inferno: The Political Theory of Capital* (Princeton, NJ: Princeton University Press, 2018).

CHAPTER 3

The economics and empirical structure of contemporary inequality are further examined in Thomas Piketty, *The Economics of Inequality* (Cambridge, MA: Belknap Press, 2015); Facundo Alvaredo et al., eds., *The World Inequality Report, 2018* (Cambridge, MA: Belknap Press, 2018); Stephen Armstrong, *The New Poverty* (London: Verso, 2017).

For a Marxist critique of egalitarian liberalism, see Alex Callinicos, *Equality* (Cambridge, UK: Polity Press, 2000); and Jeff Noonan, "Reconstructing the Normative Foundations of Socialism," *Socialist Studies* (Spring 2008), 31–55.

There is, of course, vast literature that *defends* inequality as necessary for economic growth. The classic of this genre is Milton Friedman, *Capitalism and Freedom* (Chicago: University of Chicago Press, 2002). An overview of the economic arguments can be found in Arthur M. Orkun, *Equality and Efficiency: The Big Trade-Off* (Washington, DC: Brookings Institution, 2015).

The racial dimensions of inequality, with a focus on the way in which the United States prison system is employed to ensure the suppression of black Americans, can be found in Michelle Alexander, *The New Jim Crow: Mass Incarceration in the Age of Color Blindness* (New York: The New Press, 2012). Voter suppression is another key tool used to maintain racialized political inequality. See Carol Anderson, *One Person, No Vote: How Voter Suppression Is Destroying Our Democracy* (London: Bloomsbury Publishing, 2018).

For a more general exploration of problems of sex equality, see Martha Nussbaum, *Sex and Social Justice* (Oxford, UK: Oxford University Press, 1999). Practical examples of the usefulness of the social determinants of health can be found in Alan Davidson, *Social Determinants of Health: A Comparative Approach* (Oxford, UK: Oxford University Press, 2015).

CHAPTER 4

For broader discussions of populism, see the essays in Francisco Panizza, *Populism and the Mirror of Democracy* (London: Verso, 2005).

On Trump and the American alt-right, see David Neiwert, *Alt-America: The Rise of the Radical Right in the Age of Trump* (London: Verso, 2017); Lewis Lapham, *Age of Folly: America Abandons Its Democracy* (London: Verso, 2017); Alan I. Abramowitz, *The Great Alignment: Race, Party Transformation, and the Rise of Donald Trump* (New Haven, CT: Yale University Press, 2018).

On Brexit and the European Union, see *The Brexit Crisis: A Verso Report* (London, Verso, 2016); John R. Gillingham, *The EU: An Obituary* (London, Verso, 2018); Geoffrey Evans and Anand Menon, *Brexit and British Politics* (Cambridge, UK: Polity Press, 2017).

CHAPTER 5

The philosophical foundations of the politics of difference are found in the work of Jacques Derrida. See Jacques Derrida, *Margins of Philosophy* (Chicago: University of Chicago Press, 1985), especially the essay "Différance"; Jacques Derrida, *Specters of Marx* (New York: Routledge, 2006).

Influential applications to the struggles of marginalized and oppressed communities include Iris Marion Young, *Justice and the Politics of Difference* (Princeton, NJ: Princeton University Press, 2011); Seyla Benhabib, ed., *Democracy and Difference: Contesting the Boundaries of the Political* (Princeton, NJ: Princeton University Press, 1996); and, for democracy generally, Alex Thomson, *Deconstruction and Democracy* (London: Continuum, 2007); Richard Rorty, *Contingency, Irony, Solidarity* (Cambridge, UK: Cambridge University Press, 1989).

For criticism from a democratic socialist perspective, see Norman Geras, *Solidarity in the Conversation of Humankind* (London: Verso, 1995). For a critique of the usefulness of difference as a political category, see Alain Badiou, *Ethics* (London: Verso, 2002).

On horizontalism, including case studies, see Marina Sitrin, *Horizontalism: Voices of Popular Power in Argentina* (Chico, CA: AK Press, 2006). For alternative explanations of Occupy, see Todd Gitlin, *Occupy Nation: The Roots, the Spirit, and the Promise of Occupy Wall Street* (New York: Harper Collins, 2012); Noam Chomsky, *Occupy:*

Reflections on Class War, Rebellion, and Solidarity (New York: Zucotti Park Press, 2013).

On Egypt, see Jeannie Sowers and Chris Toensing, *The Journey to Tahrir: Revolution, Protest, and Social Change in Egypt* (London: Verso, 2012). For the Arab Spring in general, see Asef Bayat, *Revolution Without Revolutionaries: Making Sense of the Arab Spring* (Stanford, CA: Stanford University Press, 2017). For a more nuanced critique of the democratic potential of the internet, see Robert W. McChesney, *Digital Disconnect: How Capitalism Is Turning the Internet against Democracy* (New York: The New Press, 2013).

CHAPTER 6

For a philosophical history of solidarity, see Hauke Brunkhorst, *Solidarity: From Civic Friendship to a Global Legal Community* (Cambridge MA: MIT Press, 2005). For a liberal interpretation of its foundations, see Keith Banting and Will Kymlicka, *The Strains of Commitment: The Political Sources of Solidarity in Diverse Societies* (Oxford, UK: Oxford University Press, 2017). For feminist interpretations of the material foundation of solidarity in the capacity for self-determination see Alison Jagger, *Feminist Politics and Human Nature* (Lanham, MD: Rowman & Littlefield, 1988); Johanna Brenner, *Women and the Politics of Class* (New York: Monthly Review Press, 2000).

On the universal political value of Black Lives Matter, see Angela Y. Davis, *Freedom Is a Constant Struggle: Ferguson, Palestine, and the Foundations of a Movement* (Chicago: Haymarket Books, 2016). For a more materialist approach to the politics of intersectionality, see Keeanga-Yahmatta Taylor, ed., *How We Get Free: Black Feminism and the Combahee River Collective* (Chicago: Haymarket Books, 2017). For an overview of the complex history between black liberation struggle and socialism, see Ahmed Shawki, *Black Liberation and Socialism* (Chicago: Haymarket Books, 2006).

The international dimensions of women's struggle are explored in Margaret A. McLaren, *Decolonizing Feminism: Transnational Feminism and Globalization* (London: Rowman & Littlefield International, 2017).

Finally, related but alternative visions of the future of a democratic socialist society are explored by Yanis Varoufakis, "Our New International Movement Will Fight Rising Fascists and Globalists," *The Guardian* (September 13, 2018); https://www.theguardian.com/co mmentisfree/ng-interactive/2018/sep/13/our-new-international-move ment-will-fight-rising-fascism-and-globalists (accessed September 13, 2018). It is part of a series *The Guardian* is running on the International Left. See also Erik Olin Wright, *Envisioning Real Utopias* (London: Verso, 2010); David Schweickart, *After Capitalism* (Lanham, MD: Rowman & Littlefield, 2011); Michael Albert, *Parecon: Life After Capitalism* (London: Verso, 2004); Anatole Anton and Richard Schmitt, eds., *Towards a New Socialism* (Washington, DC: Lexington Books, 2006).

For the socialist democratic vision of the future, see *Prosperity and Justice: Report of the Institute for Public Policy Research Commission on Economic Justice* (Cambridge, UK: Polity Press, 2018).

Bibliography

Abramson, Alana. "'I Can Be More Presidential Than Any President': Read Trump's Ohio Rally Speech." *Time*, July 26, 2017; http://time.com/4874 161/donald-trump-transcript-youngstown-ohio/ (accessed August 30, 2017).

Acemoglu, Daren, and James A. Robinson. "The Rise and Decline of General Laws of Capitalism." *Journal of Economic Perspectives*, vol. 29, no. 1 (Winter 2015): 3–28.

Adler, Seth. "By Party or Formation." *The Bullet*, July 27, 2018; https://socialistproject.ca/2018/06/by-party-or-by-formation/ (accessed July 16, 2018).

Agamben, Giorgio. *The State of Exception*. Chicago: University of Chicago Press, 2004.

Allen, Katie. "FTSE CEOs Earn 386 Times More than Workers on National Living Wage." *The Guardian*, March 22, 2017; https://www.theguard ian.com/business/2017/mar/22/uk-ceos-national-living-wage-equality-tru st-pay-gap (accessed December 20, 2017).

Anderson, Perry. *The New Old World*. London: Verso, 2009.

Aristotle, "Politics." *The Basic Works of Aristotle*. Richard McKeon, ed. New York: Random House, 1966, 1127–324.

Arneson, Richard. "Equality and Equality of Opportunity for Welfare." *Philosophical Studies*, vol. 55 (1989): 106–39.

Assange, Julien, with Jacob Appelbaum, Andy Müller-Maghun, and Jérémie Zimmermann. *Cypherpunks: Freedom and the Future of the Internet*. New York: OR Books, 2012.

Balibar, Etienne. *Politics and the Other Scene*. London: Verso, 2011.

Benkler, Yochai. *The Wealth of Networks*. New Haven, CT: Yale University Press, 2006.

Berlet, Chip, and Matthew M. Lyons. *Right Wing Populism in America: Too Close for Comfort*. New York: Guilford Press, 2000.

Bhambra, Gurminder K. "Brexit, Trump, and 'Methodological Whiteness': On the Misrecognition of Race and Class." *The British Journal of Sociology*, vol. 68, no. S1 (2017): S214–32.

Bhattacharya, Tithi, ed. *Social Reproduction Theory*. London: Pluto Press, 2017.

Black Lives Matter. "Guiding Principles." *Black Lives Matter*; https://blackli vesmatter.com/about/what-we-believe/ (accessed July 5, 2018).

Boggs, Grace Lee, and Scott Kurashige. *The Next American Revolution: Sustainable Activism for the Twenty-First Century*. Berkeley: University of California Press, 2012.

Bohman, James. *Democracy across Borders: From Demos to Demoi*. Cambridge, MA: MIT Press, 2007.

Bowman, Andrew. "An Illusion of Success: The Consequences of British Rail Privatisation." *Accounting Forum*, vol. 39 (2015): 51–63.

Brenner, Johanna. "21st Century Socialist Feminism." *Socialist Studies,* vol. 10, no. 1 (Summer 2014): 31–49.

Brown, Wendy. *Undoing the Demos*. New York: Zone Books, 2015.

Butler, Judith. *Notes Toward a Performative Theory of Assembly*. Cambridge, MA: Harvard University Press, 2015.

Cahill, Damien, and Martijn Koning. "Neoliberalism: A Useful Concept?" *The Bullet*, December 1, 2017; https://socialistproject.ca/2017/12/b1518/ (accessed December 20, 2017).

Callinicos, Alex. "The Internationalist Case against the European Union." *International Socialism Journal*, vol. 148 (October 2015); http://isj.org. uk/the-internationalist-case-against-the-european-union/ (accessed July 12, 2017).

Camfield, David. *We Can Do Better*. Halifax, NS: Fernwood Publishing, 2017.

Canadian Truth and Reconciliation Commission on Residential Schooling; http://www.trc.ca/websites/trcinstitution/index.php?p=890 (accessed August 8, 2018).

Chapman, Steve. "Why Young Americans Are Drawn to Socialism." *Reason*, May 21, 2018; https://reason.com/archives/2018/05/21/why-young-americ ans-are-drawn-to-sociali (accessed September 19, 2018).

Clayton, Dewey, M. "Black Lives Matter and the Civil Rights Movement: A Comparative Analysis of Two Social Movements in the United States." *Journal of Black Studies* (2018): 1–33. DOI: 10.1177/0021934718764099 (accessed March 12, 2018).

Cohen, G. A. *Rescuing Justice and Equality*. Cambridge, MA: Harvard University Press, 2008.

Connolly, William. *The Fragility of Things*. Durham, NC: Duke University Press, 2013.

Corlett, Adam. *Diverse Outcomes: Living Standards by Ethnicity*. London: Resolution Foundation, 2017; http://www.resolutionfoundation.org/app/uploads/2017/08/Diverse-outcomes.pdf.

Coulthard, Glen Sean. *Red Skin, White Masks: Rejecting the Colonial Politics of Recognition*. Minneapolis: University of Minnesota Press, 2014.

Credit Suisse Research Institute. *Global Wealth Report 2017*; http://publications.credit-suisse.com/tasks/render/file/index.cfm?fileid=12DFFD63-07D1-EC6 3-A3D5F67356880EF3 (accessed December 14, 2017).

Crenshaw, Kimberlé. "Demarginalizing the Intersection of Race and Sex: A Black Feminist Critique of Anti-Discrimination Doctrine, Feminist Theory, and Anti-Racist Politics." *University of Chicago Legal Forum,* vol. 139, no. 1 (1989): 139–67.

Crouch, Colin. *Post-Democracy*. Cambridge, UK: Polity Press, 2004.

Dale, Daniel. "Against the Odds." *Toronto Star*, August 6, 2017, A4.

Daremas, Georgios. "Marx's Theory of Democracy in His Critique of Hegel's Theory of the State." *Karl Marx and Contemporary Philosophy*. Andrew Chitty and Martin McIvor, eds. London: Palgrave MacMillan, 2009, 79–98.

Dean, Jodi. *Democracy and Other Neoliberal Fantasies: Communicative Capitalism and Left Politics*. Durham, NC: Duke University Press, 2009.

Department of Health and Human Services. *Health, United States, 2015: With Special Feature on Racial and Ethnic Health Inequalities* (2017); https://www.cdc.gov/nchs/data/hus/hus15.pdf (accessed December 27, 2017).

De Tocqueville, Alexis. *Democracy in America*. Richard D. Heffner, ed. New York: Mentor Books, 1956.

DeVega, Chauncey. "Idiocracy Now: Donald Trump and the Dunning-Kruger Effect—When Stupid People Don't Know They Are Stupid." *Salon*, September 30, 2016; http://www.salon.com/2016/09/30/idiocracy-now-donald-tr ump-and-the-dunning-kruger-effect-when-stupid-people-dont-know-they-ar e-stupid/ (accessed August 30, 2017).

Devine, Pat. *Democracy and Economic Planning*. Cambridge, UK: Polity Press, 1988.

Douglass, Frederick. *A Narrative of the Life of Frederick Douglass, An American Slave*. New York: Penguin, 1982.

Doyal, Len, and Ian Gough. *A Theory of Human Need*. New York: Guilford Press, 1991.

Draper, Hal. "The Two Souls of Socialism." *Marxists Internet Archive*; https ://www.marxists.org/archive/draper/1966/twosouls/ (accessed October 12, 2017).

Dunford, Robin. "Autonomous Peasant Struggles and Left Arts of Government." *Third World Quarterly,* vol. 36, no. 8 (2015): 1455–56.

Dussel, Enrique. *Ethics of Liberation in the Age of Globalization and Exclusion*. Durham, NC: Duke University Press, 2013.

Dworkin, Ronald. "Equality of Resources." *Philosophy and Public Affairs*, vol. 10 (1981): 271–302.

Edmundson, William A. *John Rawls: Reticent Socialist*. Cambridge, UK: Cambridge University Press, 2017.

Elk, Mike. "Justice in the Factory: How Black Lives Matter Breathed New Life into the Union Movement." *The Guardian*, February 10, 2018; https://www.theguardian.com/us-news/2018/feb/10/black-lives-matter-labor-unions-factory-workers-unite (accessed February 13, 2018).

Engels, Friedrich. *The Condition of the Working Class in England*. Frogmore, UK: Panther Books, 1969.

Epstein, Richard A. *The Classical Liberal Constitution: The Uncertain Quest for Limited Government*. Cambridge, MA: Harvard University Press, 2014.

Fanon, Frantz. *Wretched of the Earth*. New York: Grove Press, 1963.

Fekete, Liz. *Europe's Fault Lines: Racism and the Rise of the Right*. London: Verso, 2018.

Ferguson, Bruce. "Re-Thinking Struggle: Starting From Story." *Social Inequality and the Spectre of Social Injustice: Alternate Routes*, vol. 29 (2018): 307–19.

Fischer, Norman Arthur. *Marxist Ethics within Western Political Theory*. London: Palgrave MacMillan, 2015.

"Five Reasons the Privatization of Ontario Hydro Is a Really, Really, Bad Idea." *Press Progress*, October 29, 2015; https://pressprogress.ca/5_reasons_privatization_hydro_one_is_a_really_really_bad_idea/ (accessed September 20, 2018).

Foa, Robert Stefan, and Yascha Mounk. "The Democratic Disconnect." *Journal of Democracy,* vol. 27, no. 3 (July 2016): 5–17.

Foa, Robert Stefan, and Yascha Mounk. "The Signs of Deconsolidation." *Journal of Democracy*, vol. 28, no. 1 (January 2017): 5–17.

Fraser, Nancy. *Scales of Justice*. New York: Columbia University Press, 2010.

Fraser, Nancy, and Axel Honneth. *Redistribution or Recognition: A Political Philosophical Debate*. London: Verso, 2003.

Freeman, Jo. "The Tyranny of Structurelessness"; Personal website https://www.jofreeman.com/joreen/tyranny.htm (accessed September 20, 2018).

Gilligan, Carol, and David A. J. Richards. *The Deepening Darkness: Patriarchy, Resistance, and Democracy's Future*. New York: Cambridge University Press, 2009.

Gordon, Robert C. *The Rise and Fall of American Growth*. Princeton, NJ: Princeton University Press, 2016.

Guyatt, Gordon, et al. "A Systematic Review of Studies Comparing Health Outcomes in Canada and the United States." *Open Medicine*, April 17, 2007; https://www.ncbi.nlm.nih.gov/pmc/articles/PMC2801918/ (accessed August 9, 2018).

Habermas, Jurgen. *The Crisis of the European Union: A Response.* Cambridge, UK: Polity, 2012.

Haider, Asad. *Mistaken Identity: Race and Class in the Age of Trump.* London: Verso, 2018.

Hardt, Michael, and Antonio Negri. *Empire.* Cambridge, MA: Harvard University Press, 2000.

———. *Multitude: War and Democracy in the Age of Empire.* New York: Penguin, 2004.

———. *Commonwealth.* Cambridge, MA: Harvard University Press, 2009.

———. *Assembly.* New York: Oxford University Press, 2017.

Harvey, David. *The New Imperialism.* New York: Oxford University Press. 2003.

———. *A Brief History of Neoliberalism.* Cambridge, UK: Cambridge University Press, 2005.

———. *Seventeen Contradictions and the End of Capitalism.* Oxford, UK: Oxford University Press, 2014.

———. "Afterthoughts on Piketty's Capital." Personal website http://davidhar vey.org/2014/05/afterthoughts-pikettys-capital/ (accessed December 19, 2017).

Hedges, Chris, and Joe Sacco. *Days of Destruction, Days of Revolt.* Toronto: Knopf Canada, 2012.

Held, David. *Global Covenant.* Cambridge, UK: Polity Press, 2004.

Henkin, Louis. "International Human Rights as 'Rights.' *Human Rights.* J. Richard Pennock and John W. Chapman, eds. New York: New York University Press, 1981, 257–80.

Hewitt, Gavin. "Greece, The Dangerous Game." *British Broadcasting Corporation,* February 1, 2015; https://www.bbc.com/news/world-europe-31082656 (accessed July 8, 2017).

Hickle, Jason. *The Great Divide: A Brief Guide to Global Inequality and its Solutions.* London: Penguin Books, 2018.

Higginbotham, F. Michael. *Ghosts of Jim Crow: Ending Racism in Post-Racial America.* New York: New York University Press, 2013.

Hill, Christopher. *The World Turned Upside Down.* Harmondsworth, UK: Penguin, 1975.

Holloway, John. *Change the World without Taking Power.* London: Pluto Press, 2005.

hooks, bell. "Feminism: A Movement to End Sexist Oppression." *Feminisms.* Sandra Kemp and Judith Squires, eds. Oxford, UK: Oxford University Press, 1997, 22–26.

Horton, Myles, and Paolo Freire. *We Make the Road by Walking: Conversations on Education and Social Change.* Philadelphia: Temple University Press, 1990.

Hui, Wang, et al. "The Movement in Egypt: Dialogue with Samir Amin." *Boundary 2*, vol. 39, no. 1 (2012): 168–206; https://read.dukeupress.edu/boundary-2/article-pdf/39/1/167/232164/b2391_09Hui_Fpp.pdf (accessed April 12, 2018).

Illich, Ivan. *De-Schooling Society*. London: Marion Boyars, 2002.

Jahn, Beate. "Rethinking Democracy Promotion." *Review of International Studies*, vol. 38, no. 4 (2012): 685–705.

Judis, John B. *The Populist Explosion: How the Great Recession Transformed American and European Politics*. New York: Columbia Global Reports, 2016.

Kriner, Douglas, and Francis Shen. "Battlefield Casualties and Ballot Box Defeat: Did the Bush-Obama Wars Cost Clinton the White House?" Social Sciences Research Network; https://papers.ssrn.com/sol3/papers.cfm?abstract_id=2989040&download=yes (accessed August 31, 2017).

Krugman, Paul. "The Greatest Tax Scam in History." *New York Times*, November 27, 2017; https://www.nytimes.com/2017/11/27/opinion/senate-tax-bill-scam.html (accessed December 19, 2017).

Kuznets, Simon. "Economic Growth and Income Inequality." *The American Economic Review*, vol. 45, no. 1 (March 1955): 1–28.

Laclau, Ernesto. *On Populist Reason*. London: Verso, 2007.

Lakoff, Sanford. "Inequality as a Danger to Democracy: Reflections on Piketty's Warning." *Political Science Quarterly*, vol. 130, no. 3 (2015): 424–47.

Lefort, Claude. *The Political Forms of Modern Society: Bureaucracy, Democracy, Totalitarianism*. John B. Thompson, ed. Cambridge, MA: MIT Press, 1986.

Lendman, Stephen. "The Bank of the South: An Alternative to IMF and World Bank Dominance." *Global Research*, October 29, 2007; https://www.globalresearch.ca/the-bank-of-the-south-an-alternative-to-imf-and-world-bank-dominance/7207 (accessed August 20, 2018).

Lenin, Vladimir. *The State and Revolution*. Moscow: Progress Publishers, 1975.

Locke, John. *Second Treatise of Government*. Indianapolis, IN: Hackett, 1980.

Lotringer, Sylvère, ed. *Italy: Autonomia: Post-Political Politics*. New York: Semiotext(e), 1980.

Lovett, Frank. "The Republican Critique of Liberalism." *The Cambridge Companion to Liberalism*. Steven Wall, ed. Cambridge, UK: Cambridge University Press, 2015, 381–401.

Lugones, Maria. "Heterosexualism and the Modern Colonial/Gender System." *Hypatia*, vol. 22, no. 1 (2007): 186–209.

MacDonald, David, and Daniel Wilson. *Shameful Neglect: Indigenous Child Poverty in Canada*. Ottawa: Canadian Centre for Policy Alternatives, 2016; https://www.policyalternatives.ca/sites/default/files/upload/publications/

National Office/2016/05/Indigenous_Child Poverty.pdf (accessed December 13, 2017).

Machiavelli, Niccolò. *The History of Florence and Other Selections*. Myron P. Gilmore, ed. New York: Washington Square Press, 1970.

Madison, James. *The Federalist*. Cleveland, OH: Meridian Books, 1965.

Malthus, Thomas. *An Essay on the Principle of Population*. Amherst, NY: Prometheus Books, 1998.

Marcuse, Herbert. "The Historical Fate of Bourgeois Democracy." *Herbert Marcuse: Towards a Critical Theory of Society: Collected Papers*, vol. 2. Douglas Kellner, ed. New York: Routledge, 2001, 163–86.

Marmot, Michael. *The Health Gap: The Challenge of an Unequal World*. London: Bloomsbury Press, 2015.

Marx, Karl. "Theses on Feuerbach." *The German Ideology*. Moscow: Progress Publishers, 1976, 618–20.

———. *Capital*, vol. 1. Moscow: Progress Publishers, 1986.

Marx, Karl, and Friedrich Engels. *Karl Marx Friedrich Engels: Collected Works*, vol. 3. New York: International Publishers, 1978.

———. *The Marx-Engels Reader*. Robert C. Tucker, ed. New York: W. W. Norton, 1978.

———. *Manifesto of the Communist Party*. Moscow: Progress Publishers, 1986.

McMurtry, John. *Unequal Freedoms*. Toronto: Garamond, 1998.

———. *Philosophy and World Problems, Volume 1: What is Good? What is Bad? The Value of all Values Through Time, Place, and Theories*. Oxford: EOLSS Publishers, 2011.

———. *The Cancer Stage of Capitalism: From Crisis to Cure*, second edition. London: Pluto Press, 2013.

McNally, David. *Global Slump: The Economics and Politics of Crisis and Resistance*. Oakland, CA: PM Press, 2011.

Mill, John Stuart. *Considerations on Representative Government*. Indianapolis, IN: Bobbs-Merrill, 1958.

———. *On Socialism*. Buffalo, NY: Prometheus Books, 1987.

Mill, John Stuart, and Harriet Taylor Mill. *Essays on Sex Equality*. Alice S. Rossi, ed. Chicago: University of Chicago Press, 1970.

Miller, Greg, Julie Vitkovskaya, and Reuben Fischer-Baum. "'This Deal Will Make Me Look Terrible': Full Transcript of Trump's Calls with Australia and Mexico." *Washington Post*, August 3, 2017; https://www.was hingtonpost.com/graphics/2017/politics/australia-mexico-transcripts/?utm_ term=.cadded59c572 (accessed August 30, 2017).

Miller, Sarah Clark. *The Ethics of Need: Agency, Dignity, and Obligation*. London: Routledge, 2012.

Morozov, Evgeny. *To Save Everything, Click Here.* New York: Public Affairs, 2013.

Mouffe, Chantal. *The Democratic Paradox.* London: Verso, 2000.

———. *Agonistics.* London: Verso, 2013.

———. *For a Left Populism.* London: Verso, 2018.

Mutua, Makau. *Human Rights: A Political and Economic Critique.* Philadelphia: University of Pennsylvania Press, 2002.

Nimtz, August H. Jr. *Marx and Engels: Their Contribution to the Democratic Breakthrough.* Albany, NY: State University of New York Press, 2000.

Noonan, Jeff. *Democratic Society and Human Needs.* Montreal: McGill-Queen's University Press, 2006.

———. "The Contradictions of Nussbaum's Liberalism." *International Critical Thought*, vol. 1, no. 4 (2011): 427–36.

———. *Materialist Ethics and Life-Value.* Montreal: McGill-Queen's University Press, 2012.

———. "The Historical and Contemporary Life-Value of the Canadian Labour Movement." *Labour/Le Travail*, vol. 71 (Spring 2013): 9–27.

———. *Embodiment and the Meaning of Life.* Montreal: McGill-Queen's University Press, 2018.

Nove, Alex. *The Economics of Feasible Socialism.* London: Allen and Unwin, 1983.

Nussbaum, Martha. *Women and Human Development.* Cambridge, UK: Cambridge University Press, 2000.

———. *Creating Capabilities: The Human Development Approach.* Cambridge, MA: Harvard University Press, 2011.

O'Rourke, Lindsey A. "The US Government Tried to Change Other Countries' Governments 72 Times during the Cold War." *Washington Post*, December 23, 2016; https://www.washingtonpost.com/news/monkey-cage/wp/2016/12/23/the-cia-says-russia-hacked-the-u-s-election-here-are-6-things-to-learn-from-cold-war-attempts-to-change-regimes/?noredirect=on&utm_term=.00a1ba21c77f (accessed July 17, 2018).

Pettit, Phillip. *On the People's Terms: A Republican Theory and Model of Democracy.* Cambridge, UK: Cambridge University Press, 2012.

Pickett, Kate, and Richard Wilkinson. *The Spirit Level: Why Equality Is Better for Everyone.* Harmondsworth, UK: Penguin, 2010.

Piketty, Thomas. *Capital in the Twenty-first Century.* Cambridge, MA: Harvard University Press, 2014.

Piketty, Thomas, and Emmanuel Saez. *World Income Database*; http://wid.world/ (accessed December 14, 2017).

Plato. *The Republic.* G. M. A. Grube, trans., revised by C. D. C. Reeve. Indianapolis, IN: Hackett, 1992.

Rancière, Jacques. *Hatred of Democracy.* London: Verso, 2006.

Rawls, John. *A Theory of Justice*, revised edition. Cambridge, MA: Harvard University Press, 1999.

———. *Political Liberalism*. New York: Columbia University Press, 1996.

Reilly, Katie. "Read Hillary Clinton's 'Basket of Deplorables' Remarks about Donald Trump's Supporters." *Time*, September 10, 2016; http://time.com /4486502/hillary-clinton-basket-of-deplorables-transcript/ (accessed August 25, 2017).

Roediger, David. *Class, Race, and Marxism*. London: Verso, 2017.

Rosa, Hartmut. *Social Acceleration: A New Theory of Modernity*. New York: Columbia University Press, 2015.

Rowbotham, Sheila. "Women: Linking Lives with Democracy." *Rethinking Democracy: Socialist Register 2018*. Leo Panitch and Greg Albo, eds. London: Merlin Press, 2018, 28–47.

Sawyer, Bradley, and Selena Gomez. "How Does the Quality of the US Healthcare System Compare to Other Countries?" *Health System Tracker*, May 22, 2017; https://www.healthsystemtracker.org/chart-collection/quality-u-s-healthcare-system-compare-countries/#item-hospital-admissions-preventa ble-diseases-frequent-u-s-comparable-countries (accessed August 9, 2018).

Schmidt, Ingo. "Introduction: Social Democracy and Uneven Development: Theoretical Reflections on the Three Worlds of Social Democracy." *The Three Worlds of Social Democracy*. Ingo Schmidt, ed. London: Pluto Press, 2016, 1–28.

Sears, Alan. *The Next New Left: A History of the Future*. Halifax, NS: Fernwood, 2014.

———. "Body Politics: The Social Reproduction of Sexualitie." *Social Reproduction Theory*. Thithi Bhattacharya, ed. London: Pluto, 2017, 171–91.

Sen, Amartya. *Equality of What? The Tanner Lectures on Human Values*. Scott McMurrin, ed. Cambridge, UK: Cambridge University Press, 1980.

———. *Development as Freedom*. New York: Knopf, 1999.

Seymour, Richard. "UKIP and the Crisis of Britain." *Socialist Register 2016: The Politics of the Right*. London: Merlin Press, 2016, 24–50.

Sitrin, Marina. *Everyday Revolutions: Horizontalism and Autonomy in Argentina*. London: Zed Books, 2012.

South African Federation of Trade Unions. "Working Class Movement Must Be Independent." *The Bullet*, August 5, 2018; https://socialistproject.ca/20 18/08/working-class-movement-must-be-independent/ (accessed August 5, 2018).

Srnicek, Nick, and Alex Williams. *Re-inventing the Future: Post-Capitalism and a World without Work*. London: Verso, 2015.

Stavrakakis, Yannis, et al. "Contemporary Left-wing Populism in Latin America: Leadership, Horizontalism, and Postdemocracy in Chávez's Venezuela." *Latin American Politics and Society*, vol. 58, no. 3 (2016): 51–76.

Stephens, Bret. "Presidency without Guardrails." *New York Times International Weekly* (included in the *Toronto Star*), August 5–6, 2017, 15.

Stiglitz, Joseph. *The Price of Inequality.* New York: Norton, 2013.

———. *The Great Divide: Unequal Societies and What We Can Do about Them.* New York: W. W. Norton, 2015.

Thucydides. "Melian Dialogue"; https://www.shsu.edu/~his_ncp/Melian.html (accessed April 4, 2017).

———. "Pericles Funeral Oration." University of Minnesota Human Rights Library; http://hrlibrary.umn.edu/thucydides.html (accessed March 22, 2017.

Tyson, Alec, and Shiva Maniam. "Behind Trump's Victory: Divisions by Race, Gender, Education." Pew Research Center, November 9, 2016; http://www.pewresearch.org/fact-tank/2016/11/09/behind-trumps-victory-divisions-by-race-gender-education/ (accessed August 30, 2017).

Virno, Paolo. *A Grammar of the Multitude.* Los Angeles: Semiotext(e), 2004.

Wagner, Peter, and Bernadette Rabuy. "Mass Incarceration: The Whole Pie 2017." *Prison Policy Initiative*, March 14, 2017; https://www.prisonpolicy.org/reports/pie2017.html (accessed August 28, 2017).

Wainwright, Hilary. "Radicalising the Party-Movement Relationship: From Ralph Miliband to Jeremy Corbyn and Beyond." *Rethinking Revolution: Socialist Register 2017.* London: Merlin Press, 2017, 80–101.

Wenman, Mark. *Agonistic Democracy: Constitutive Power in the Era of Globalisation.* Cambridge, UK: Cambridge University Press, 2013.

Wilpert, Greg. *Changing Venezuela by Taking Power.* London: Verso, 2007.

Wilson, Valerie, et al. "Black Women Have to Work 7 Months into 2017 to Be Paid the Same as White Men in 2016." *Economic Policy Institute*, July 28, 2017; http://www.epi.org/blog/black-women-have-to-work-7-months-into-2017-to-be-paid-the-same-as-white-men-in-2016/ (accessed December 14, 2017).

Wolin, Sheldon. *Fugitive Democracy and Other Essays.* Nicolas Xenos, ed. Princeton NJ: Princeton University Press, 2016.

Wood, Ellen Meiksins. *Citizens to Lords: A Social History of Western Political Thought from Antiquity to the Middle Ages.* London: Verso, 2008.

Index

About the Author

Jeff Noonan is professor of philosophy at the University of Windsor in Ontario, Canada. He is the author of four previous books, the most recent being *Embodiment and the Meaning of Life* (2018). He has published a wide variety of scholarly papers on problems of democratic theory and practice, the future of socialism, materialist ethics, life-value philosophy, and issues related to meaningful lives. He has also written extensively for community-based publications and political websites, publishes a blog at www.jeffnoonan.org and is a long-time activist in the academic labor movement in Canada.